George South
Record Book
Highway Run into the Midnight Sun

Jason Freeman

George South

ISBN:
ISBN-13: 9781729183328

DEDICATION

JASON FREEMAN

I WANT TO DECICATE THIS BOOK TO THE GIRL I STARTED CHASING IN THE SEVENTH GRADE AND THE WOMAN I WAS LUCKY ENOUGH TO MARRY. MY BEST FRIEND, MY NORTH STAR RACHEL FREMAN AND TO MY HERO – MY SON AUSTIN FREEMAN. MARTHA FREEMAN (1937 – 2010) THE GREATEST HUMAN BEING I HAVE EVERY KNOWN. I MISS YOU EVERYDAY

SPECIAL THANKS
MICHAEL ELLIOTT: FOR HELP ME WITH EVERY CRARY IDEA I COME UP WITH.
DONNIE WEBB, JEFF PATTON & JAMES HARBISON FOR GETTING ME STARTED
MARK HENDERSON FOR BEING A GREAT FRIEND AND TAKING ME TO THE NEXT LEVEL.
DAVE & TAMMY MONROE, TRENT HUDSON, BUDDY PORTER, GUS BOLICK, DANNY DEESE, DEON JOHNSON, DIGGER BROWN, JEREMY BENGE (TC3), SCOTTY MCKEEVER, DAVID LYNCH, CJ BENTLEY, BOOGIE, SCOTTY BLACK, DANNY PARIS, TONY BENGE, JAMES CHILDERS AND COUNTLESS OTHERS I WILL BE REMINDED I FORGOT.

GEORGE SOUTH

" THOUGH YOUR BEGINNING WAS INSIGNIFICANT, YET YOUR END WILL INCREASE GREATLY. " - JOB 8:7

WHEN MY GREAT FRIEND JASON FREEMAN FIRST ASK ME TO SEE ALL MY WRESTLING MATCH RESULTS BOOKS, I THOUGHT HE WAS EITHER CRAZY, OR ONE HUGE WRESTLING FAN. I WANT TO THANK HIM FOR BEING BRAVE ENOUGH TO SPEND HOURS AND HOURS LOOKING AT ALL MY OLD NOTES, WRITTEN ON POPCORN BOXES, AND OLD YELLOW STAINED PAGES FULL OF NOTEBOOKS SO THAT WE COULD GET THIS BOOK FINISHED. FOR OVER 40 YEARS I HAVE BEEN DOING SOMETHING THAT I LOVE. PRO WRESTLING IS THE ONLY JOB I HAVE EVER HAD AND WHEN I THINK ABOUT ALL THE LONG 'HIGHWAY RUN' MILES, ALL THE LEGENDS I HAVE BEEN IN THE RING WITH THAT ARE NO LONGER HERE, I AM REMINDED JUST HOW REAL JESUS IS! TO MY BEAUTIFUL KIDS THAT HAVE HAD TO MISS OUT ON SO MUCH 'DAD' TIME, THANK YOU FOR STILL LOVING ME.I HAVE SO MANY WONDERFUL FRIENDS THAT HAVE BEEN A PART OF MY JOURNEY AND I AM GOING TO TRY AND THANK THEM HERE. I HOPE THIS BOOK IS A BLESSING TO EVERYONE THAT READS IT. AND, MAYBE SOME OF YOU HAVE NOT TRUSTED JESUS CHRIST AS YOUR PERSONAL FRIEND, CAN I ENCOURAGE YOU TO DO THAT TODAY? HE CHANGED MY LIFE AND I HAVE NEVER LOOKED BACK. GOD BLESS AND REMEMBER, ' DON'T STOP BELIEVING.'

I WANT TO DEDICATE THIS BOOK TO JESUS CHRIST WHO DIED FOR MY SINS, MY BEAUTIFUL KIDS AND GRAND BABY'S. MY FAVORITE WRESTLER OF ALL TIME, MR. NO. 1 PAUL JONES, MY MOM, SISTER SHIRLEY, BROTHERS WAYNE AND DEAN WHO ALL HAVE GONE ON TO HEAVEN. I WILL SEE YOU SOON.

THANK YOU TO THESE PEOPLE FOR HELPING MAKE EVERY TOWN WITH ME.
JESUS CHRIST, JASON FREEMAN, (ABIGAIL - SCARLET - BROCK - GARRETT - LITTLE GEORGE - MAKAYLA - MAVERICK - DALLAS, -AXL AND BABY COLT SOUTH), DICK BOURNE, PREACHER AND CAROLYN WILSON, PASTOR JIM PALMER, PAUL JONES, RUSTY ROBERTS, BRAD ARMSTRONG, DUSTY RHODES, GARY ROYAL, JIM CROCKETT, MIKE JACKSON, OLE AND GENE ANDERSON, RICKY STEAMBOAT, AL SNOW, RIC FLAIR, REID FLAIR, MAGNUM T.A., TESSA BLANCHARD, CHAD AND VICKY ADAMS, MARK JAMES, JIMMY AND ANGEL VALIANT, STEVE PERRY AND JOURNEY, J. J. DILLON, TED DIBIASE, TRACY MYERS, BRIAN HAWKS, SUSAN GREEN, TERRY FUNK, JAY EAGLE, JOHNNY HUNTER, STEVE PERKINS, SCOTTY MCKEEVER, TERRY TAYLOR, BARRY DARSOW, BILL EADIE, GARY DAMRON, CODY GREEN, ERIC LESTER, ERIC FOSTER, LORI AND JILLIAN JAMES, THE ARMSTRONG FAMILY, SHANE DOUGLAS AND TO EVERY PRO WRESTLER I HAVE BEEN IN THE RING WITH, I LOVE YOU ALL.

" THEREFORE, IF ANYONE IS IN CHRIST, HE IS A NEW CREATION, OLD THINGS HAVE PASSED AWAY, BEHOLD, ALL THINGS HAVE BECOME NEW. " - 2 CORINTHIANS 5:7

CONTENTS

	Forward	i
1	1982 - 1983	8
2	1984	12
3	1985	18
4	1986	30
5	1987	45
6	1988	59
7	1989	72
8	1990	84
9	1991	95
10	1992	107
11	1993	120
12	1994	131
13	1995	140
14	1996	150
15	1997	165
16	1998	178
17	1999	188
18	2000	196
19	2001	205
20	2002	211
21	2003	218
22	2004	226
23	2005	234
24	2006	240
25	2007	247
26	2008	253

27	2009	258
28	2010	263
29	2011	271
30	2012	279
31	2013	286
32	2014	292
33	2015	298
34	2016	304
35	2017	309
36	2018	313
37	Quotes	317

Highway Run into the Midnight Sun

FORWARD

When I was asked to write this forward to say that I was honored would be an understatement.

To have a request from a true legend of the sport of wrestling made me feel both intimidated and proud at the same time .

Intimidated by my desire to do justice to the incredible talent and the priceless role that this legend has played through several decades in the sport .

Proud because someone of that stature would hold me in enough regard to want me to do this for him .

Isaac Newton said "If I have seen further than others it is upon standing on the shoulders of giants " and through George South's selfless dedication and passion for the true art form that is professional wrestling there have been many who have seen further and been far more including myself by standing upon George's shoulders .

George South truly is a giant in professional wrestling .
With a very long and storied career .
That at first glance as just a fan and without any true knowledge of the art of wrestling you would be quick to dismiss , but for those of us who know and truly understand that career . We know just how amazing and priceless all of George's contributions have been .

I first met George personally in 1995 when started in Smoky Mountain Wrestling and George was my first and second match in the territory.

I mean by saying I met him personally because everyone who has been involved with professional wrestling from a fan to a promoter have all known of George South for quite literally several decades .

From the moment I stepped inside that ring I knew I was in with a true master and I was more than happy to be an apprentice and learn everything George had to teach me .

Not only did I have the honor to work with George that day but was also blessed to make a lifelong friend .

In professional wrestling the etiquette is to always shake each other's hands and say sincerely thank you .

The purpose for this is quite simple . It's to always reinforce that no one person is bigger than the show and that we all need each other to perform and make a living .

In saying that I will always shake George South's hand and say sincerely thank you for those reasons and also for the following,
One : because he has always been a wrestler I've admired , Two : for all that he's done for both myself and the entirety of professional wrestling , Three: for all of the things he continues to teach me about the art of professional wrestling and finally for being the type of man we can all aspire to be .

From myself and all of wrestling thank you George sincerely .

Al Snow

EASTERN CHAMPIONSHIP WRESTLING

KELLY LYNN PROMOTIONS

Exclusive right to manage Agreement

_12-20-82_ DATE

George South , hereby agrees to be represented exclusively in his or her career by EASTERN CHAMPIONSHIP WRESTLING and KELLY LYNN PROMOTIONS under the following articles of this agreement. The duration of this contract is _12-20-83 (RB)_ .

EASTERN CHAMPIONSHIP WRESTLING and KELLY LYNN PROMOTIONS will arrange and negotiate all bouts and matches, pre and post fight interviews and publicity, all public and private appearances, all television and radio appearances, all training schedules, and all purses, expenses, moneys, and or benefits to be considered compensation for services rendered.

No interviews, public or private, for any media(television, radio, newspaper, etc or personal appearances for any group, organization, club, or etc. shall be granted without first being approved by EASTERN CHAMPIONSHIP WRESTLING And KELLY LYNN PROMOTIONS.

EASTERN CHAMPIONSHIP WRESTLING and KELLY LYNN PROMOTIONS reserves the right to all pictures, still or moving, taken of the undersigned party during the duration of this agreement.

Rusty Roberts (Lonnie Bonghead)

EASTERN CHAMPIONSHIP WRESTLING

REPRESENTATIVE

George South

PRENCIPLE PARTY

Lee D. Ramey

WITNESS

Ray Stepp

KELLY LYNN PROMOTIONS REPRESENTATIVE

Tony Locklear

WITNESS

December 11, 1982
Gastonia, NC
First Pro Wrestling Workout

December 18, 1982
Bessemer City, NC – High School
Eastern Championship Wrestling (Kelly Lynn)
- Iron Man Mark Thunder vs. Blonde Sweetheart

First Pro Match. December 18, 1982
Photo: George South collection

January 8, 1983
Central, SC – Central Jr. High School
- Iron Man Mark Thunder vs. The Caveman

January 22, 1983
Clover, SC- Armory
- Iron Man Mark Thunder vs. The Hawaiian

February 4, 1983
Newport, TN – Armory
- Iron Man Mark Thunder vs. Chic White

February 5, 1983
Gaffney, SC – Armory
- Iron Man Mark Thunder vs. Black Angel II

February 19, 1983
Clover, SC – Armory
- Iron Man Mark Thunder &? vs. Islander II &Bad Boy Sula

March 5, 1983
Clover, SC – Armory
- Iron Man Mark Thunder &? vs. J.T. Jaggers & The Islanders

March 12, 1983
Kings Mountain, NC – Armory
- Iron Man Mark Thunder &? Vs. Islanders I & II

March 19, 1983
Clover, SC – Armory
- Iron Man Mark Thunder &? Vs. Mike Ivey & Black Angel I

March 26, 1983
Shallotte, NC – Armory
- Iron Man Mark Thunder vs. J.T. Jaggers

March 27, 1983
Whitesville, NC – Armory
Iron Man Mark Thunder &? Vs. Black Widow & Black Angel I

April 9, 1983
York, SC – Armory
- Iron Man Mark Thunder &? Vs. The Islander & Black Angel II

April 23, 1983
Clover, SC -Armory
- Iron Man Mark Thunder vs. Chic White

April 30, 1983
Belwood, NC – High School
- Iron Man Mark Thunder vs. Chris Gardan

May 7, 1983
Lookout, WV – Nuttall Middle School
- Iron Man Mark Thunder vs. The Assassin

May 14, 1983
Marshville, NC – East Union High School
- Iron Man Mark Thunder vs. The Rebel

May 21, 1983
Kings Mountain, NC – Armory
- Iron Man Mark Thunder vs. The Assassin

May 28, 1983
Clover, SC – Armory
- Iron Man Mark Thunder vs. The Rebel

June 4, 1983
Belwood, NC – High School
- Iron Man Mark Thunder vs. The Rebel

June 17, 1983
Gastonia, NC – Longhorn Supper Club
- Iron Man Mark Thunder vs. Blonde Sweetheart

June 18, 1983
Clover, SC – Armory
- Iron Man Mark Thunder vs. Jimmy Ingle

July 16, 1983
Lincolnton, NC – Armory
- Iron Man Mark Thunder vs. Jimmy Ingle

July 23, 1983
Clover, SC – Armory
- Iron Man Mark Thunder vs. Ron Rossi

August 20, 1983
Lincolnton, NC – Armory
- Iron Man Mark Thunder &? Vs. Jimmy Ingle & The Assassin

Highway Run into the Midnight Sun

September 24, 1983
Lincolnton, NC – Armory
- Iron Man Mark Thunder vs. Ed Jones

October 1, 1983
Mooresboro, NC – High School
- Iron Man Mark Thunder &? vs. Billy Eagle & Eddie Dean

October 4, 1983
Johnson City, TN – Rec Center
- Iron Man Mark Thunder &? Vs. John Savage & Johnny Hayes

October 11, 1983
Johnson City, TN – Rec Center
- Iron Man Mark Thunder &? Vs. The Assassin & The Superstar

October 18, 1983
Johnson City, TN – Rec Center
- Iron Man Mark Thunder vs. Winter Hawk

October 22, 1983
Monroe, NC – Armory
- Iron Man Mark Thunder vs. Ed Jones
- Iron Man Mark Thunder &? vs. Jimmy Ingle & Danny Jackson

November 2, 1983
Pageland, SC – B & W Auction Barn
- Iron Man Mark Thunder vs. Damen Smith

November 3, 1983
Batesburg, SC – Leesville Civic Center
- Iron Man Mark Thunder vs. Jay Eagle

November 17, 1983
Batesburg, SC – Leesville Civic Center
- Iron Man Mark Thunder vs. Jay Eagle

December 7, 1983
Pageland, SC – B & W Auction Barn
- Iron Man Mark Thunder &? Vs. Jay Eagle & Mitch Stevens

December 15, 1983
Clinton, SC – Armory
- Iron Man Mark Thunder &? Vs. Jim Tucker & Brute Bernard

December 22, 1983
Pageland, SC – B & W Auction Barn
- Iron Man Mark Thunder vs. Damen Smith

1984

January 7, 1984
Lincolnton, NC – Armory
• Iron Man Mark Thunder vs. Brute Bernard

January 14, 1984
Woodruff, SC – Abby Gym
• Iron Man Mark Thunder vs. Jay Eagle

January 19, 1984
Pageland, SC – B & W Auction Barn
Iron Man Mark Thunder &? vs. Jay Eagle & Mitch Stevens

January 21, 1984
Ft. Bragg, NC – Lee Field House
• Iron Man Mark Thunder vs. Jay Eagle

February 2, 1984
Inman, SC – Armory
• Iron Man Mark Thunder &? vs. Jay Eagle & Winter Hawk

February 12, 1984
Gastonia, NC – Hillview House
• Iron Man Mark Thunder vs. Damen Blake

February 25, 1984
Columbia, SC – Keenan High School
• Iron Man Mark Thunder &? vs. Jay Eagle & Winter Hawk

March 3, 1984
Belwood, NC – High School
• Iron Man Mark Thunder vs. Damen Blake
• Iron Man Mark Thunder vs. The Islander

March 11, 1984
Gastonia, NC – Hillview House
• Iron Man Mark Thunder &? vs. Jay Eagle & Mitch Stevens

March 30, 1984
Columbia, SC – Keenan High School
• Iron Man Mark Thunder vs. Dana Breck

March 31, 1984
Lincolnton, NC – Armory
• Iron Man Mark Thunder vs. The Samoan

Match # 50
April 7, 1984
Concord, NC – Logan Center
• Iron Man Mark Thunder &? vs. Jay Eagle & John Savage

April 8, 1984
Gastonia, NC – Hillview House
• Iron Man Mark Thunder &? vs. Jay Eagle & John Savage

April 20, 1984
Elgin, SC – Elgin Gym
• Iron Man Mark Thunder vs. Mitch Stallion
• 12-Man Battle Royal

April 28, 1984
Lincolnton, NC – Armory
• Iron Man Mark Thunder &? vs. Jay Eagle & Mitch Stallion

April 29, 1984
Gastonia, NC – Hillview House
• Iron Man Mark Thunder vs. Jay Eagle

May 3, 1984
Goldsboro, NC – Roadies
• Iron Man Mark Thunder vs. Boom Boom Bullet

May 10, 1984
Greenville, NC – Greenleaf Ent. Center
• Iron Man Mark Thunder vs. Boom Boom Bullet
• Battle Royal

May 12, 1984
Hickory, NC – Armory
• Iron Man Mark Thunder &? vs. Jay Eagle & Mitch Stallion

May 18, 1984
Drexel, NC – Community Center
• Iron Man Mark Thunder vs. Doc Garrison

May 19, 1984
York, SC – Armory
• Iron Man Mark Thunder vs. Mitch Stallion

May 20, 1984
Campbells, SC – Redland Rhythm Ranch
• Iron Man Mark Thunder vs. Jay Eagle

May 28, 1984
Gastonia, NC – Hillview House
• Iron Man Mark Thunder vs. Mitch Stallion

June 2, 1984
Monroe, NC – Armory
• Iron Man Mark Thunder vs. Sweet Ebony Diamond

June 8, 1984
Pacolet, SC – Old Amphitheatre
• Iron Man Mark Thunder &? vs. Jay Eagle & Winter Hawk

June 9, 1984
Lincolnton, NC – Armory
• Iron Man Mark Thunder vs. Jay Eagle

June 15, 1984
Pacolet, SC – Old Amphitheatre
• Iron Man Mark Thunder vs. Jay Eagle

June 17, 1984
Gastonia, NC – Hillview House
• Iron Man Mark Thunder vs. Billy Eagle

June 22, 1984
Hickory, NC – Armory
• Iron Man Mark Thunder vs. Sweet Ebony Diamond
• Battle Royal

June 23, 1984
Belmont, NC – Armory
• Iron Man Mark Thunder vs. Sweet Ebony Diamond

June 29, 1984
Marion, NC – Rec Center
• Iron Man Mark Thunder vs. Jay Eagle
• Iron Man Mark Thunder &? vs. Jay Eagle & Lisa Darnell

June 30, 1984
Lincolnton, NC - Armory
• Iron Man Mark Thunder vs. Jay Eagle

July 1, 1984
Gastonia, NC – Hillview House
• 6 Man Tag: Iron Man Mark Thunder &?? vs. Jay Eagle, The Islander & Sweet Ebony Diamond

July 6, 1984
North Wilkesboro, NC – Armory
• Iron Man Mark Thunder vs. Jay Eagle
• Iron Man Mark Thunder &? vs. Jay Eagle & Lisa Darnell

July 7, 1984
Eden, NC – YMCA
• Iron Man Mark Thunder vs. Jay Eagle
• Iron Man Mark Thunder &? vs. Jay Eagle & Lis Darnell

July 14, 1984
Gastonia, NC – Clay Street Gym
• Iron Man Mark Thunder &? vs. Danny Jackson & Mitch Stallion

July 28, 1984
Belmont, NC – Armory
• Iron Man Mark Thunder &? vs. Ed Jones & Sweet Ebony Diamond

August 2, 1984
Monroe, NC – Armory
• Iron Man Mark Thunder &? vs. Danny Jackson & Sweet Ebony Diamond

August 4, 1984
Lincolnton, NC – Armory
• Iron Man Mark Thunder vs. Jay Eagle

August 9, 1984
Elgin, SC – Elgin Gym
• Iron Man Mark Thunder &? vs. Masked Invaders
• Iron Man Mark Thunder vs. Jay Eagle

August 11, 1984
Burlington, NC – North Park Community Center
• Iron Man Mark Thunder &? vs. Big Valley & Dave Forrester

August 17, 1984
Monroe, NC – Sweet Union Playhouse
• Iron Man Mark Thunder vs. Sweet Ebony Diamond

August 24, 1984
Spartanburg, SC – Armory
• Iron Man Mark Thunder vs. Jay Eagle

August 25, 1984
Gastonia, NC – Clay Street Gym
• Iron Man Mark Thunder&? vs. The Islanders & Sweet Ebony Diamond

August 31, 1984
Shallotte, NC – Armory
• Iron Man Mark Thunder vs. Jay Eagle
• Iron Man Mark Thunder vs. Miguel Feliciano

September 1, 1984
Wallace, NC – Armory
• Iron Man Mark Thunder vs. Jay Eagle
• Iron Man Mark Thunder vs. Miguel Feliciano

September 8, 1984
Pageland, SC- Bingo House
• Iron Man Mark Thunder vs. Sweet Brown Sugar

September 15, 1984
Lexington, NC – Churchland School Gym
• Iron Man Mark Thunder vs. Jay Eagle
• Battle Royal

September 16, 1984
Gastonia, NC – Hillview House
• Iron Man Mark Thunder &? vs. Jay Eagle & Billy Eagle

September 17,1984
Hartsville, GA – Shoal Creek Music Hall
• Iron Man Mark Thunder vs The Avenger
• Battle Royal

Match # 100
September 21, 1984
Monroe, NC – Sweet Union Music Hall
• Iron Man Mark Thunder &? vs. Terry Flynn & Mitch Stallion

September 22, 1984
Lenoir, NC – West Caldwell High School
• Iron Man Mark Thunder vs. Jay Eagle

September 23, 1984
North Wilkesboro, NC – Armory
• Iron Man Mark Thunder vs. Jay Eagle
• Battle Royal

September 29, 1984
North Wilkesboro, NC – Armory
• Iron Man Mark Thunder vs. Jay Eagle
• Battle Royal

WRESTLING
NORTH WILKESBORO ARMORY
SATURDAY, SEPT. 29 8:15 P.M.
Concessions: National Guard N.C.O. Club
8 BIG MATCHES

MAIN EVENT 10-Man Over The Top Rope Blindfold Battle Royal

Man Mountain Rick Link and Johnny Hunter (317 lbs.)
VS.
Masked Super Star and Buddy Shane

Girls' Match!!
Lisa Darnell VS. Jackie Bradley

Super Destroyer I & II
VS.
Mr. Wrestling and Joe Blevins

The Masked Assassins I & II
VS.
Sweet Ebony Diamond & Scufflin' Hillbillie

JACKIE BRADLEY

El Lobo VS. Jim Gallagher

Jim "Big Cat" Ladd VS. Ken Ruff

Chief Jay Eagle VS. "Iron Man" Thunder

TO SPONSOR WRESTLING CALL (704) 249-7909

October 6, 1984
Pageland, SC – Bingo Hall
CWA
• Indian Strap Match: Iron Man Mark Thunder vs. Jay Eagle

October 13, 1984
Gastonia, NC – Clay Street Gym
• Iron Man Mark Thunder &? vs. Hawaiian Giant & Sweet Ebony Diamond

October 20, 1984
Hartsville, SC – Armory
• Iron Man Mark Thunder &? vs. Jay Eagle & Mr. Wrestling

October 21, 1984
Gastonia, NC – Hillview House
• Iron Man Mark Thunder vs. Jim Holiday

October 22, 1984
Hartwell, GA – Shoal Creek Music Park
• Iron Man Mark Thunder vs. Jay Eagle

October 27, 1984
Mill Springs, NC – Polk Central High School
• Iron Man Mark Thunder beat Jay Eagle

November 3, 1984
Lenoir, NC – West Caldwell High School
• Iron Man Mark Thunder vs. Jay Eagle
• Iron Man Mark Thunder &? vs. Jay Eagle & Lisa Darnell

November 4, 1984
Gastonia, NC – Hillview House
• Iron Man Mark Thunder vs. Dale Starr

November 9, 1984
Wallace, NC – Armory
• Iron Man Mark Thunder &? vs. John Savage & Mitch Stallion

November 10, 1984
North Wilkesboro, NC – Armory
• Iron Man Mark Thunder vs. Jay Eagle
• Iron Man Mark Thunder vs. Jay Eagle & Lisa Darnell

November 12, 1984
Hartwell, GA – Shoal Creek Music Park
• Iron Man Mark Thunder &? vs. Jay Eagle & The Average

November 14, 1984
Atlanta, GA – WBTS Studio
George Championship Wrestling TV Taping
• Jerry Lawler & Jimmy Valiant beat George South & Italian Stallion

November 17, 1984
Spartanburg, SC – Brame High School
• George South vs. Donnie Gilbert

November 22, 1984
Pageland, SC – Bingo Hall
• George South &? vs. Jay Eagle & John Savage

November 25, 1984
Gastonia, NC – Hillview House
• George South &? vs. Dale Starr & Dave Porter
• George South &? Vs. Steve Young & Terry Flynn
• George South & &? Vs. John Savage & Billy Becker

November 27, 1984
Misenheimer, NC – Phiffier College
JCP TV Taping
• Buzz Tyler beat George South
• Assassin I beat George South

November 29, 1984
Atlanta, GA – WBTS Studio
George Championship Wrestling TV Taping
• Tommy Rich & Brad Armstrong beat George South & Italian Stallion
• Brian Adias & Ron Richie beat George South & Randy Barber

December 1, 1984
Union, SC – New High School
• George South vs. Jay Eagle

December 6, 1984
Harlem, GA – High School
• The Sheik beat George South

December 7, 1984
Camedon, SC – Armory
Atlantic Coast Wrestling
• George South vs. John Savage

December 8, 1984
Douglas, GA – Douglas Gym
• The Sheik beat George South

December 12, 1984
Atlanta, GA – WBTS Studio
George Championship Wrestling TV Taping
• Tommy Rich beat George South
• Ron Richie beat George South

December 15, 1984
Landrum, SC – Landrum High School
• George South &? Vs. Jay Eagle & Don Gilbert

December 22, 1984
Gastonia, NC – Clay Street Gym
• George South &? vs. Gerry Austin & Mitch Stallion

December 26, 1984
Tampa, FL
Championship Wrestling from Florida (Eddie Graham)
• The P.Y.T. Express beat George South &?

December 29, 1984
Belmont, NC – Armory
• George South &? Vs. The Islander & John Savage

1985

January 2, 1985
Shreveport, LA
Mid – South (Bill Watts)
TV Taping
• Kamala beat George South

January 5, 1985
Eden, NC – YMCA
Johnny Hunter
• George South vs. Chief Jay Eagle
• George South &? vs. Jay Eagle & John Savage
• Battle Royal

January 6, 1985
Drexel, NC – Community Center
• George South &? vs. The Islander & Terry Flynn

January 11, 1985
Hartwell, GA – Shoal Creek Music Park
• 6 Man Tag: George South & ?? vs. The Avenger, Mr. Wrestling & Bobcat Wright
• Battle Royal

January 12, 1985
Lincolnton, NC - Armory
• George South vs. Jay Eagle

January 16, 1985
Atlanta, GA – WBTS Studio
George Championship Wrestling TV Taping
• Tommy Rich beat George South
• Doug Sommers beat George South

January 17, 1985
Spartanburg, SC – Armory
• George South vs. Mr. Wrestling
• George South &? vs. The Montana Brothers

January 19, 1985
Tignall, GA – Gym
• George South vs. Bob Cat Brown
• Battle Royal

January 26, 1985
Chesnee, SC – YMCA
• George South vs. Jay Eagle
• George South &? vs. Jay Eagle & Hawaiian Giant

January 28, 1985
Augusta, GA – Armory
• George South &? vs. The Dirty White Boys

January 30, 1985
Atlanta, GA – WBTS Studio
George Championship Wrestling TV Taping
• Rock n Roll RPM's (Mike Davis & Tommy Lane) beat George South & Mike Starbuck
• Ron Star beat George South

February 1, 1985
Hartwell, GA – Shoal Creek Music Park
• George South vs. Mr. X
• George South &? vs. Montana Brothers

February 2, 1985
Concord, NC – Logan Center
• George South vs. Fred Carpenter
• Battle Royal
• George South &? vs. Jay Eagle & John Savage

February 8, 1985
Drexel, NC – Community Center
Piedmont Championship Wrestling (Dean Willard)
• 6 Man Tag: Iron Man Mark Thunder, The Islander & T. G. Rhodes
vs. Jay Eagle, Mr. Wrestling & Cowboy Terry Flynn

SPONSORED BY BURKE COUNTY WARRIORS
★ PIEDMONT CHAMPIONSHIP ★
WRESTLING
FRI. NITE—FEB. 8th
AT 8:00 P.M.
DREXEL COMMUNITY CENTER
DREXEL, NORTH CAROLINA
★ ★ MAIN EVENT — SIX MAN TAG TEAM ★ ★
Cowboy Terry Flynn, Mr. Wrestling
And Chief Jay Eagle
VS.
Iron Man Mark Thunder, The Islander
And T. G. Rhodes
★ ★ SEMI MAIN EVENT ★ ★
Rock-N-Roll Johnny Savage vs. Assassin II
LADIES MATCH
PENNY JACKSON vs. THE DIRTY BLONDE
★ ★ PLUS OTHER MATCHES ★ ★
SPONSORED BY DREXEL COMMUNITY CENTER
Tickets on Sale At: Drexel Community Center
ADVANCE TICKETS $4.00—DOOR TICKETS $5.00—CHILDREN 5-10 $2.50
★ ★ PROMOTER DEAN WILLARD ★ ★

February 9, 1985
Eden, NC – YMCA
Johnny Hunter
• Lou Thesz beat George South
• Street Fight: George South & Terry Slater vs. Jay Eagle & John Savage

Bouts set

Professional wrestling returns to the area tonight with a slate at the Eden (N.C.) YMCA gym. Belltime is 8:15 p.m. with six big championship matches, sponsored by the Y's men's club, scheduled.

The International World's Heavyweight Title will be on the line when Lou Thesz (right) risks his title against "Iron Man" thunder. Thesz has been world champ for 18½ years. North American Heavyweight champ Buddy Shane battle Mr. Wrestling No. 2 in a title match. Eastern United States heavyweight champion Johnny Hunter lays his title on the line against Mike Shane.

A "Street Fight" finds Mark Thunder and Terry Slater tackling Chief Jay Eagle and Johnny Savage, while 420-lb. Rick Link puts his World's Brass Knucks title on the line against newcomer Bob Brandon. Southern Heavyweight champ Chief Jay Eagle goes head to head again with Terry Slater in a title clash.

Doors open at 7 p.m. Plenty of free parking space is available.

Lou Thesz will wrestle in Eden tonight.

February 10, 1985
Colombia, SC
• George South & Terry Slater vs. Jay Eagle & John Savage

February 13, 1985
Atlanta, GA – WBTS Studio
George Championship Wrestling TV Taping
• Blue Devil beat George South
• Bob Roop & Ron Star beat George South & Henry Mills

February 15, 1985
Winder, GA – Armory
• George South vs. Jay Eagle

February 16, 1985
Tignall, GA – Gym
• George South vs. Jay Eagle

February 22, 1985
Batesburg, SC – Armory
• George South &? vs. Jay Eagle & Mr. Wrestling

February 23, 1985
Gastonia, NC – Clay Street Gym
• George South vs. Don Gilbert

Highway Run into the Midnight Sun

February 25, 1985
Hartwell, GA – Shoal Creek Music Park
• George South &? vs. The Assassins

February 27, 1985
Atlanta, GA – WBTS Studio
George Championship Wrestling TV Taping
• Rip Rogers beat George South
• Italian Stallion & Paul Diamond beat George South & Terry Ellis

March 2, 1985
Washington, GA – Middle School
• George South vs. Jay Eagle

March 9, 1985
Eden, NC – YMCA
Johnny Hunter
• George South vs Fred Carpenter
• 6 Man Tag: George South, Terry Slater &Rick Link Vs. Jay Eagle, Johnny Hunter & Jim Gallagher

March 13, 1985
Atlanta, GA – WTBS Studio
Georgia Championship Wrestling TV Taping
• Rip Rogers beat George South
• Scott Irwin & Kareem Muhammed beat George South &?

March 15, 1985
Batesburg, SC – Armory
• George South vs. Jay Eagle

March 16, 1985
Charleston, SC – Stall High School
• George South vs. Jay Eagle
• Battle Royal

March 21, 1985
Greenville, SC – Southside High School
• George South vs. Don Gilbert

March 23, 1985
Mocksville, NC – Rec Center
• George South vs. Jay Eagle
• George South &? vs. Jay Eagle & Rick Link

March 25, 1985
Hartwell, GA – Shoal Creek Music Hall
• George South &? vs. Assassins

March 27, 1985
Atlanta, GA – WTBS Studio
JCP TV Taping
• Magnum TA beat George South
• Tully Blanchard beat George South

March 29, 1985
Greenville, SC – Parker High School
• George South vs. Jay Eagle

March 30, 1985
Danielsville, GA – Elementary School
• George South vs. Jay Eagle

April 6, 1985
Atlanta, GA – WBTS Studio
JCP TV Taping
• Black Bart beat George South
• Ivan & Nikita Koloff beat George South & Greg Stone

CHAMPIONSHIP WRESTLING

SAT., APRIL 6 - 1985

8:15 P. M.

LOGAN CENTER

CONCORD, NORTH CAROLINA

Main Event ★ Steel Cage Match

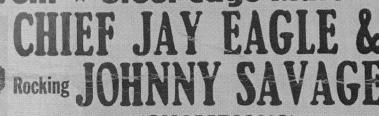

CHIEF JAY EAGLE &
Rocking **JOHNNY SAVAGE**

vs. (CHAMPIONS)

IRONMAN THUNDER
& HANDSOME TERRY SLADER

★ ★ **SEMI-MAIN EVENT** ★ ★

SWEET BROWN SUGAR
vs. 450 POUNDS ....
MAN EATING BEAST

PLUS 6 MAN TAG TEAM & OTHERS

BREAK DANCE CONTEST AT INTERMISSION FOR CASH PRIZE - EVERYONE WELCOME TO ENTER - FOR MORE INFORMATION CALL: 786-0613

Advance Tickets on Sale at Logan Center and Ski Racquet in Kannoplis

.April 6, 1985
Concord, NC – Logan Center
• George South &? vs. Jay Eagle & John Savage

April 13, 1985
Atlanta, GA – WBTS Studio
JCP TV Taping
• Magnum TA beat George South
• Ole & Arn Anderson beat George South & Rocky King

April 13, 1985
Lexington, NC – North Davidson High School
Johnny Hunter
• George South vs. Chief Jay Eagle
• George South vs. Rick Link

April 20, 1985
Atlanta, GA – WBTS Studio
JCP TV Taping
• Ole & Arn Anderson beat George South & Rocky King
• 6 Man Tag: Krusher Khruschev , Ivan & Nikita Koloff beat George South, &??

Match # 200
April 20, 1985
Tignall, GA – Gym
• George South vs. Jay Eagle

April 22, 1985
Camber, GA – Madison Co. Fairgrounds
• George South vs. John Savage

April 26, 1985
Hickory, NC – Elks Lodge
• George South vs. Terry Flynn

April 27, 1985
Atlanta, GA – WTBS Studio
JCP TV Taping
• Ron Garvin beat George South
• Bob Roop beat George South

May 3, 1985
Drexel, NC – Community Center
• George South vs. John Savage

May 11. 1985
Atlanta – WTBS Studio
JCP TV Taping

May 11, 1985
Macon, GA – Coliseum
JCP
• Ron Rossi beat George South

May 21, 1985
Greenwood, SC – Civic Center
JCP TV Taping
Ole & Arn Anderson beat George South &?

May 25, 1985
Elkin, NC – Armory
• George South vs. Jay Eagle

May 28, 1985
Lincolnton, NC – West Lincolnton High School
JCP TV Taping
• Buddy Landel beat George South
• Magnum TA beat George South

June 1, 1985
Atlanta, GA – WTBS Studio
JCP TV Taping
• NWA World Title: Ric Flair* beat George South
• Dick Slater beat George South

June 1, 1985
Lexington, NC – Cow Palace
Johnny Hunter
• George South vs. Jay Eagle

June 3, 1985
Hartwell, GA – Shoal Creek Music Hall
• George South &? vs. Jay Eagle & The Islander

June 8, 1985
Atlanta, GA – WTBS Studio
JCP TV Taping
• Manny Fernandez beat George South
• Thunderbolt Patterson & Pez Whatley beat George South &?

June 9, 1985
Roanoke, VA – Civic Center
JCP
• The Barbarian beat George South

June 10, 1985
Tignall, GA – Gym
• George South vs. Jay Eagle

June 11, 1985
Shelby, NC – Rec Center
• NWA World Title: Ric Flair* beat George South
• Sam Houston beat George South

June 15, 1985
Lexington, NC – Cow Palace
Johnny Hunter
• George South vs. Jay Eagle

June 16, 1985
Asheville, NC – Civic Center
JCP
• Road Warriors (Hawk & Animal) beat George South & Ron Rossi
• Buddy Landel beat George South

June 18, 1985
Burgaw, NC – Pender High School
JCP
• George South vs. Pat Tanaka

June 22, 1985
Lexington, NC – Cow Palace
Johnny Hunter
• Texas Death Match: George South vs. Jay Eagle
• George South &? vs. Jay Eagle, Johnny Hunter & Rick Link

July 6, 1985
Highland, SC – Civic Center
• George South vs. Jay Eagle

July 12, 1985
Columbia, SC – Township Auditorium
JCP
- Gene Ligon beat George South

July 13, 1985
Atlanta, GA – WTBS Studio
JCP TV Taping
- Buzz & Brett Sawyer beat George South &?

July 13, 1985
Florence, SC – American Legion Stadium
JCP
- George South vs. Ricky Reeves

July 16, 1985
Gaffney, SC – Timken Center
JCP TV Taping
- NWA World Tag Team Title: Rock & Roll Express* (Ricky Morton & Robert Gibson)
beat George South & Gene Ligon (5:26)

July 19, 1985
Tignall, GA – Gym
- George South &? vs. Jay Eagle & John Savage

July 20, 1985
Lexington, NC – Cow Palace
Johnny Hunter
- George South vs. Mitch Stallion

July 27, 1985
Atlanta, GA – WTBS Studio
JCP TV Taping
- Abdullah the Butcher beat George South
- Tully Blanchard beat George South

July 27, 1985
Greensboro, NC – Greensboro Coliseum
JCP
- Sam Houston beat George South

July 29, 1985
Greenville, SC – Memorial Auditorium
JCP
- Sam Houston beat George South

July 30, 1985
Salisbury, NC – Catawba College
JCP
- Magnum TA beat George South

August 3, 1985
Lock Heart, SC – High School
- George South &? vs. Mad Bull & Jim Tucker

August 6, 1985
Rock Hill, SC – Winthrop Coliseum
JCP TV Taping
- Nikita Koloff & Krusher Khrushchev beat George South & Denny Brown
- Buddy Landel beat George South

August 9, 1985
Hanea Park, SC
- George South vs. Jay Eagle

Jason Freeman & George South

August 10, 1985
Atlanta, GA – WTBS Studio
JCP TV Taping
• Harley Race beat George South

August 10, 1985
Florence, SC – Legion Stadium
JCP
• George South vs. Ben Alexander

August 11, 1985
Asheville, NC – Civic Center
JCP
• George South vs. Ron Rossi

August 12, 1985
Greenville, SC – Memorial Auditorium
JCP TV Taping
• Superstar Billy Graham beat George South
• The Barbarian & Abdullah the Butcher beat George South &?

August 13, 1985
Shelby, NC – Community Center
JCP TV Taping
• Abdullah the Butcher & The Barbarian beat George South & Denny Brown
• The Rock & Roll Express beat George South &?

August 16, 1985
Charleston, SC – County Hall
JCP
• George South vs. Lee Ramsey

August 24, 1985
Atlanta, GA – WTBS Studio
JCP TV Taping
• Buzz & Brett Sawyer beat George South &?

August 24, 1985
Greensboro, NC – Greensboro Coliseum
JCP
• Stoney Burke beat George South

August 27, 1985
Greenwood, SC – Civic Center
JCP TV Taping
• Krusher Khruschev beat George South
• Ole & Arn Anderson beat George South &?

August 30, 1985
Charleston, SC – County Hall
JCP
• George South vs. Ron Rossi

August 31, 1985
Florence, SC – Legion Stadium
• George South &? vs. Rising Sun I & II

September 1, 1985
Atlanta, GA – WTBS Studio
JCP TV Taping
• Denny Brown beat George South
• Sam Houston beat George South

September 3, 1985
Gaffney, SC – Timken Center
JCP TV Taping
• Billy Graham beat George South

September 10, 1985
Shelby, NC – Community Center
JCP TV Taping
• NWA World Tag Team Title: Rock & Roll Express* beat George South & Golden Terror
• Abdullah the Butcher beat George South

September 14, 1985
Columbus, GA – Municipal Auditorium
JCP
• George South beat Mac Jeffers

September 15, 1985
Atlanta, GA – WTBS Studio
JCP TV Taping
• Tully Blanchard beat George South

September 15, 1985
College Park, GA – Henderson's Arena
JCP
• George South vs. Italian Stallion

September 17, 1985
Greenwood, SC – Civic Center
JCP TV Taping
• The Barbarian & Abdullah the Butcher beat George South &?
• Jimmy Valiant & Rocky King beat George South &?

September 20, 1985
Columbia, SC – Township Auditorium
JCP
• Starship Eagle beat George South

September 22, 1985
Atlanta, GA – WTBS Studio
JCP TV Taping
• Buddy Landell w/ JJ Dillion beat George South

September 28, 1985
Columbus, GA – Municipal Auditorium
JCP
• Ricky Reeves beat George South

September 29, 1985
Atlanta, GA – WTBS Studio
JCP TV Taping
• Denny Brown beat George South
• Don Kernodle beat George South

October 8, 1985
Shelby, NC – Rec Center
JCP TV Taping
• The Rock & Roll Express beat George South &?
• The Midnight Express w/ Jim Cornette beat George South &?

October 11, 1985
Macon, GA – Coliseum
JCP
• George South vs. Stoney Burke

October 13, 1985
Atlanta, GA – WTBS Studio
JCP TV Taping
• Abdullah the Butcher beat George South

October 15, 1985
Greenwood, SC – Civic Center
JCP
• George South vs. Italian Stallion

October 20, 1985
Savannah, GA – Civic Center
JCP
• George South vs. Stoney Burke

October 27, 1985
Atlanta, GA – WTBS Studio
JCP TV Taping
• Rock & Roll Express beat George South &?
• 6 Man Tag: Krusher Khruschev, Ivan & Nikita Koloff beat George South &??

October 28, 1985
Marietta, GA – Cobb Co. Civic Center
JCP
• The Barbarian w/ Paul Jones beat George South

November 10, 1985
Atlanta, GA – WTBS Studios
JCP TV Taping
• The Barbarian beat George South
• The Road Warriors beat George South &?

November 11, 1985
Fayetteville, NC – Cumberland County Memorial Auditorium
JCP
• George South vs. Don Kernodle

November 12, 1985
Shelby, NC – Rec Center
JCP TV Taping
• Buddy Landel beat George South
• Midnight Express w/ Jim Cornette beat George South &?

November 19, 1985
Greenwood, SC – Civic Center
JCP TV Taping
• Midnight Express w/ Jim Cornette beat George South &?

November 24, 1985
Atlanta, GA – WTBS Studio
JCP TV Taping
• Midnight Express w/ Jim Cornette beat George South &?

November 25, 1985
Easley, SC – Easley High School
JCP
• George South vs. Ron Garvin

December 1, 1985
Atlanta, GA – WTBS Studios (9am)
JCP TV Taping
• Terry Taylor beat George South
• The Barbarian beat George South

December 1, 1985 (3pm)
Asheville, NC – Civic Center
JCP
• George South beat Gerald Finley

December 1, 1985 (8pm)
Greenville, SC – Memorial Auditorium
JCP
- George South beat Gerald Finley

December 8, 1985
Atlanta, GA – WTBS Studio
JCP TV Taping
- Rock & Roll Express beat George South &?

December 9, 1985
Greenwood, SC – Civic Center
- Ivan & Nikita Koloff beat George South &?

December 11, 1985
Rock Hill, SC – Winthrop Coliseum
JCP TV Taping
- Ivan & Nikita Koloff beat George South & Pat Tanaka
Match # 300
- The Barbarian beat George South

December 14, 1985
Atlanta, GA – WTBS Studio
JCP TV Taping
- Magnum TA beat George South
- Rock & Roll Express vs. George South &?
- Rock & Roll Express vs. George South &?

December 15, 1985
Atlanta, GA – WTBS Studio
JCP TV Taping
- Arn Anderson beat George South
- Black Bart beat George South

December 15, 1985
Marietta, GA – Cobb Co. Civic Center
JCP
- Italian Stallion beat George South

December 28, 1985
Greensboro, NC – Greensboro Coliseum
Gate: $116,000
JCP TV Taping
- NWA World Tag Team Titles: Rock & Roll Express* beat George South & Gene Ligon (2:59)

December 29, 1985
Asheville, NC – Civic Center
Gate: $13,000
JCP
- Don Kernodle beat George South

1986

January 7, 1986
Spartanburg, SC – Memorial Auditorium
JCP TV Taping
Gate: $10,000
• Ron Bass & Don Kernodle beat George South & Mark Fleming

January 13, 1986
Greenwood, SC – Flora Civic Center
JCP TV Taping
• Jimmy Valiant beat George South

January 19, 1986
Asheville, NC – Civic Center
JCP
• Jim Jeffers beat George South

January 21, 1986
Shelby, NC – Community Center
JCP TV Taping
• Black Bart beat George South

January 26, 1986
Atlanta, GA – WTBS Studio
JCP TV Taping
• The Barbarian w/Paul Jones beat George South
• Rock & Roll Express beat George South &?

January 26, 1986
Columbus, GA – Civic Center
JCP
George South vs. Italian Stallion

January 28, 1986
Rock Hill, SC – Winthrop Coliseum
JCP
• Road Warriors (Hawk & Animal) beat George South & Mike Somaini

February 4, 1986
Spartanburg, SC – Memorial Auditorium
JCP TV Taping
• Black Bart beat George South
• Rock & Roll Express beat George South &?

February 8, 1986
Atlanta, GA – WTBS Studio
JCP TV Taping
• Baron Von Raschke beat George South
• Ron Bass beat George South

February 16, 1986
Macon, GA – Macon Coliseum
JCP
• Black Bart beat George South

February 17, 1986
Fayetteville, NC – Cumberland County Memorial Auditorium
JCP TV Taping
Gate: $30,731
• Tully Blanchard w/ JJ Dillion beat George South
• Rock & Roll Express beat George South &?

February 21, 1986
Sumpter, SC – Civic Center
JCP
- George South vs. Rocky King

February 22, 1986
Atlanta, GA – WTBS Studio
JCP TV Taping
- Tijo Khan w/ Paul Jones beat George South
- Denny Brown beat George South

February 23, 1986
Atlanta, GA – WTBS Studios (9am)
JCP TV Taping
- Barron Von Raschke w/ Paul Jones beat George South
- Rock & Roll Express beat George South &?

February 25, 1986
Greenwood, SC – Flora County Civic Center
JCP TV Taping
Gate: $13,300
- Black Bart beat George South
- George South &? vs. Gene Ligon & Todd Bridges
- Tijo Khan & The Barbarian w/ Paul Jones beat George South &?

March 1, 1986
Conway, SC – High School
JCP
- Pez Whatley beat George South

March 4, 1986
Spartanburg, SC – Memorial Auditorium att. sell out
Gate: $11,700
JCP TV Taping
- Jimmy Valiant beat George South
- Ron Garvin beat George South

March 5, 1986
Raleigh, NC – Dorton Arena
Gate: $18,600
JCP
- Ben Alexander beat George South

March 6, 1986
Lenoir, NC – West Caldwell High School
JCP
- Rocky King beat George South

March 8, 1986
Atlanta, GA – WTBS Studios (9am)
JCP TV Taping
- Leo Burke beat George South

March 9, 1986
Savannah, GA – Civic Center
JCP
Pat Tanaka beat George South

March 10, 1986
Greenville, SC – Memorial Auditorium
JCP
- Midnight Express (Bobby Eaton & Dennis Condrey) w/ Jim Cornette beat George South & Don Kernodle
- Jimmy Valiant beat George South

March 14, 1986
Bassett, VA - High School
JCP
Rocky Kernodle beat George South

March 16, 1986
Asheville, NC – Civic Center
JCP
• Rocky Kernodle beat George South

March 17, 1986
Greenville, SC – Memorial Auditorium
Gate: $16,000
JCP
• Rocky Kernodle beat George South

March 18, 1986
Mooresville, NC -Lake Norman High School
Gate: $14,000
JCP TV Taping
• Tully Blanchard w/ JJ Dillion beat George South
• Rock & Roll Express beat George South &?

March 19, 1986
Raleigh, NC – Dorton Arena
Gate: $14,600
JCP
• Manny Fernandez beat George South

March 20, 1986
Harrisonburg, VA – Harrisonburg High School
JCP
• George South vs. Don Kernodle

March 22, 1986
Rocky Mount, VA – High School
JCP
• George South vs. Italian Stallion

March 23, 1986
Greenville, SC – Memorial Auditorium
JCP TV Taping
• Arn Anderson & Tully Blanchard / JJ Dillion beat George South &?
• George South vs. Todd Bridges
• Jimmy Garvin w/ Precious beat George South

March 27, 1986
Norfolk, VA – Norfolk Scope
Gate: $34,000
JCP
• Denny Brown beat George South

March 29, 1986
Greensboro, NC – Greensboro Coliseum att, 12,339
Gate: $95,000
JCP
• Nelson Royal beat George South

April 1, 1986
Spartanburg, SC – Memorial Auditorium
JCP TV Taping
• Hector Guerrero beat George South
• 6 Man Tag: Ric Flair, Arn Anderson & Tully Blanchard w/ JJ Dillion beat George South &??

April 2, 1986
Misenheimer, NC – Pheifer College
JCP
- Hector Guerrero beat George South

April 4, 1986
Albany, GA – Civic Center
JCP
- Nelson Royal beat George South

April 7, 1986
Gaffney, SC – Limestone College
Gate: $89,000
JCP TV Taping
- Hector Guerrero beat George South

April 8, 1986
Greenwood, SC – Flora Civic Center
JCP TV Taping
- Manny Fernandez & Hector Guerrero beat George South & Denny Brown
  - Black Bart beat George South

April 10, 1986
Kershaw, NC – North Central High School
JCP
- Rocky Kernodle beat George South

April 12, 1986
Atlanta, GA – WTBS Studios
JCP TV Taping
- Manny Fernandez & Hector Guerrero beat George South & Tony Zane
  - Jimmy Garvin w/ Precious beat George South

April 15, 1986
Rock Hill, SC – Winthrop Coliseum
JCP TV Taping
- Nelson Royal & Sam Houston beat George South & Gene Ligon
  - Shaska Whatley beat George South

April 18, 1986
Charleston, SC – St. Mary's High School
JCP
Nelson Royal beat George South

April 21, 1986
Greenwood, SC – Civic Center
JCP TV Taping
- Midnight Express w/ Jim Cornette beat George South &?
  - Hector Guerrero beat George South

April 26, 1986
Atlanta, GA – WTBS Studios
JCP TV Taping
- NWA World Tag Team Title: Midnight Express (Bobby Eaton & Dennis Condrey)* w/ Jim Cornette beat George South & Rocky King

April 28, 1986
Forest City, NC – Chase High School
JCP
- Rocky King beat George South

April 29, 1986
Macon, GA – Macon Coliseum
JCP
- George South vs. Frank Dusek

May 2, 1986
Norfolk, VA – Scope Arena
JCP
- George South vs. Rocky Kernodle

May 5, 1986
Greenville, SC – Memorial Auditorium
JCP
- Rocky Kernodle beat George South

May 6, 1986
Spartanburg, SC – Memorial Auditorium
JCP TV Taping
- Midnight Express w/ Jim Cornette beat George South &?
- The Road Warriors w/ Paul Ellering beat George South &?

May 7, 1986
Rhonda, NC – High School
JCP
- George South vs. Rocky Kernodle

May 8, 1986
Kannapolis, NC – Northwest Cabarrus High School
JCP
- George South vs. Golden Terror

May 10, 1986
Florence, SC – Legion Stadium
JCP
- George South vs. Brody Chase

May 13, 1986
Richburg, SC – Lewisville High School
JCP TV Taping
- Arn Anderson & Tully Blanchard w/ JJ Dillion beat George South &?
- Todd Champion beat George South

May 17, 1986
Union, SC – Union County Stadium
JCP
- George South vs. Hector Guerrero

May 23, 1986
Columbia, SC – Township Auditorium
JCP
Don Kernodle beat George South

May 24, 1986
Atlanta, GA – WTBS Studios
JCP TV Taping
- Steve Regal beat George South
- Midnight Express w/ Jim Cornette beat George South &?

May 27, 1986
Greenwood, SC – Flora Civic Center
Gate: $9,500
JCP TV Taping
- Ivan & Nikita Koloff beat George South & Mike Schiavone
- Tully Blanchard & Steve Regal beat George South & Rocky Kernodle

May 31, 1986
Atlanta, GA – WTBS Studio
JCP TV Taping
- Shaska Whatley w/ Paul Jones beat George South

June 2, 1986
Fayetteville, NC – Cumberland County Memorial Auditorium
JCP
- Rocky King beat George South

June 3, 1986
Spartanburg, SC – Memorial Auditorium
JCP
- Shaska Whatley & Baron Von Raschke w/ Paul Jones beat George South &?

June 5, 1986
WADESBORO, SC – Anen Jr High School
JCP
- Nelson Royal beat George South

June 7, 1986
Atlanta, GA – WTBS Studio
JCP TV Taping
- Arn Anderson & Tully Blanchard w/ JJ Dillion beat George South &?
- Rock & Roll Express beat George South &?

June 10, 1986
Salisbury, NC – Catawba College
JCP TV Taping
- Rock & Roll Express beat George South &?
- Warlord w/ Baby Doll beat George South

June 14, 1986
Atlanta, GA – WBTS Studio
JCP TV Taping
- 6 Man Tag: Krusher Khruschev, Ivan & Nikita Koloff beat George South &??

June 17, 1986
Greenwood, SC – Flora Civic Center
JCP TV Taping
- Steve Regal beat George South
- Jimmy Garvin w/ Precious beat George South

June 22, 1986
Atlanta, GA – WTBS Studios
JCP TV Taping
- NWA World Tag Team Title: Midnight Express (Bobby Eaton & Dennis Condrey)*w/ Jim Cornette beat George South

June 22, 1986
Asheville, NC – Civic Center
JCP
- George South vs. Ben Alexender

June 23, 1986
Fayetteville, NC – Cumberland Arena
JCP TV Taping
- 6 ManTag: The Barbarian, Shaska Whatley & Baron Von Raschke w/ Paul Jones beat George South &??
- Midnight Express w/ Jim Cornette beat George South &?

June 24, 1986
Rock Hill, SC – Winthrop Coliseum
Gate: $16,000
JCP TV Taping
- Krusker Khrushchev, Ivan & Nikita Koloff beat George South, Rocky King, & Italian Stallion
- Rock & Roll Express beat George South &?

June 26, 1986
Troy, NC – West Montgomery High School
JCP
- George South vs. Rocky King

June 27, 1986
Atlanta, GA – WTBS Studio
JCP TV Taping
- Midnight Express w/ Jim Cornette beat George South &?
  - Black Bart beat George South

June 28, 1986
Savannah, GA – Civic Center
JCP
- The Warlord beat George South

June 29, 1986
Greenville, SC – Memorial Auditorium
JCP
- The Warlord beat George South

July 6, 1986
Raleigh, NC – Civic Center
Gate: $74,000
JCP
- Sam Houston beat George South

July 15, 1986
Gaffney, SC – Limestone College
Gate: $17,800
JCP TV Taping
- Steve Regel & Jimmy Garvin w/ Precious beat George South &?
  - Jimmy Garvin w/ Precious beat George South

July 22, 1986
Greenwood, SC – Flora County Civic Center
JCP TV Taping
- The Warlord w/ Baby Doll beat George South
- Midnight Express w/ Jim Cornette beat George South &?

July 24, 1986
Hendersonville, NC – Dietz Field
JCP
- The Warlord beat George South

July 26, 1986
Atlanta, GA – WTBS Studio
JCP TV Taping
- Buddy Landel w/ Bill Dundee beat George South

July 28, 1986
Wilmington, NC – Legion Stadium att. 2,000
Gate: $15,900
JCP
- Krusher Khruschev beat George South

July 29, 1986
Rock Hill, SC – Winthrop Coliseum
JCP TV Taping
- Rock & Roll Express beat George South & Ben Alexander
  - Buddy Landel w/ Bill Dundee beat George South

August 9, 1986
Atlanta, GA – WTBS Studio
JCP TV Taping
- Warlord w/ Baby Doll beat George South
- Arn & Ole Anderson beat George South &?

August 16, 1986
Atlanta, GA – WTBS Studio
JCP TV Taping
- Kansas Jayhawks (Bobby Jaggers & Dutch Mantel) beat George South &?
- Buddy Landel & Bill Dundee beat George South &?

August 24, 1986
Atlanta, GA – WTBS Studio
JCP TV Taping
- Ronnie Garvin beat George South
- Arn & Ole Anderson beat George South &?

August 26, 1986
Greenville, SC – Memorial Auditorium
- Steve Regal beat George South

August 27, 1986
Rock Hill, SC – Winthrop Coliseum
JCP TV Taping
- Shaska Whatley beat George South
- Baron Von Rashke beat George South
- George South & Rocky King beat Randy & Bill Mulkey

September 1, 1986
Greenville, SC – Memorial Auditorium
JCP
- Rocky King beat George South

September 2, 1986
Spartanburg, SC – Memorial Auditorium
JCP
- Shaka Whatley w/ Paul Jones beat George South

September 4, 1986
Cincinnati, OH – Cincinnati Gardens
JCP
- George South vs. Todd Champion

September 5, 1986
Richmond, VA – Richmond Coliseum
Gate: $42,000
JCP
- Italian Stallion beat George South

September 6, 1986
Baltimore, MD – Arena
JCP
- Denny Brown beat George South

September 7, 1986
Asheville, NC – Civic Center
JCP
- Nelson Royal beat George South

September 12, 1986
Richwood, WV – Junior High School
JCP
- Sam Houston beat George South

September 13, 1986
Conway, SC- High School
JCP
- Rocky Kernodle beat George South

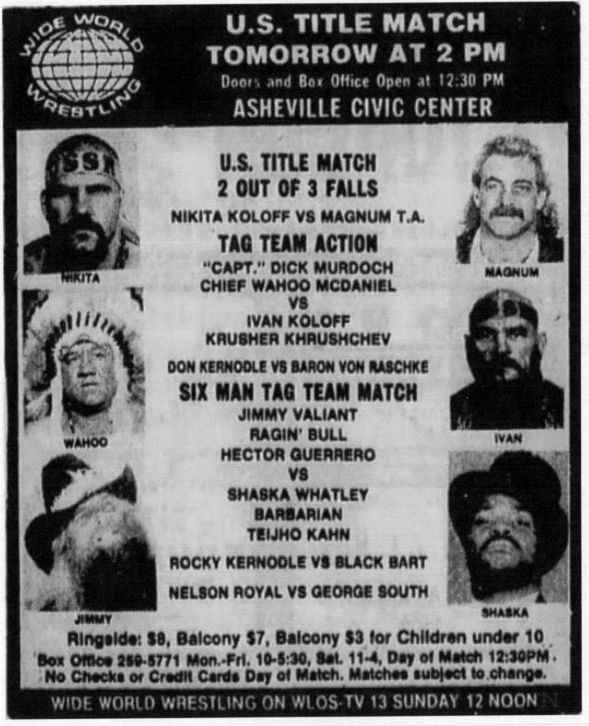

September 14, 1986
Atlanta, GA – WTBS Studio
JCP TV Taping
- Midnight Express w/ Jim Cornette beat George South &?
- Ivan Koloff & Krusher Khruschev beat George South &?

September 20, 1986
Columbus, GA – Civic Center
JCP
- George South vs. Vernon Deaton

September 26, 1986
Concordia, KS – Bryant Gymnasium
JCP/ Central States
- George South, Rocky King, & Rufus R. Jones vs. Teijo Khan & The Mod Squad (Basher & Spike)

September 26, 1986
Kanas City, MO – Memorial Hall
JCP/ Central States
- The Mod Squad & Colt Steele beat George South, Rufus R. Jones & Mitch Snow

September 29, 1986
Wichita, KS – Century II
JCP/ Central States
- The Mod Squad w/ JD Costello beat George South & Rocky King

September 30, 1986
St. Joseph, MO – Civic Arena
JCP/ Central States
- The Mod Squad w/ JD Costello beat George South & Rocky King

October 2, 1986
Des Moines, IA – Memorial Auditorium
JCP/ Central States
- The Mod Squad w/ JD Costello beat George South & Rocky King

October 4, 1986
Fulton, MO – High School
JCP/Central States
- George South & Rocky King vs. The Mod Squad w/ JD Costello

October 5, 1986
Louisiana, MO – High School
JCP/Central States
- George South & Rocky King vs. The Mod Squad w/ JD Costello

October 7, 1986
Emporia, KS – Civic Auditorium
JCP/Central States
- George South & Rocky King vs. The Mod Squad w/ JD Costello

October 8, 1986
Chilicothe, MO – Fieldhouse
JCP/Central States
- George South & Rocky King vs. The Mod Squad w/ JD Costello

October 9, 1986
Union, MO – High School
JCP/Central States
- George South & Rocky King vs. The Mod Squad w/ JD Costello

October 10, 1986
Quincy, IL – High School
JCP/Central States
- George South & Rocky King vs. The Mod Squad w/ JD Costello

October 11, 1986
Topeka, KS – Auditorium
JCP/Central States
- George South & Rocky King vs. The Mod Squad w/ JD Costello

October 13, 1986
Scott City, KS – High School
JCP/Central States
- George South & Rocky King vs. The Mod Squad w/ JD Costello

October 14, 1986
Hoisington, KS – Civic Auditorium
JCP/Central States
• George South & Rocky King vs. The Mod Squad w/ JD Costello

October 15, 1986
Tangansine, KS – Middle School
JCP/Central States
• George South & Rocky King vs. The Mod Squad w/ JD Costello

October 16, 1986
Arkansas City, KS – Cauley Auditorium
JCP/Central States
• George South & Rocky King vs. The Mod Squad w/ JD Costello

October 18, 1986
Ft. Scott, KS - Civic Center
JCP/Central States
• George South vs. Mitch Snow

October 19, 1986
Des Moines, IA
JCP/ Central States
• George South vs. Mark Fleming

October 20, 1986
Wichita, KS – Century II Civic Center
JCP/Central States
• 6 Man: George South, Rocky King, & Rufus R. Jones vs. Colt Steele & The Mod Squad (Basher & Spike) w/ JD Costello

October 21, 1986
Joplin, MO – Municipal Auditorium
JCP/Central States
• 6 Man: George South, Rocky King, & Rufus R. Jones vs. Colt Steele & The Mod Squad (Basher & Spike) w/ JD Costello

October 22, 1986
Topeka, KS – Auditorium
JCP/Central States
• 6 Man: George South, Rocky King, & Rufus R. Jones vs. Colt Steele & The Mod Squad (Basher & Spike) w/ JD Costello

October 23, 1986
Concordia, KS – Bryant Gymnasium
JCP/ Central States
• 6 Man: George South, Rocky King, & Rufus R. Jones vs. Teijo Khan & The Mod Squad (Basher & Spike)

October 24, 1986
Kanas City, KA – Memorial Hall
JCP/ Central States
• George South beat Colt Steele

October 26, 1986
St. Joseph, MO – Civic Arena
JCP/ Central States
• George South beat Mark Fleming

October 27, 1986
St. Joseph, MO – Civic Center
JCP/Central States
• George South vs. Colt Steele

October 28, 1986
Minneapolis, KS – High School
JCP/Central States
• George South &Rocky King vs. The Mod Squad w/ JD Costello

November 1, 1986
Ft. Levanworth, KS – Fieldhouse
JCP/Central States
- George South & Rocky King vs. Tijo Khan & Mark Fleming

November 2, 1986
Omaha, NE – Omaha Civic Auditorium
JCP/ Central States
- The Mod Squad & Superstar Bill Dundee beat George South, Rocky King, & Italian Stallion

November 3, 1986
Kirksville, MO – Missouri State College
JCP/Central States
- George South& Rocky King vs. Tijo Khan & Mark Fleming

November 6, 1986
Montgomery City, MO
JCP/Central States
- 6 Man: George South, Rocky King & Italian Stallion vs. Colt Steele & The Mod Squad w/ JD Costello

November 7, 1986
Kanas City, MO – Memorial Hall
JCP/ Central States
- Mod Squad Spike beat George South

November 8, 1986
Ft. Scott, KS – Civic Center
JCP/Central States
- 6 Man: George South, Rocky King & Italian Stallion vs. Colt Steele & The Mod Squad w/ JD Costello

November 9, 1986
Topeka, KS – Memorial Auditorium
JCP/Central States
- George South vs. Mod Squad Spike

November 11, 1986
Hutchinson, KS – Convention Hall
JCP/ Central States
- George South vs. Mod Squad Spike

November 13, 1986
Ft. Riley, KS – Fieldhouse
JCP/Central States
- 6 Man: George South, Rocky King & Italian Stallion vs. Colt Steele & The Mod Squad w/ JD Costello

November 14, 1986
Kanas City, MO – Memorial Hall
JCP/ Central States
- Bob Brown beat George South
- The Mod Squad beat George South & Rocky King (dq)

November 15, 1986
Greenville, IL – High School
JCP/Central States
- George South& Rocky King vs. The Mod Squad

November 16, 1986
St. Louis, MO – St. Louis Arena
JCP/ Central States
- The Mod Squad & Colt Stele beat George South, Rufus R. Jones & Rocky King

November 17, 1986
Waterloo, IL – High School
JCP/Central States
- George South & Rocky King vs. The Mod Squad

November 19, 1986
Salina, KS
JCP/Central States
•   George South vs. Mod Squad Basher

November 21, 1986
Kanas City, MO – Memorial Hall
JCP/ Central States
•   Colt Steele beat George South

November 22, 1986
Des Moines, IA – Memorial Auditorium
JCP/ Central States
•   George South vs. Colt Stele

November 23, 1986
Topeka, KS – Municipal Auditorium
JCP/Central States
•   George South vs. Colt Steele

November 25, 1986
Joplin, MO – Municipal Auditorium
JCP/Central States
•   George South vs. Colt Steele

November 26, 1986
Malta Bend, MO – High School
JCP/Central States
George South vs. Mod Squad Spike

November 27, 1986
Kanas City, MO – Memorial Hall
JCP/ Central States
•   George South beat Colt Steele

November 28, 1986
Pratt, KS – Community College
JCP/Central States
•   George South vs. Colt Steele

November 29, 1986
Wichita, KS – Century II Center
JCP/Central States
•   George South vs. Colt Steele

November 30, 1986
St. Joseph, MO – Civic Arena
JCP/ Central States
•   George South, Rocky King & Rufus R. Jones beat The Mod Squad & Mark Fleming (22:00)

WRESTLING
SUNDAY NOVEMBER 30 — 8 P.M.

ST. JOSEPH CIVIC ARENA

MAIN EVENT

SAM
HOUSTON
vs.
BULLDOG
BOB BROWN

CENTRAL STATES TAG TITLE
Champions
DAVE PETERSON
TODD CHAMPION
vs.
THE WARLORD
COLT STEELE
Managed by BABY DOLL

RUFUS R. JONES
ROCKY KING
GEORGE SOUTH
vs.
THE MOD SQUAD
MARK FLEMING
Managed by J.B COSTELLO

MITCH
SNOW
vs.
TEIJHO
KAHN

THE ITALIAN STALLION
DENNY BROWN
vs.
THUNDERFOOT
NO 1 & NO. 2

ADMISSION RINGSIDE — $10, Gen. Adm — $8 (Children under 10 Gen. Adm — $4)
ADVANCE TICKET SALES AT ST JOSEPH CIVIC ARENA

Brown defeats Houston

Bulldog Bob Brown took down Sam Houston at 21 minutes in the feature match of Sunday's Central States Wrestling Alliance action at the St. Joseph Civic Arena.

In the no-disqualification match, Brown used a pair of brass knuckles to nail Houston.

Earlier, Rufus R. Jones, Rocky King and George South teamed to defeat the Mod Squad and Mark Fleming. Jones pinned Fleming at 22 minutes.

The Central States Champions Dave Peterson and Todd Champion defeated the War Lords and Colt Steele to retain their title. Peterson body pressed Steele at 19 minutes for the victory.

Mitch Snow pinned Teijo Kahn with a side suplex at 12 minutes and the Italian Stallion and Denny Brown defeated Thunderfoot I and II in other matches.

Nov.30,1986 - St.Joseph,Missouri

Match # 500
December 2, 1986
Jefferson City, MO – Lincoln College
JCP/ Central States
- Warlord w/ Baby Doll beat George South

December 9, 1986
Spartanburg, SC – Memorial Auditorium
JCP TV Taping
- Midnight Express w/ Jim Cornette beat George South & Rocky King
  - Jimmy Garvin w/ Precious beat George South

December 12, 1986
Charlotte, NC – Old Charlotte Coliseum
Gate: $80,000
JCP TV Taping
- Midnight Express w/ Jim Cornette beat George South & Rocky King

December 13, 1986
Atlanta, GA – WTBS Studios
JCP TV Taping
- Midnight Express w/ Jim Cornette beat George South & Rocky King
  - Arn & Ole Anderson beat George South & Rocky King

December 15, 1986
Greenville, SC – Memorial Auditorium
JCP TV Taping
- Rick Rude & Manny Fernandez w/ Paul Jones beat George South & Rocky King
- 6 Man: Midnight Express & Big Bubba Rogers w/ Jim Cornette beat George South, Rocky King &?

December 25, 1986
Greenville, SC – Memorial Auditorium att.3,566
Gate: $10,700
JCP
- Thunderfoot 1 & 2 beat George South & Rocky King
Note: Fan appreciation night. All ticket $3

December 27, 1986
Norfolk, VA – Scope
JCP
- George South & Rocky King vs. Alan West & Eddie Roberts

1987

January 3, 1987
Atlanta, GA – WTBS Studio
JCP TV Taping
• Midnight Express w/ Jim Cornette beat George South & Rocky King
• Lighting Express (Brad Armstrong & Tim Horner) beat George South &?

January 6, 1987
Spartanburg, SC – Memorial Auditorium
JCP
• Vladimir Petrov w/ Ivan Koloff beat George South

January 10, 1987
Atlanta, GA – WTBS Studio
JCP TV Taping
• Bill Dundee beat George South
• Vladimir w/ Ivan Koloff beat George South
• Ivan Koloff & Vladimir Petrov beat George South & Rocky King

January 13, 1987
Columbia, SC – Township Auditorium
JCP TV Taping
• Midnight Express w/ Jim Cornette beat George South & Rocky King
• Rock & Roll Express beat George South & Rocky King

January 16, 1987
Columbus, GA – Civic Center
JCP
• George South vs. Rocky King

January 17, 1987
Atlanta, GA – WTBS Studio
JCP TV Taping
• Lex Luger bet George South
• Midnight Express w/ Jim Cornette beat George South & Rocky King

January 24, 1987
Atlanta, GA – WTBS Studio
JCP TV Taping
• 6 Man: Big Budda Rogers & The Midnight Express w/ Jim Cornette beat George South &??
• Tim Horner beat George South

January 27, 1987
Rock Hill, SC – Winthrop Coliseum
JCP TV Taping
• Arn Anderson & Tully Blanchard w/ JJ Dillion beat George South & Rocky King

January 31, 1987
Atlanta, GA – WTBS Studio
JCP TV Taping
• Jimmy Garvin w/ Precious beat George South
• Lex Luger & Tully Blanchard w/ JJ Dillion beat George South & Rocky King

February 2, 1987
Greenville, SC – Memorial Auditorium
JCP
• Shaska Whatley beat George South

February 3, 1987
Spartanburg, SC – Memorial Auditorium
JCP TV Taping
• Lex Luger w/ JJ Dillion beat George South
• Ronnie Garvin & Barry Windham beat George South & Rocky King

February 4, 1987
Elberton, GA – Middle School
JCP
• George South & Rocky King vs. Randy Mulkey & Brody Chase

February 5, 1987
Clinton, SC – YMCA
JCP
• George South vs. Brody Chase

February 10, 1987
Columbia, SC – Township Auditorium
JCP TV Taping
• Bob Armstrong beat George South
• George South vs. John Savage

February 11, 1987
Marion, NC – McDowell High School
JCP
• Bob Armstrong beat George South

February 14, 1987
Atlanta, GA – WTBS Studio
JCP TV Taping
• Big Bubba Rogers w/ Jim Cornette beat George South

February 14, 1987
Charlotte, NC – Charlotte Coliseum
JCP
• Jimmy Garvin w/ Precious beat George South

February 20, 1987
North Wilkesboro, NC – YMCA
JCP
• Nelson Royal beat George South

February 21, 1987
Atlanta, GA – WTBS Studio
JCP TV Taping
• Ivan Koloff & Dick Murdoch beat George South & Rocky King

February 21, 1987
Gainesville, GA – Civic Center
JCP
• George South & Rocky King vs. Randy Mulkey & Brody Chase

February 23, 1987
Greenville, SC – Memorial Auditorium
JCP
• George South & Rocky King vs. Randy & Bill Mulkey

February 24, 1987
Rock Hill, SC – Winthrop Coliseum
JCP TV Taping
• Ivan Koloff & Dick Murdoch beat George South & Rocky King
• 6 Man: Ivan Koloff, Vladimir Petrov & Dick Murdoch beat George South &??

February 27, 1987
Albany, GA – Civic Center
JCP
• George South & Rocky King vs. John Savage & Randy Mulkey

February 28, 1987
Atlanta, GA – WTBS Studio
JCP TV Taping
• Big Bubba Rogers w/ Jim Cornette beat George South
• Tim Horner beat George South

March 4, 1987
Spartanburg, SC – Memorial Auditorium
JCP TV Taping
• 6 Man: Ivan Koloff, Vladimir Petrov & Dick Murdoch beat George South &??
• Lex Luger w/ JJ Dillion beat George South

March 7, 1987
Atlanta, GA – WTBS Studio
JCP TV Taping
• The Mod Squad w/ Bill Dundee bet George South &?

March 9, 1987
Fayetteville, NC – Cumberland Arena
JCP
• Bob & Brad Armstrong beat George South &?

March 15, 1987
Huntington, WV – Civic Center
JCP
• Lazor-Tron beat George South

March 16, 1987
Lenoir, NC – West Caldwell High School
JCP
• Lazor-Tron beat George South

March 17, 1987
China Grove, NC – High School
JCP TV Taping
• Midnight Express w/ Jim Cornette beat George South &?
• Bob & Brad Armstrong beat George South &?

March 18, 1987
Monroe, NC – High School
JCP
• George South vs. Italian Stallion

March 19, 1987
Oakwood, VA – High School
JCP
• George South vs. Italian Stallion

March 20, 1987
Norwood, NC – High School
JCP
• George South vs. Italian Stallion

March 22, 1987
Columbus, GA – Municipal Auditorium
JCP
• Barron Von Raschke beat George South

March 23, 1987
Greenville, SC – Municipal Auditorium
JCP TV Taping
• Rock & Roll Express beat George South &?

March 24, 1987
Lincolnton, NC – High School
JCP TV Taping
• NWA World Tag Team Title: Manny Fernandez & Rick Rude* w/ Paul Jones beat George South & Rocky King

March 25, 1987
Oxford, NC – J.F. Webb High School
JCP
• George South vs. Todd Champion

March 26, 1987
Macon, GA - Coliseum
JCP
• George South vs. Todd Champion

March 27, 1987
Atlanta, GA – The Omni att. 4,500
JCP
• Denny Brown beat George South

March 28, 1987
Atlanta, GA – WTBS Studio
JCP TV Taping
• Randy & Bill Mulkey beat The Gladiators (George South & Gary Royal)
Note: This match was the birth of Mulkey Mania

March 29, 1987
Charlotte, NC – Charlotte Coliseum
JCP
• Tim Horner beat George South

March 30, 1987
Biscoe, NC – East Montgomery High School
JCP
• Barron Von Raschke beat George South

March 31, 1987
Gastonia, NC – Hunter Huss High School
JCP TV Taping
• Ronnie & Jimmy Garvin w/ Precious beat George South &?
• Bobby Jaggers beat George South

April 2, 1987
Robbins, NC – North Moore High School
JCP
• The Gladiators vs. Italian Stallion & Bobby Jaggers

April 7, 1987
Spartanburg, SC – Memorial Auditorium
JCP TV Taping
• The Road Warriors beat George South & Gary Royal
• New Breed beat George South & Rocky King

April 10, 1987
Baltimore, MD – Arena att. 9,300
Gate: $111,000
JCP Crockett Cup Day 1
• George South & Steve Keirn drew Mike Graham & Nelson Royal (20:00)

April,12, 1987
Charlotte, NC – Charlotte Coliseum
JCP
• George South vs. Nelson Royal

April 16, 1987
Harrisonburg, VA – High School
JCP
• George South vs. Lazon-Tron

April 17, 1987
Macon, GA – Coliseum
JCP
• George South vs. Rocky King

April 18, 1987
Roanoke, VA – Civic Center
JCP
• Brad Armstrong beat George South

April 19, 1987
Huntington, WV – Civic Center
JCP
• Jimmy Garvin w/ Precious beat George South

April 21, 1987
Columbia, SC – Township Auditorium
JCP TV Taping
• Ivan Koloff & Vladimir Petrov beat George South & Rocky King
• Brad Armstrong beat George South

April 26, 1987
Rock Hill, SC – Winthrop Coliseum
JCP TV Taping
• Jimmy Garvin w/Precious beat George South
• Ron Garvin beat George South

May 4, 1987
Greenville, SC – Memorial Auditorium
JCP
• George South vs. Thunderfoot I

May 5, 1987
Spartanburg, SC – Memorial Auditorium
JCP TV Taping
• Rock & Roll Express vs. George South &?

May 6, 1987
Cheraw, SC – High School
JCP
• George South vs. Italian Stallion

May 11, 1987
Newton, NC – High School
JCP
• George South vs. Thunderfoot I

May 12, 1987
Columbia, SC – Township Auditorium
JCP
• George South vs. Shawn Royal

May 14, 1987
Charleston, SC – High School
JCP
• George South vs. Dexter Wesscote

May 15, 1987
Johnson City, TN – Freedom Hall
JCP
• George South vs. Nelson Royal

May 19, 1987
Raleigh, NC – Dorton Arena
JCP TV Taping
• Ron Garvin beat George South
• Todd Champion beat George South

May 20, 1987
Savannah, GA – Civic Center
JCP
• George South vs. Tim Horner

May 21, 1987
Bessemer City, NC – High School
JCP
• Bob Armstrong beat George South

May 22, 1987
Macon, GA – Coliseum
JCP
• The Gladiators vs. Italian Stallion & Rocky King

May 23, 1987
Atlanta, GA – WTBS Studio
JCP TV Taping
• Fabulous Freebirds beat George South &?

May 23, 1987
Columbus, GA – Civic Center
JCP
• George South vs. Mike Forest

May 24, 1987
Wilmington, NC – Legion Stadium
JCP
• George South vs. Mark Fleming

May 26, 1987
Greenwood, SC – Civic Center
JCP TV Taping
• Tully Blanchard w/JJ Dillion beat George South
• Midnight Express w/ Jim Cornette beat The Gladiators

May 28, 1987
Syler City, NC – High School
JCP
• Gladiator # 2 vs. Rocky King

May 30, 1987
Florence, SC – Legion Stadium
JCP
• The Gladiators vs. Jimmy Valiant & Lazon-Tron

May 31, 1987
Asheville, NC – Civic Center
JCP
• Barron Von Raschke beat George South

June 1, 1987
Fayetteville, NC – Cumberland Arena
JCP
• Gladiator # 2 vs. Mark Fleming

June 2, 1987
Spartanburg, SC – Memorial Auditorium
JCP
Midnight Express w/Jim Cornette beat The Gladiators

June 6, 1987
Atlanta, GA – WBTS Studio
• Barry Windham beat Gladiator # 2 (0:15)

June 11, 1987
Albany, GA – Civic Center
JCP
• Gladiator # 2 vs. Denny Brown

NWA WRESTLING
ALBANY JAMES H. GRAY, SR. CIVIC CENTER
THURSDAY, JUNE 11th   8:15 P.M.

MAIN EVENT

"THE RAGING BULL"
VLADIMIR PETROV   VS.   "ROCK & ROLL EXPRESS"

★ ★ ★ ★ ★ ★ ★ ★ ★ ★ ★ ★

FOUR MAN TAG TEAM EVENT

"THE NEW BREED"   "BOOGIE WOOGIE MAN"
CHRIS CHAMPION   JIMMY VALIANT
AND SHAWN ROYAL   VS.   AND LAZERTRON

SPECIAL FEATURE EVENT

GLADIATOR #1   VS.   NELSON ROYAL

PLUS

GLADIATOR #2   VS.   DENNY BROWN

LARRY STEPHENS VS.   PLUS   RANDY SAVAGE VS.
DEXTER WESCOTT   AND   RICKY NELSON

TICKETS:
RINGSIDE $10⁰⁰   PLUS
GEN. ADMISSION $8⁰⁰   SERVICE CHARGE
CHILDREN UNDER 12 $4⁰⁰
FOR INFORMATION: (912)432-2230

Albany Civic Center

June 12, 1987
Norfolk, VA – Norfolk Scope
Gate: $52,000
JCP
• Tommy Angel beat Gladiator # 2

June 13, 1987
Florence, SC – Legion Stadium
JCP
• Gladiator # 2 vs. John Savage
• Battle Royal

June 14, 1987 (2pm)
Asheville, NC – Civic Center
JCP
• Gladiator # 2 vs. Lazertron

June 14, 1987 (8pm)
Charlotte, NC – Old Charlotte Coliseum
Gate: $62,700
JCP
• Jimmy Valiant & Lazertron beat Gladiator # 1 & 2

June 15, 1987
Greenville, SC – Memorial Auditorium
JCP
• Lazertron beat Gladiator # 2

June 16, 1987
Fayetteville, NC – Cumberland Arena
JCP
• Midnight Express w/ Jim Cornette beat The Gladiators

June 18, 1987
Columbus, GA – Civic Center
JCP
• Gladiator # 2 vs. Kendell Windham

June 22, 1987
Greenville, SC – Memorial Auditorium
JCP TV Taping
• Jimmy Valiant beat Gladiator # 2
• Midnight Express w/Jim Cornette beat The Gladiators

June 23, 1987
Carnsville, GA – High School
JCP
• Gladiator # 2 vs. Rocky King

June 26, 1987
Greenville, SC – Memorial Auditorium
JCP
• Gladiator # 2 vs. Larry Stevens

June 28, 1987
Rock Hill, SC – Winthrop Coliseum
JCP TV Taping
• NWA World Tag Team Title: Rock & Roll Express* beat Gladiator # 2 & Rick Sullivan
• Jimmy Garvin beat Gladiator # 2

June 29, 1987
Greenville, SC – Memorial Auditorium
JCP
• Gladiator # 2 beat Ricky Nelson

June 30, 1987
Columbia, SC – Township Auditorium
JCP
• Gladiator # 2 vs. Kendell Windham

July 2, 1987
Raleigh, NC – Dorton Arena
JCP
• 8 Man Battle Royal

July 5, 1987
Charleston, WV – Civic Center
Gate: $95,000
JCP Great American Bash Tour
• Italian Stallion beat Gladiator # 2

July 7, 1987
Hickory, NC – High School
JCP
• Gladiator # 2 vs. John Savage

July 11, 1987
Greensboro, NC – Greensboro Coliseum
JCP
• Gladiator # 2 vs. Barry Windham

July 12, 1987
Asheville, NC – Civic Center
JCP Great American Bash
• Gladiator # 2 beat Rick Savage
• George South vs. Todd Champion

July 14, 1987
Gaffney, SC – Limestone College
JCP Great American Bash Tour
• George South beat Gladiator # 1

July 15,1987
Atlanta, GA – WTBS Studio
JCP TV Taping
• Jimmy Valiant beat Gladiator # 2

July 16, 1987
Johnson City, TN – Freedom Hall
Gate: $72,000
JCP Great American Bash Tour
• The Gladiators vs. Italian Stallion & Todd Champion

July 17, 1987
Norfolk, VA – The Scope
Gate; $180,000
JCP Great American Bash Tour
• The Gladiators vs. Italian Stallion & Todd Champion
Note: This event broke the all-time gate record for the state of Virginia.

July 18, 1987
Charlotte, NC – Memorial Stadium att. 15,000
Gate: $174,000
JCP Great American Bash Tour
• Jimmy Valiant, Lazer-Tron, & Kendall Windham beat Gladiator # 1 & 2, and Sean Royal

July 23, 1987
Harrisonburg, VA – High School
JCP Great American Bash Tour
• Italian Stallion beat Gladiator # 2

July 29, 1987
Atlanta, GA – WTBS Studio
JCP TV Taping
• Midnight Express w/ Jim Cornette beat The Gladiators
• Lex Luger w/JJ Dillion beat George South

August 2, 1987
Huntington, WV – Civic Center
Gate: $34,000
JCP
• Gladiator # 2 vs. John Savage

August 4, 1987
Spartanburg, SC – Memorial Auditorium
JCP TV Taping
• Ronnie Garvin beat Gladiator # 2
• Midnight Express w/ Jim Cornette beat The Gladiators

August 5, 1987
Atlanta, GA – WTBS Studio
JCP TV Taping
• Gladiator # 2 vs. Shawn Royal

August 9, 1987
Atlanta, GA – The Omni att. 14,100
Gate: $80,000
JCP
• Denny Brown beat George South

August 21, 1987
Macon, GA – Macon Coliseum
JCP TV Taping
• Ivan Koloff & Manny Fernandez beat George South & Rocky King (3:35)

August 22, 1987
Philadelphia, PA – Convention Hall
Gate: $48,000
JCP
• Lazertron beat Gladiator # 2

August 25, 1987
Rock Hill, SC – Winthrop Coliseum
JCP TV Taping
• The Barbarian, Ivan Koloff & Manny Fernandez beat George South, Ricky Nelson & Rocky King

August 26, 1987
Atlanta, GA – WTBS Studio
JCP TV Taping
• Lex Luger w/ JJ Dillion beat George South

September 1, 1987
Spartanburg, SC – Memorial Auditorium
JCP
Ivan Koloff w/ Paul Jones beat George South

September 2, 1987
Cherryville, NC – Rudsill Stadium
JCP
• Gladiator # 2 vs. Mod Squad Basher

September 3, 1987
Farmville, VA – Longwood College
JCP
• Gladiator # 2 vs. Gary Royal

September 4, 1987
Albany, GA – Civic Center
JCP
• Gladiator # 2 beat Larry Stevens

September 6, 1987
Asheville, NC – Civic Center
JCP TV Taping
• NWA World Tag Team Title: Rock & Roll Express* beat Gladiator # 1 & 2 (0:45)
Ronnie Garvin beat George South

September 7, 1987
Greenville, SC – Memorial Auditorium
JCP
• Denny Brown beat Gladiator # 2

September 8, 1987
Amherst, VA – High Scholl
JCP
• Gladiator # 2 vs. Mark Fleming

September 10, 1987
Raleigh, NC – Dorton Arena
JCP
• Ivan Koloff w/ Paul Jones beat George South

September 11, 1987
Charleston, WV – Civic Center
JCP
• George South beat Mark Fleming

September 12, 1987
Greensboro, NC – Greensboro Coliseum att. 3,725
JCP
• The Barbarian beat George South

September 18, 1987
Columbus, GA – Civic Center
JCP
• Gladiator # 2 vs. Chance McQuade

September 19, 1987
Charlotte, NC – Old Coliseum
JCP TV Taping
• The Barbarian beat George South
• The Warlord beat George South
• The Midnight Express (Bobby Eaton & Stan Lane) beat George South & Ricky Nelson

September 20, 1987
Atlanta, GA – The Omni
JCP
• Todd Champion beat Gladiator # 2

September 21, 1987
Winnsboro, SC – Fairfield Central High School
JCP
• Gladiator # 2 drew Ricky Nelson (10:00)

September 22, 1987
Fayetteville, NC – Cumberland Co. Memorial Auditorium
• Gladiator # 2 beat Larry Stevens

September 24, 1987
Macon, GA – Coliseum
JCP
• Gladiator # 2 vs. Mod Squad Basher

September 26, 1987
Clayton, GA – High School
JCP
• Gladiator # 2 vs. Thunderfoot I

September 28, 1987
Darlington, SC – High School
JCP
• George South vs. The Warlord

September 29, 1987
Misenheimer, NC – Pheifer College
JCP
• Gladiator # 2 vs. Chris Champion

September 30, 1987
Atlanta, GA – WTBS Studio
JCP TV Taping
• Kevin Sullivan beat George South

October 2, 1987
Asheboro, NC – High School
JCP
• George South &? vs. Samurai Warriors

October 6, 1987
Spartanburg, SC – Memorial Auditorium
JCP TV Taping
• Arn Anderson & Tully Blanchard w/ JJ Dillion beat George South & Rocky King
• Ivan Koloff & Mighty Wilber w/ Paul Jones beat George South & Rocky King

Jason Freeman & George South

October 9, 1987
Albany, GA – Civic Center
JCP
• The Gladiators vs. Cuban Connection
• Big Bubba w/ Jim Cornette beat George South

October 13, 1987
Shelby, NC – Rec Center
JCP TV Taping
• Barry Windham beat George South
• Jimmy Valiant & Bugsy McGraw beat The Gladiators

October 14, 1987
Atlanta, GA – WTBS Studio
JCP
• NWA World Tag Team Title: Arn Anderson & Tully Blanchard * w/JJ Dillion beat George South & Rocky King (3:12)
• Ivan Koloff & The Warlord w/ Paul Jones beat George South &?
• The Midnight Express w/ Jim Cornette best George South &?

October 18, 1987
Roanoke, VA - Civic Center
JCP
• Kendall Windham beat George South

October 20, 1987
Fayetteville, NC – Cumberland Arena
JCP
• Ron Garvin beat George South

October 27, 1987
Columbia, SC – Township Auditorium
JCP TV Taping
• Midnight Express beat George Royal & George South
• Kevin Sullivan beat George South

October 28, 1987
Atlanta, GA – WTBS Studio
JCP Taping
• Michael Hayes & Jimmy Garvin w/ Precious beat George South &?

November 1, 1987
Salisbury, MD – Wicomico Co. Youth & Civic Center
JCP – UWF TV Taping
• Rock & Roll Express beat Gladiator # 1 & 2
• Ivan Koloff & The Warlord beat George South & Gary Royal

November 3, 1987
Winston- Salem, NC- Coliseum
JCP
• Jimmy Valiant & Bugsy McGraw beat The Gladiators

November 6, 1987
Marion, NC – McDowell High School
JCP
• The Gladiators vs. Italian Stallion & Denny Brown

November 8, 1987
Atlanta, GA – The Omni
Gate: $43,000
JCP
• Handicap Match: Ron Garvin beat Gladiator # 1 & 2

November 10, 1988
Jacksonville, NC – high School
JCP
• George South vs. Rocky King

November 11, 1987
Burlington, NC – High School
JCP
• George South vs. Italian Stallion

November 12, 1987
Kings Mountain, NC – Community Center
• Jimmy Valiant & Bugsy McGraw beat George South & Thunderfoot # 1

November 14, 1987
Huntington, WV – Civic Center
JCP
• Gladiator # 2 & Thunderfot # 1 vs. Italian Stallion & Kendell Windham

November 16, 1987
Wadesboro, NC – High School
JCP
• Jimmy Valiant & Bugsy McGraw vs. Gladiator # 2 & Thunderfoot # 1

November 17, 1987
Columbia, SC – Township Auditorium
JCP TV Taping
• Rick Steiner beat George South (2:28)
• Jimmy Valiant & Bugsy McGraw beat George South & Thunderfoot # 1

November 18, 1987
Richburg, SC – High School
JCP
• Gladiator # 2 & Thunderfoot # 1 vs. David Isley & Tommy Angel

November 23, 1987
Bennettsville, SC
JCP
• Jimmy Valiant & Bugsy McGraw beat George South & Thunderfoot # 1

November 28, 1987
Atlanta, GA – WTBS Studio
JCP TV Taping
• Michael Hayes & Jimmy Garvin w/ Precious beat George South &?

December 1, 1987
Dallas, NC – North Gaston High School
JCP
• Nelson Royal beat George South

December 3, 1987
Atlanta, GA – WTBS Studio
JCP TV Taping
• Steve Williams beat Gladiator # 2
• The Midnight Express w/ Jim Cornette beat George South &?

December 5, 1987
Clinton, NC – YMCA
JCP
• George South vs. Denny Brown

December 6, 1987
Charlotte, NC – Old Charlotte Coliseum
JCP TV Taping
• Sting beat Gladiator # 2
• The Road Warriors beat Gladiator # 2 & Thunderfoot # 1
• Steve Williams beat Gladiator # 2

December 9, 1987
Atlanta, GA – WTBS Studio
JCP TV Taping
• Michael Hayes & Jimmy Garvin w/ Precious beat Gladiator # 2 &?

December 10, 1987
Raleigh, NC -Dorton Arena
JCP TV Taping
• Eddie Gilbert beat George South (4:34)

December 11, 1987
Columbus, GA - Civic Center
JCP
• Gladiator # 2 vs. Ricky Santana

December 12, 1987
Greensboro, NC – Greensboro Coliseum att. 6,000
JCP TV Taping
• The Warlord beat George South
• Eddie Gilbert beat George South

December 13, 1987
Albany, GA -Civic Center
Gate: $22,000
JCP TV Taping
• NWA United States Tag Team Title: Midnight Express* beat George South & Denny Brown
• Sting beat George South
• The Warlord w/ Paul Jones beat George South
• Bunkhouse Stampede

December 26, 1987
Richmond, VA – Coliseum
JCP TV Taping
• Pez Whatley & Tiger Conway Jr. beat The Gladiators
• Kevin Sullivan beat George South

December 27, 1987
Charleston, WV – Civic Center
Gate: $31,000
JCP
• Black Bart beat George South
• 25 Man Bunkhouse Stampede

1988

January 2, 1988
Greensboro, NC – Greensboro Coliseum
JCP
- Brad Armstrong & Tim Horner beat Gladiator # 1 & 2

January 3, 1988
Baltimore, MD – Baltimore Arena
Gate: $72,000
JCP TV Taping
- Sting & Barry Windham beat George South & Gary Royal (2:33)
- The Road Warriors w/ Paul Ellering beat George South & Gary Royal

January 4, 1988
Ceno Gordo, NC – High School
JCP
- George South vs. John Savage

January 10, 1988
Charlotte, NC – Charlotte Coliseum
JCP TV Taping
- Sting beat Gladiator # 2
- Barry Windham beat George South

January 12, 1988
North Wilkesboro, NC – YMCA
JCP
- Gladiator # 2 vs. Rocky King

January 13, 1988
Atlanta, GA – WTBS Studio
JCP
- Michael Hayes & Jimmy Garvin w/ Precious beat George South & Tony Surber
- Dick Murdoch w/ Jim Cornette beat George South

January 14, 1988
Norfolk, VA – Norfolk Scope
JCP TV Taping
- Rock & Roll Express beat George South & Gene Ligon (2:32)

January 15, 1988
Richmond, VA – The Scope
JCP
- Arn Anderson beat George South

January 19, 1988
Charleston, SC – St. Andrews High School
JCP
- Jimmy Valiant beat George South

January 20, 1988
Atlanta, GA – WTBS Studio
JCP
- Arn Anderson beat George South

January 25, 1988
Greenville, SC – Memorial Auditorium
JCP
- Butch Miller beat George South

January 26, 1988
Raleigh, NC – Dorton Arena
JCP TV Taping
- The Warlord & The Barbarian beat George South & Gary Royal
- Larry Zbyszko w/ Baby Doll beat George South

January 28, 1988
Harrisonburg, VA – High School
JCP
• Rick Steiner beat George South

January 30, 1988
Greensboro, NC – Greensboro Coliseum
JCP TV Taping
• Rick Steiner & Mike Rotundo beat George South & Gary Royal

February 1, 1988
Newton, NC – High School
JCP
• Gladiator # 2 vs. Kendall Windham

February 3, 1988
Laurinburg, NC – St. Andrews College
JCP
• Gladiator # 2 vs. Tiger Conway Jr

February 5, 1988
Johnson City, TN – Freedom Hall
JCP
• Dick Murdoch beat George South

February 7, 1988
Fayetteville, NC – Cumberland Arena
JCP TV Taping
• Rick Steiner & Mike Rotundo w/ Kevin Sullivan beat George South & Gary Royal
• The Warlord & The Barbarian beat George South & Gary Royal

February 8, 1988
Macon, GA – Coliseum
JCP
• George South vs. The Terminator (Johnny Ace)

February 10, 1988
Atlanta, GA – WTBS Studio
JCP
• Shane Douglas beat George South
• Sting, Barry Windham & Lex Luger beat George South, Gary Royal & Tommy Angel (3:22)

February 12, 1988
Walterboro, SC – Rec Center
JCP
• George South vs. John Savage

February 13, 1988
Bentonville, SC – High School
JCP
• George South vs. John Savage

February 14, 1988
Greenville, SC – Memorial Auditorium
JCP
• The Terminator beat George South

February 15, 1988
Atlanta, GA – WTBS Studio
JCP TV Taping
• Eddie Gilbert beat George South
• Arn Anderson & Tully Blanchard w/ JJ Dillion beat George South & Gary Royal

February 19, 1988
Richmond, VA – Coliseum
JCP TV Taping
• Shane Douglas & Ricky Santana beat George South & Gary Royal
• Ivan Koloff, The Warlord & The Barbarian w/ Paul Jones beat George South &??

February 22, 1988
Fayetteville, NC – Cumberland Arena
JCP TV Taping
• The Warlord & The Barbarian w/ Paul Jones beat George South &?

February 23, 1988
Savannah, GA – Civic Center
JCP
The Warlord, The Barbarian & Ivan Koloff w/ Paul Jones beat George South &??

February 24, 1988
Atlanta, GA – WTBS Studio
JCP TV Taping
• Shane Douglas & Ricky Santana beat George South &?
• Barry Windham beat George South

February 26, 1988
Lynchburg, VA – Armory
JCP
George South vs. Gary Royal

February 29, 1988
Washington, NC – High School
JCP
• George South vs. Chris Champion

March 1, 1988
Gainesville, GA – Georgia Mountain Center
JCP
• George South vs. The Terminator

March 3, 1988
Harrisonburg, VA – High School
JCP
• George South vs. The Terminator

March 5, 1988
Louisville, KY – Comm. Convention Center
JCP TV Taping
• Sting, Lex Luger & Barry Windham beat George South &??
• The Warlord & The Barbarian w/ Paul Jones beat George South & Gary Royal
• Tully Blanchard w/ JJ Dillion beat George South

March 6, 1988
Kingsport, TN – Dobyns-Bennett Dome
JCP
• George South vs. Nelson Royal

March 7, 1988
Macon, GA – Macon Coliseum
JCP
• George South double count out Nelson Royal

March 8, 1988
Columbus, GA – Municipal Auditorium
JCP
• George South vs. Nelson Royal

March 12, 1988
Norfolk, VA – Scope
JCP TV Taping
• The Fantastic's (Bobby Fulton & Tommy Rogers beat Cruel Connection I & II (Gary Royal & George South)

March 14, 1988
Fayetteville, NC – Cumberland Arena
JCP
• George South vs. Nelson Royal

March 17, 1988
Canton, NC – High School
JCP
• Cruel Connection II vs. Rocky King

March 18, 1988
Franklin, NC – High School
JCP
• Cruel Connection II vs. Italian Stallion

March 19, 1988
Oakwood, VA – High School
JCP
• Cruel Connection II vs. Ron Simmons

March 21, 1988
Hallsboro, NC – High School
JCP
• Cruel Connection I & II vs. Nelson Royal & Jimmy Valiant

March 22, 1988
Athens, GA – High School
JCP
• Cruel Connection II vs. Pez Whatley

March 23, 1988
Gastonia, NC – High School
JCP
• Cruel Connection II vs. Rick Steiner
March 25, 1988
Bisco, NC – High School
JCP
Cruel Connection II vs. Nelson Royal

March 26, 1988
Farmville, VA – Longwood College
JCP
Cruel Connection I & II vs. Italian Stallion & Kendell Windham

March 28, 1988
Greenville, SC – Memorial Auditorium
JCP
• Nelson Royal beat George South

March 29, 1988
North Wilkesboro, NC – YMCA
JCP
• Ron Simmons beat Cruel Connection II

March 30, 1988
Atlanta, GA – WTBS Studio
JCP
• Mike Rotundo, Rick Steiner & Kevin Sullivan beat George South, Larry Davis & Bob Riddle

March 31, 1988
Dergetown, SC – High School
JCP
• Cruel Connection II vs. Rocky King

April 1, 1988
Huntington, WV – Civic Center
JCP
• Cruel Connection II vs. Ron Simmons

April 2, 1988
Charlotte, NC – Charlotte Coliseum
JCP TV Taping
• Sting beat Cruel Connection II
• Steve Williams beat George South

April 4, 1988
Columbus, GA – Municipal Auditorium
JCP
• Cruel Connection II vs. Chris Champion

April 5, 1988
Macon, GA – Coliseum
JCP
• Cruel Connection II vs. Tony Surber

April 6, 1988
Atlanta, GA – WTBS Studio
JCP TV Taping
• Sting beat Cruel Connection II

April 7, 1988
Kings Mountain, NC – Community Center
JCP
• Cruel Connection II vs. Curtis Thompson

April 13, 1988
Atlanta, GA – WTBS Studio
JCP TV Taping
• Midnight Express w/ Jim Cornette beat Cruel Connection I & II
• Ricky Santana beat George South

April 17, 1988
Asheville, NC – Civic Center
JCP TV Taping
• The Fantastics beat Cruel Connection I & II
• Arn Anderson & Tully Blanchard w/ JJ Dillion beat George South & Gary Royal
• Dick Murdoch beat George South

April 21, 1988
Harrisonburg, VA – High School
JCP
• Chris Champion beat Cruel Connection II

April 22, 1988
Greenville, SC – Memorial Auditorium
JCP Crockett Cup Round One
• Luke Williams & Butch Miller bet George South & Garry Royal (7:20)

April 24, 1988
Charleston, WV – Civic Center
JCP TV Taping
• Sting & Nikita Koloff beat Cruel Connection I & II

April 26, 1988
Chattanooga, TN – UTC Arena
JCP
• NWA United States Title: Barry Windham* beat George South

April 27, 1988
Atlanta, GA – WTBS Studio
JCP TV Taping
• Al Perez beat George South (3:17)

May 2, 1988
Bishopville, SC – McGraw Stadium
JCP
• Cruel Connection I & II vs. Jimmy Valiant & Bugsy McGraw

May 3, 1988
Shallotte, NC – High School
JCP
• Cruel Connection II vs. Mighty Wilbur

May 5, 1988
Raleigh, NC – Dorton Arena
JCP TV Taping
• Nikita Koloff & Steve Williams beat Cruel Connection I & II
• Steve Williams beat George South

Highway Run into the Midnight Sun

May 6, 1988
Marion, NC – McDowell High School
JCP
Cruel Connection II vs. Ricky Santana

May 12, 1988
Walterboro, SC – Rec Center
JCP
• Cruel Connection II vs. Ricky Santana

May 14, 1988
Florence, SC – Legion Stadium
JCP
• Cruel Connection II vs. Jimmy Valiant

May 15, 1988
Asheville, NC – Civic Center
JCP TV Taping
• Arn Anderson & Tully Blanchard w/ JJ Dillion beat Cruel Connection I & II
• Sting & Nikita Koloff beat George South & Gary Royal

May 17, 1988
Columbia, SC – Township Auditorium
JCP
• Bugsy McGraw beat Cruel Connection II

May 19, 1988
Fisherville, VA – Augusta Expo
JCP
• Jimmy Valiant & Bugsy McGraw beat Cruel Connection I & II

May 20, 1988
Norfolk, VA – The Scope
JCP TV Taping
• Al Perez w/ Gary Hart beat George South
• Ivan Koloff, The Warlord & The barbarian w/ Paul Jones beat George South, Gary Royal & Rocky King

May 21, 1988
Richmond, VA – Richmond Coliseum
JCP
• Ron Simmons & Bugsy McGraw beat beat Cruel Connection I & II

May 23, 1988
Hartsville, SC – Kellytown Stadium
JCP
• Tiger Conway Jr beat George South

May 24, 1988
Hillsville, VA – High School
JCP
• Butch Miller & Luke Williams beat George South & Gary Royal

May 30, 1988
Union, SC – High School Football Stadium
JCP
• Bugsy McGraw beat Cruel Connection II

May 31, 1988
Erwin, NC – High School
JCP
• Chris Champion beat George South

June 2, 1988
Bluefield, WV – Brush Fork National Guard Armory
JCP
• Ron Simmons beat Cruel Connection II

June 3, 1988
Richmond, VA – Richmond Coliseum
JCP
• Mighty Wilber beat Cruel Connection II

June 5, 1988
Roanoke, VA – Civic Center
JCP TV Taping
• Arn Anderson & Tully Blanchard w/ JJ Dillion beat George South & Gary Royal
• Sting, Nikita Koloff & Steve Williams beat Cruel Connection I & II &?
• Ron Garvin beat George South
• Steve Williams & Sting beat George South & Gary Royal

June 6, 1988
Fayetteville, NC – Cumberland Arena
JCP
• Ron Simmons beat George South

June 7, 1988
Columbia, SC – Township Auditorium
JCP
George South vs. Rip Morgan

June 9, 1988
Dunn, NC – High School
JCP
• Chris Champion beat Cruel Connection II

June 11, 1988
Florence, SC – Legion Stadium
JCP
• George South vs. Rip Morgan

June 16, 1988
Harrison, VA – High School
JCP
• Italian Stallion beat Cruel Connection II

June 17, 1988
Charleston, WV – Civic Center
JCP
• Sting & Steve Williams beat Cruel Connection II & Larry Zbyszko

June 18, 1988
Buckingham, VA – High School
JCP
• Ron Simmons beat George South

June 19, 1988
Fayetteville, NC – Cumberland Arena
JCP
• Bugsy McGraw beat Cruel Connection II

June 22, 1988
Atlanta, GA – WTBS Studio
JCP
• Brad Armstrong, Tim Horner & Kendall Windham beat Cruel Connection I & II and Max MacGyver

June 27, 1988
Greenville, SC – Memorial Auditorium
JCP
• The Sheepherders w/ Rip Morgan beat Cruel Connection I & II

Highway Run into the Midnight Sun

June 28, 1988
Columbia, SC – Township Auditorium
JCP TV Taping
• Arn Anderson & Tully Blanchard w JJ Dillion beat George South & Gary Royal
• Brad Armstrong beat George South

June 29, 1988
Atlanta, GA – WTBS Studio
JCP
• Al Perez w/ Gary Hart beat George South
• Rick Steiner & Mike Rotundo w/ Kevin Sullivan beat George South & Rick Allen

July 2, 1988
Charlotte, NC – Memorial Stadium
JCP Great American Bash Tour
• Brad Armstrong, Tim Horner & Bugsy McGraw beat Cruel Connection II, Tiger Conway Jr. & Chris Champion (7:49)

July 7, 1988
Raleigh, NC – Dorton Arena
JCP
• Brad Armstrong beat Cruel Connection II

July 20, 1988
Atlanta, GA – WTBS Studio
JCP
• Rock & Roll Express beat George South & Agent Steel
• Sting, Nikita Koloff & Steve Williams beat Cruel Connection II, Larry Stevens & Green Hornet

July 24, 1988
Johnson City, TN – Freedom Hall
JCP Great American Bash Tour
• Cruel Connection II vs. Italian Stallion

July 26, 1988
Savannah, GA – Civic Center
Gate: $58,00
JCP Great American Bash Tour
• NWA United States Tag Team Title: Midnight Express* beat George South & Kendall Windham (1:36)
• Ron Simmons beat Cruel Connection II

July 27, 1988
Jacksonville, FL – Veterans Memorial Coliseum
Gate: $66,000
JCP Great American Bash Tour
• NWA United States Tag Team Title: Midnight Express* beat George South & Gary Royal (2:37)

August 2, 1988
Trotwood, OH – Hara Arena att. 8,000
WWF TV Taping
• Intercontinental Title: Honky Tonk Man* w/ Jimmy Hart beat George South (3:24)

August 3, 1988
Wheeling, WV – Civic Center att. 7,200 sell out
WWF TV Taping
• Hercules w/Bobby Heenan beat George South (0:59)

August 12, 1988
Norfolk, VA – The Scope
Gate: $98,000
JCP TV Taping
• Rick Steiner beat George South

August 23, 1988
Providence, RI – Civic Center att. 13,800 sell out
WWF TV Taping
• Sam Houston & Hillbilly Jim beat George South & Gene Ligon (7:02)
• Jake Roberts beat George South (3:00)

August 24, 1988
Hartford, CT – Civic Center att. 16,000 sell out
WWF TV Taping
• The Blue Blazer (Owen Hart) beat George South (2:02)
• The British Bulldogs (Davey Boy Smith & Dynamite Kid) beat George South & Trent Knight (3:08)

August 28, 1988
Greensboro, NC – Greensboro Coliseum
JCP TV Taping
• Arn Anderson & Tully Blanchard w/JJ Dillion beat George South &?
• Al Perez & Kevin Sullivan beat George South &?

August 30, 1988
Savannah, GA – Civic Center
JCP
• Russian Assassin w/ Paul Jones beat George South

August 31, 1988
Atlanta, GA – WTBS Studio
JCP TV Taping
• The Fantastics beat George South &?
• Ivan Koloff & The Russian Assassins w/ Paul Jones beat George South, Gary Royal & Rick Savage

September 1, 1988
Raleigh, NC – Dorton Arena
JCP
• Ivan Koloff beat George South

September 5, 1988
Covington, GA - Fairgrounds
JCP
• George South beat Rip Morgan w/ Larry Zbyszko

September 11, 1988
Fayetteville, NC – Cumberland Co. Memorial Auditorium
JCP TV Taping
• Midnight Express beat George South & John Savage (0:58)
• Kevin Sullivan beat George South

September 13, 1988
Indianapolis, IN – Market Square Arena
WWF TV Taping
• Brutus "The Barber" Beefcake beat George South (1:46)

September 14, 1988
Louisville, KY – Louisville Garden
WWF TV Taping
• The British Bulldogs beat George South & Barry Horowitz (2:40)

September 16, 1988
Shelby, NC – Rec Center
• George South vs Ricky Starr

September 26, 1988
Greenville, SC – Memorial Auditorium
JCP
• Russian Assassin # 1 w/ Paul Jones beat George South

September 27, 1988
Columbus, GA – Municipal Auditorium
JCP
• Bam Bam Bigelow w/ Sir Oliver Humperdink beat George South

September 28, 1988
Atlanta, GA – WTBS Studio
JCP TV Taping
• Barry Windham w/ JJ Dillion beat George South

October 5, 1988
Fort Wayne, IN – Allen Co. War Memorial Coliseum
WWF TV Taping
• Intercontinental Title: Ultimate Warrior* beat George South (2:40)

October 6, 1988
Toledo, OH – Sports Arena att. 9,500
WWF TV Taping
• Sam Houston beat George South (2:08)

October 8, 1988
Charlotte, NC – Coliseum
JCP
• Luke Williams w/ Rip Morgan beat George South

October 11, 1988
Fayetteville, NC – Cumberland Arena
JCP TV Taping
• Midnight Express w/ Jim Cornette beat cruel Connection I & II
• The Sheepherders w/ Rip Morgan beat George South &?

October 13, 1988
Sumpter, SC - Arena
JCP
• Rick Steiner beat George South

October 17, 1988
Atlanta, GA – WTBS Studio
JCP TV Taping
• Ron Simmons beat George South

October 21, 1988
Richmond, VA – The Showplace
VWA
• George South vs. The Bounty Hunter

October 22, 1988
Falmouth, VA – High School
VWA
• George South vs. The Bounty Hunter

October 25, 1988
Baltimore, MD – Baltimore Arena
WWF TV Taping
The Rockers (Shawn Michaels & Marty Jannetty) beat George South & Gene Ligon (2:34)

October 26, 1988
Salisbury, MD – Civic Center
WWF TV Taping
• The Blue Blazer (Owen Hart) beat George South

November 1, 1988
Savanah, GA - Civic Center
JCP TV Taping
• George South vs. Rip Morgan
• The Russian Assassins w/ Paul Jones beat George South &?

November 2, 1988
Atlanta, GA – WTBS Studio
JCP TV Taping
• The Fantastics beat George South &?

November 3, 1988
Atlanta, GA – WTBS Studio
JCP TV Taping
• NWA World Title: Ric Flair* beat George South

69

November 6, 1988
Johnson City, TN – Freedom Hall
JCP
• George South vs. Mike Justice

November 9, 1988
Greenwood, SC – Civic Center
JCP TV Taping
• Mike Rotundo w/ Kevin Sullivan beat George South
• Ric Flair & Barry Windham w/ JJ Dillion beat George South & Italian Stallion

November 14, 1988
Atlanta, GA – WTBS Studio
JCP TV Taping
• Ivan & Nikita Koloff beat George South &?
• The Commando's beat George South &?

November 16, 1988
Mooresville, NC – High School
Atlantic Coast Wrestling (Nelson Royal)
TV Taping
• The Rock & Roll Express beat George South &
• Ricky Nelson & Todd Champion beat George South &

November 17, 1988
Norfolk, VA – The Scope
JCP
• Rick Steiner beat George South

November 19, 1988
Roanoke Rapids, NC – High School
• George South vs. Cruel Connection I (Gary Royal)

November 22, 1988
Sumpter, SC – Civic Center
WCW TV Taping
• Sting beat Cruel Connection II

November 24, 1988
Atlanta, GA – WTBS Studio
WCW TV Taping
The Fantastics beat Cruel Connection I & II
Ivan & Nikita Koloff beat George South &?

November 25, 1988
Charlotte, NC – Charlotte Coliseum
Gate: $57,000
WCW
• Midnight Express beat Cruel Connection I & II (5:00)

November 26, 1988
Greensboro, NC – Greensboro Coliseum att. 7,500
WCW
• Midnight Express beat Cruel Connection I & II

November 27, 1988
Richmond, VA – Richmond Coliseum
WCW
• Midnight Express beat Cruel Connection I & II

November 28, 1988
Macon, GA – Coliseum
WCW TV Taping
• Barry Windham w/ JJ Dillion beat George South

Highway Run into the Midnight Sun

December 6, 1988
Daytona Beach, FL – Ocean Center att. 10,000 sell out
WWF TV Taping
The Brain Busters (Arn Anderson & Tully Blanchard) w/ Bobby Heenan beat George South & Tim Horner (2:21)

December 7, 1988
Tampa, FL – USF Sun Dome att. 9,176
WWF TV Taping
• Honky Tonk Man & Greg Valentine beat George South & Jose Luis Rivera (3:30)

December 8, 1988
Atlanta, GA – WTBS Studio
WCW TV Taping
• Rick Steiner beat George South
• Ivan Koloff, Rick Steiner & Junkyard Dog beat George South &??

December 10, 1988
Jackson, NC – High School
WCW
• Lazor-Tron beat George South

December 13, 1988
Gainesville, GA – Georgia Mountain Center
WCW TV Taping
• Dustin Rhodes & Kendell Windham beat Cruel Connection I &II
• The Midnight Express w/Jim Cornette beat George South & Gary Royal

December 14, 1988
Spartanburg, SC – Memorial Auditorium
WCW
• Dustin Rhodes beat Cruel Connection II

December 16, 1988
Winston-Salem, NC
WCW
• Dustin Rhodes & Kendall Windham beat Cruel Connection I & II

December 25, 1988
Greenville, SC – Memorial Auditorium
WCW 2pm
• Dustin Rhodes & Kendell Windham beat Cruel Connection I & II

December 25, 1988
Charlotte, NC - Coliseum
WCW 8pm
• Bunkhouse Stampede

December 31, 1988
North Wilkesboro, NC – Armory
Johnny Hunter
• George South & Gene Ligon vs. Brad & Brett Hoilday
• Nikita Koloff beat Cruel Connection II

1989

January 2, 1989
Columbus, GA
WCW TV Taping
- Michael Hayes & Junkyard Dog beat George South & Gary Royal

January 3, 1989
Albany, GA – Civic Center
WCW
- Eddie Gilbert beat George South

January 4, 1989
Atlanta, GA – WTBS Studio
WCW TV Taping
- Larry Zbyszko & Al Perez beat George South & Curtis Thompson (2:50)

January 5, 1989
Atlanta, GA – WTBS Studio
WCW TV Taping
- Larry Zbyszko & Al Perez beat George South &?
- Larry Zbyszko beat Cruel Connection I & II

January 8, 1989
Greensboro, NC – Greensboro Coliseum
WCW
- Bunkhouse Stampede

January 13, 1989
Taylorsville, NC – Alexander Central High School
Atlantic Coast Wrestling (Nelson Royal)
TV Taping
- Tommy Angel & Todd Champion beat George South &
- Mitch Snow & Scott Armstrong beat George South &

January 16, 1989
Macon, GA – Coliseum
WCW
- George South vs. Steve Casey

January 17, 1989
Savannah, Ga – Civic Center
WCW
- Al Perez beat George South

January 18, 1989
Atlanta, GA – WTBS Studio
WCW TV Taping
- Butch Reed beat George South

January 19, 1989
Atlanta, GA – WTBS Studio
WCW TV Taping
- Kendell Windham beat George South
- Original Midnight Express w/ Paul E Dangerously beat George South &?

January 20, 1989
Georgetown, SC – High School
WCW
- Dustin Rhodes & Kendell Windham beat Cruel Connection I & II

January 21, 1989
Sumpter, SC – Exhibition Center
WCW
- Dustin Rhodes & Kendell Windham beat Cruel Connection I & II

January 23, 1989
Elberton, GA – High School
WCW
- Kendell Windham beat Cruel Connection II

January 26, 1989
Roanoke, VA – Civic Center
WCW
- The Fantastics beat Cruel Connection I & II
  - Bunkhouse Stampede

January 27, 1989
Norfolk, VA – Norfolk Scope
Gate: $12,000
WCW
- Bobby Fulton & Tommy Rogers beat Cruel Connection I & II

January 28. 1989
Richmond, VA – Coliseum
Gate: $36,000
WCW
- Bunkhouse Stampede

January 30, 1989
Chattanooga, TN – UTC Arena
WCW TV Taping
- Midnight Express w/ jim Cornete beat Georg South & Gary Royal
  - Barry & Kendell Windham beat George South &?

January 31, 1989
Marietta, GA – Cobb Co. Civic Center
WCW TV Taping
- Sting & Lex Luger beat Cruel Connection I & II
  - The Fantastics beat George South &?

February 1, 1989
Atlanta, GA – WBTS Studio
WCW
- NWA United States Tag Team Title: Kevin Sullivan & Steve Williams* beat George South & Bob Emery (5:55)
  - Sting. Junkyard Dog & Michael Hayes beat Cruel Connection I & II and Max McGiver (2:50)
  - Kevin Sullivan, Steve Williams & Mike Rotundo beat George South, Gary Royal & Bob Emery

February 2, 1989
Atlanta, GA – WTBS Studio
WCW TV Taping
- Midnight Express w/ Jim Cornette beat George South &?

February 4, 1989
Denton, NC – High School
- George South vs. Jay Eagle

February 9, 1989
Lawrenceville, VA – High School
Atlantic Coast Wrestling (Nelson Royal)
- The Rock & Roll Express beat George South & Gene Ligon

February 11, 1989
Wilkesboro, NC – Wilks Central High School
Atlantic Coast Wrestling (Nelson Royal)
- Nelson Royal beat George South

February 12, 1989
Atlanta, GA – WTBS Studio
WCW TV Taping
- Kevin Sullivan, Steve Williams & Mike Rotundo beat George South &??
  - Rick Steiner & Eddie Gilbert beat Cruel Connection I & II (3:15)

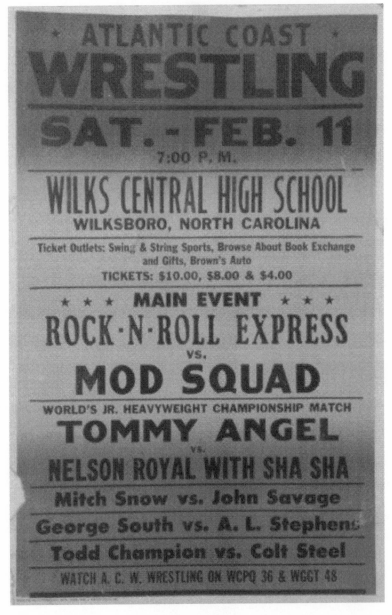

February 13, 1989
Columbus, GA - Auditorium
WCW TV Taping
• Eddie Gilbert & Vince Young beat Cruel Connection I & II
• Vince Young beat George South

February 14, 1989
Gainesville, GA – Georgia Mountain Center
WCW TV Taping
• Rick Steiner & Eddie Gilbert beat Cruel Connection I & II
• Dan Spivey & Kevin Sullivan beat George South &?

February 16, 1989
Hildebran, NC – Hildebran Gym
Atlantic Coast Wrestling (Nelson Royal)
TV Taping
• The Mod Squad (Spike & Basher) beat George South & Gene Ligon
• Tommy Angel beat George South
• George South beat Rusty Riddle

February 17, 1989
Athens, GA – High School
WCW
- Midnight Express w/ Jim Cornette beat George South & Randy Rose

February 19, 1989
Atlanta, GA – WTBS Studio
WCW
- Ron Simmons & Junkyard Dog beat Cruel Connection I & II
- The Fantastics beat George South & Gary Royal

February 21, 1989
Forest City, NC – High School
WCW
- Ivan Koloff & Junkyard Dog beat Cruel Connection I & II

February 23, 1989
Shallotte, NC – High Scholl
WCW
- The Fantastics beat Cruel Connection I & II

February 24, 1989
Waterboro, SC
Gate: $3,500
WCW
- George South beat Mike Justice

February 25, 1989
Newton, NC – Newton Conover High School
Gate: $4,600
WCW
- George South vs. Mike Justice

February 27, 1989
Macon, GA – Coliseum
WCW TV Taping
- George South vs Mike Justice

February 28, 1989
Columbia, SC – Township Auditorium
WCW TV Taping
- Rick Steiner & Eddie Gilbert beat George South &?
- Dan Spivey & Mike Rotundo beat George South &?

March 1, 1989
Atlanta, GA – WTBS Studio
WCW TV Taping
- Barry Windham beat George South

March 2, 1989
Atlanta, GA – WTBS Studio
WCW TV Taping
- Iron Sheik beat George South
- Vince Young, Michael Hayes & Junkyard Dog beat Cruel Connection I & II &?

March 4, 1989
Roanoke Rapids, NC – High School
- George South vs. Cruel Connection I

March 12, 1989
Statesville, NC – Armory
- George South vs. Cruel Connection I

March 17, 1989
Marion, NC – McDowell High School
- George South vs Russian Assassin

75

March 18, 1989
Conway, SC - High School
- George South vs The Raider

March 20, 1989
Chesterfield, SC - High School
- George South vs The Raider

March 21, 1989
Marion, VA - High School
- George South vs The Raider

March 23, 1989
Raleigh, NC – Dorton Arena
WCW
- The Great Muta w/Gary Hart beat George South

March 25, 1989
Traphill, NC – High Scholl
- George South vs Mitch Stallion
- George South vs. Jimmy Valiant

March 29, 1989
Atlanta, GA – WTBS Studio
WCW TV Taping
Handicap match: The Great Muta w/ Gary Hart beat Cruel Connection I & II

March 30, 1989
Atlanta, GA – Center Stage
WCW TV Taping
- The Great Muta w/ Gary Hart beat George South

April 4, 1989
Glen Falls, NY – Civic Center
WWF TV Taping
- "Hacksaw" Jim Duggan beat George South (1:49)
- The Rockers beat George South & Boris Zhukov (4:04)

April 5, 1989
Syracuse, NY – Onondaga War Memorial
WWF TV Taping
- "Superfly" Jimmy Snuka beat George South (3:45)
- The Ultimate Warrior beat George South

April 7, 1989
Goosecreek, SC – High School
WCW
- Ranger Ross beat George South

April 9, 1989
Charlotte, NC – Coliseum
WCW
- The Great Muta w/ Gary Hart beat George South

Match # 1000
April 10, 1989
Atlanta, GA – Center Stage
WCW TV Taping
- Ron Simmons beat George South

April 14, 1989
Milwaukee, WI – MECCA Arena
WCW
- Shane Douglas beat George South

Highway Run into the Midnight Sun

April 15, 1989
Chicago, IL – UIC Pavilion
WCW
- Shane Douglas beat George South

April 16, 1989
Indianapolis, IN – Convention Center
WCW
- Shane Douglas beat George South

April 19, 1989
Little Rock, AR – Barton Coliseum
WCW
The Great Muta w/ Gary Hart beat George South

April 20, 1989
Memphis, TN – Mid South Coliseum
WCW
- The Great Muta beat George South

April 21, 1989
St. Louis, MO – Kiel Auditorium
WCW
- The Great Muta w/ Gary Hart beat George South

April 22, 1989
Louisville, KY – Convention Center
WCW
- Shane Douglas beat George South

April 23, 1989 (2pm show)
Columbus, OH - Fairgrounds
WCW
- Shane Douglas beat George South

April 23, 1989
Huntington, WV (8pm show)
WCW
- Shane Douglas beat George South

April 24, 1989
Dayton, OH - Arena
WCW
- The Great Muta w/ Gary Hart beat George South

April 25, 1989
Johnson City, TN – Freedom Hall
WCW
- The Great Muta w/ Gary Hart beat George South

April 27, 1989
Atlanta, GA – Center Stage
WCW TV Taping
- Randy Rose beat George South
- Samoan Swat Team w/ Paul E Dangerously beat George South &?
- The Dynamic Dudes beat George South &?

April 29, 1989
Elkin, NC – Armory
- George South vs. Rip Holiday
- George South vs. Mitch Stallion

May 9, 1989
Atlanta, GA – Center Stage
WCW TV Taping
- Randy Rose beat George South
- The Fabulous Freebirds beat George South &?

May 10, 1989
Atlanta, GA – Center Stage
WCW TV Taping
- Brian Pillman beat George South

May 12, 1989
Albemarle, NC – Albe Center
- Cruel Connection I & II vs. Eddie & Hector Guerrero

May 19, 1989
Lynchburg, VA – Armory
- George South vs Trent Knight

Match # 1000
May 20, 1989
Burlington, NC – Community Center
- George South vs. The Assassin

May 22, 1989
Bluefield, WV – Bluefield Armory
WCW
- The Great Muta w/ Gary Hart beat George South

May 23, 1989
Asheville, NC – Civic Center
WCW TV Taping
- Brian Pillman beat George South
- The Dynamic Dudes beat George South & Rip Rogers

May 24, 1989
Atlanta, GA – Center Stage
WCW TV Taping
- Dick Murdoch beat George South

June 5, 1989
Columbus, GA – Municipal Auditorium
WCW TV Taping
- Brian Pillman beat George South
- Butch Reed beat George South

June 6, 1989
Albany, GA – Civic Center
WCW TV Taping
- New Zealand Militia beat George South &?
- Brian Pillman beat George South

June 7, 1989
Atlanta, GA – WTBS Studio
Music Video for "Fan Night Tracks" on TBS
- Michael Hayes vs. Cruel Connection II

June 14, 1989
Fort Bragg, NC – Ritz-Epps Fitness Center
WCW Clash of the Champions VII: Guts & Glory
- The Ding Dongs (Greg Evans & Richard Sartain) beat George South & Cougar Jay (5:00)
- George South vs. Butch Reed

June 19, 1989
Macon, GA – Macon Coliseum
WCW
- Dan Spivey & Sid Vicious beat George South &?

June 20, 1989
Savannah, GA – Civic Center
WCW TV Taping
- Ranger Ross beat George South
- Tommy Rich beat George South

Highway Run into the Midnight Sun

June 21, 1989
Atlanta, GA – Center Stage
WCW TV Taping
- Dan Spivey & Sid Vicious beat George South &?
- Rick & Scott Steiner beat George South &?

June 24, 1989
Charlotte, NC – Park Center
All-Star Wrestling (Greg Price)
- Cruel Connection I & II vs. Vic Steamboat & Jumpin Joe Savoldi

July 1, 1989
Charlotte, NC – Charlotte Coliseum
Gate: $37,000
WCW Great American Bash
- Triple Crown Battle Royal

July 2, 1989
Atlanta, GA – The Omni att. 6,800
WCW Great American Bash Tour
- Sky Scrapper's (Sid Vicious & Dan Spivey) beat George South & Trent Knight
- Triple Crown Battle Royal

July 3, 1989
Columbia, SC – Coliseum
WCW TV Taping
- Rick & Scott Steiner beat George South &?
- The Midnight Express & Steve Williams w/ Jim Cornete beat George South &??

July 4, 1989
Fayetteville, NC – Cumberland Arena
WCW TV Taping
- The Skyscrapers w/ Teddy Long beat George South &?
- The Dynamic Dudes beat George South &?

July 5, 1989
Charleston, SC – Citadel Football Stadium
WCW Great American Bash Tour
- Triple Crown Battle

July 6, 1989
Marietta, GA – Cobb Co. Civic Center
WCW TV Taping
- Brian Pillman beat George South
- The Ding Dongs beat George South &?

July 7, 1989
Roanoke, VA – Civic Center
WCW Great American Bash Tour
- Triple Crown Battle Royal

July 19, 1989
Atlanta, GA – Center Stage
WCW TV Taping
- Joe Kapchuk w/ Hiro Matsuda beat George South
- Tommy, Johnny & Davey Rich beat George South &??
- Gangsters of Love beat George South & Gary Royal

July 31, 1989
New Orleans, LA – Municipal Auditorium
WCW TV Taping
- Tommy Rich & Brian Pillman beat George South &?
- New Zealand Militia beat George South &?

NIKITA KOLOFF "THE BOSS" BARRY WINDHAM
MAGNUM T.A.

SATURDAY JUNE 24 8:15 P.M.

ALL STAR CHAMPIONSHIP

WRESTLING

GRADY COLE CENTER, CHARLOTTE, N.C.
NIKITA KOLOFF vs. BARRY WINDHAM

FANS AUTOGRAPH SESSION
6:30-7:30 FEATURING **MAGNUM T.A.**

JUNKYARD DOG vs MANNY FERNANDEZ

IVAN KOLOFF VS. RUSSIAN ASSASSIN
(IF KOLOFF WINS, HE GETS 5 MINUTES WITH PAUL JONES)

TOMMY RICH vs. **TOM ZENK** | GIRLS / **BAMBI** VS **PEGGY LEE LEATHER**

TAG TEAM MATCH *** **JOHNNY & DAVEY RICH** VERSUS **KENDALL WINDHAM & TOM PRICHARD**

VIC STEAMBOAT & JUMPIN JOE SAVOLDI -VS- CRUEL CONNECTION	GEN. ADM. $6	RESERVED $8	RINGSIDE $10

ORDER TICKETS 24 HOURS BY PHONE (704) 551-4131
BOX OFFICE OPENS AT NOON ON DAY OF MATCH

August 1, 1989
Baton Rouge, LA – Civic Center
WCW TV Taping
- New Zealand Militia beat George South &?
- The Road Warriors w/Paul Ellering beat George South &?

August 2, 1989
Atlanta, GA – Center Stage
WCW TV Taping
- Sky Scrapper's w/ Teddy Long beat George South & Bob Emery (1:55)
- George South vs. Bill Loyd
- New Zealand Militia beat George South &?

August 12, 1989
Wentworth, NC – High School
- George South vs. Bob Emery

August 14, 1989
Charleston, WV – Civic Center
WCW TV Taping
- The Skyscrapers w/ Teddy Long beat George South &?
- The Midnight Express w/ Jim Cornette beat George South &?

August 15, 1989
Cleveland, OH – Convention Center
WCW
- Brian Pillman beat George South

August 16, 1989
Atlanta, GA – Center Stage
WCW TV Taping
- Kevin Kelly beat George South
- Dick Slater beat George South
- Rick & Scott Steiner   beat George South &?

August 26, 1989
Fort Pickett, VA – Fieldhouse
VWA
- George South vs. The Phantom
- George South &? vs The Cream Team

September 1, 1989
Fayetteville, NC – Cumberland Arena
WCW
- George South vs. Trent Knight

September 2, 1989
Myrtle Beach, NC – Convention Center
WCW
- George South vs Trent Knight

September 19, 1989
Roanoke, VA – Civic Center
WCW
- Rick & Scott Steiner w/ Missy Hyatt beat George South &?

September 20, 1989
Atlanta, GA – Center Stage
WCW TV Taping
- Rick & Scott Steiner w/ Missy Hyatt beat George South &?
- Brian Pillman beat George South
- Midnight Express w/ Jim Cornette beat George South &?

September 23, 1989
Fort Pickett, VA – Fieldhouse
VWA
• George South vs. The Eliminator

September 25, 1989
Johnstown, PA – War Memorial
WCW
Steve Williams & Midnight Express w/ Jim Cornette beat George South &??

October 2, 1989
Wheeling, WV – Wheeling Civic Center
WWF TV Taping
• Al Perez beat George South

October 2, 1989
Wheeling, WV – Wheeling Civic Center
WWF TV Taping
• Dusty Rhodes beat George South (2:30)
• Hercules beat George South (3:47)

October 7, 1989
Drexel, NC – Community Center
Southern Championship Wrestling
• George South vs. Cruel Connection # 1

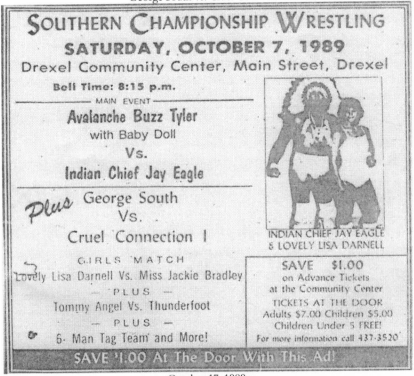

October 17, 1989
Marietta, GA – Cobb County Civic Center
WCW TV Taping
• Twin Towers (Sid Vicious & Dan Spivey) beat George South & Mark Kyle (0:55)
• Doom (Ron Simmons & Butch Reed) beat George South & Johnny Kennedy (4:06)

October 19, 1989
Murphy, NC – High School
• George South vs. Batman
• Blind Fold Battle Royal

October 30, 1989
Gainesville, GA – George Mountain Center
WCW
• The Dynamic Dudes beat George South &?

Highway Run into the Midnight Sun

November 1, 1989
Atlanta, GA – Center Stage
WCW TV Taping
- Midnight Express w/ Jim Cornette beat George South &?

November 3, 1989
Bluefield, WV – Armory
Pro Wrestling Federation (George South & Gary Sabaugh)
- Italian Stallion w/ Princess beat George South
- Bunkhouse Stampede

November 10, 1989
Charlotte, NC – Park Center
- George South vs. Jay Eagle

November 14, 1989
McAdenville, NC – Community Center
- George South vs. David Three Feathers
- Battle Royal

November 20, 1989
Columbus, OH – Fairgrounds
WCW
- The Dynamic Dudes vs. George South &?

November 22, 1989
Charlotte, NC – Charlotte Coliseum
WCW
- The Dynamic Dudes vs. George South &?

November 24, 1989
Monroe, NC – Armory
Pro Wrestling Federation (George South & Gary Sabaugh)
- George South vs. Rocky Mills
- George South vs. Ricky Nelson
- Battle Royal

November 25, 1989
Roanoke Rapids, NC – High School
- George South vs. Rocky Mills
- George South vs. Ricky Nelson

November 30, 1989
Norfolk, VA – Naval Base
- George South vs. Dan Casannova
- George South &? Vs. The Fantastics

December 12, 1989
Nashville, TN – Municipal Auditorium
WWF TV Taping
- Jake "The Snake" Roberts beat George South

December 13, 1989
Huntsville, AL – Von Braun Civic Center
- Brutus "The Barber" Beefcake beat George South (2:04)

December 22, 1989
Kings Mountain, NC – Community Center
- George South vs Jay Eagle
- Battle Royal

December 30, 1989
North Wilkesboro, NC – YMCA
- George South vs. Jackie Fulton
- George South vs. Ricky Nelson
- Battle Royal

1990

January 2, 1990
Birmingham, AL – Civic Center
WWF TV Taping
- Demolition (Ax & Smash) beat George South & Alan Martin

January 3, 1990
Chattanooga, TN – UTC Arena
WWF TV Taping
- The Rockers beat George South & Mike Davis (2:58)

January 6, 1990
Hickory, NC – Fred T Ford High School
Pro Wrestling Federation (George South & Gary Sabaugh)
- George South vs Jay Eagle

January 12, 1990
McAdenville, NC – Community Center
PWF
- George South &? vs. Jay Eagle & David Three Feathers

January 20, 1990
Leland, NC – High School
- George South vs. Marc Watkins

January 27, 1990
Kings Mountain, NC – Community Center
PWF
- George South vs Jake Steele
- George South vs Jay Eagle
- Bunkhouse Stampede

February 2, 1990
Monroe, NC – Armory
PWF
- George South vs. Jay Eagle
- Bunkhouse Stampede

February 9, 1990
Denver, NC – Elementary School
PWF
- George South vs Kenny Herd
- George South vs Jay Eagle
- Bunkhouse Stampede

February 10, 1990
Statesville, NC – Armory
PWF
- George South vs. Italian Stallion

February 24, 1990
Kings Mountain, NC – Armory
PWF
- George South vs Kenny Herd
- George South vs Italian Stallion

March 3, 1990
Princeton, WV – Junior High School
PWF
- George South vs Ricky Nelson
- Bunkhouse Stampede

March 10, 1990
Gastonia, NC – Armory
PWF
- George South vs Ricky Nelson

March 15, 1990
Cherryville, NC – Nixon Gym
PWF
- George South vs John Savage
- George South vs. Ricky Nelson
  - Bunkhouse Stampede

March 17, 1990
McAdenville, NC – Community Center
PWF
- George South vs Kenny Herd
- George South vs. Ricky Nelson
  - Bunkhouse Stampede

March 22, 1990
Denver, NC – East Lincoln High School
PWF
- George South vs Kenny Herd
- George South vs Ricky Nelson
  - Bunkhouse Stampede

March 30, 1990
Greensboro, NC - Armory
PWF
- George South vs Ricky Nelson

March 31, 1990
Concord, NC - Rec Center
- George South vs Gary Royal
- George South vs Ricky Nelson

April 6, 1990
Monroe, NC – Armory
PWF
- George South vs Hillbilly
  - Ricky Nelson

April 10, 1990
Mocksville, NC – Gym
- George South vs Rick Link

April 18, 1990
Concord, NC – Rec Center
- George South vs. Hillbilly

April 20, 1990
North Wilkesboro, NC – Armory
PWF
- George South vs Hillbilly
- George South vs Ricky Nelson

April 21, 1990
Princeton, WV – Junior High School
PWF
- George South vs Hillbilly
- Cage Match: George South & Russian Assassin vs Italian Stallion & Claudio Montrosse

May 9, 1990
Concord, NC – Rec Center
- George South vs Gene Legon

May 10, 1990
Salisbury, NC – Catawba College
PWF
- George South vs Ricky Nelson

May 11, 1990
Norwood, NC – High School
PWF
- George South vs Hillbilly
- George South vs Ricky Nelson

May 12, 1990
Pineville, WV – High School
PWF
- George South vs. Hillbilly
- George South vs Ricky Nelson

May 13, 1990
Mt. Airy, NC - Armory
PWF
- George South vs Italian Stallion

May 18, 1990
Monroe, NC – High School
PWF
- George South vs Hillbilly Willie
- Bunkhouse Stampede

May 19, 1990
Concord, NC – High School - 2pm
- George South &? Vs David Isley & Ricky Nelson

May 19, 1990
Rocky Gap, VA – High School – 8pm
PWF
- George South vs Hillbilly Willie
- George South vs Ricky Nelson
- Bunkhouse Stampede

May 25, 1990
Fries, VA – Rec Center
PWF
- George South vs David Isley
- George South vs Italian Stallion
- Bunkhouse Stampede

May 26, 1990
Sugar Grove, NC – Cove Creek Gym
PWF
- George South vs. John Savage
- Bunkhouse Stampede

June 1, 1990
North Wilkesboro, NC - Armory
PWF
- George South vs. David Isley
- Bunkhouse Stampede

June 2, 1990
Elizabethtown, NC - Armory
PWF
- George South vs Hillbilly Willie
- George South vs Italian Stallion
- Bunkhouse Stampede

June 5, 1990
McAdenville, NC – Community Center
PWF
• George South vs. David Isley
• George South & Russian Assassin vs. Scott & Bobby Bradley

June 6, 1990
Concord, NC – Rec Center
• George South vs. Trent Knight

June 8, 1990
Herndon, WV – High School
PWF
• George South vs David Taylor
• Bunkhouse Stampede

June 9, 1990
Kings Mountain, NC – Armory
PWF
- George South vs David Taylor
  - Bunkhouse Stampede

June 15, 1990
Monroe, NC – Armory
PWF
- George South vs Italian Stallion

June 16, 1990
Bluefield, WV – Youth Center
PWF
- George South vs Italian Stallion
  - Bunkhouse Stampede

June 22, 1990
Albemarle, NC – Armory
PWF
- George South vs David Taylor
  - Battle Royal

June 23, 1990
Wallace, NC – Armory
PWF
- George South vs David Taylor
  - Battle Royal

June 30, 1990
Concord, NC -Armory
- George South vs Ricky Nelson

July 4, 1990
Princeton, WV – Princeton High School
PWF
- George South vs Italian Stallion

July 5, 1990
Fries, VA – Baseball Field
PWF
- George South & Russian Assassin vs Italian Stallion & David Taylor

July 6, 1990
North Wilkesboro, NC – Armory
PWF
- George South vs David Taylor

July 7, 1990
Concord, NC – Rec Center
- George South vs Ricky Nelson

July 18, 1990
Gaffney, SC – College
PWF
- George South vs The Assassin

July 19, 1990
Monroe, NC – Armory
PWF
- George South vs Italian Stallion

July 20, 1990
Elizabethtown, NC – Armory
PWF
- George South vs David Taylor
  - Battle Royal

July 21, 1990
Bluefield, WV – Junior High School
PWF
- George South vs Italian Stallion

July 26, 1990
Albemarle, NC – Armory
PWF
- George South vs Benji

July 27, 1990
Herndon, WV – High School
PWF
- George South & Russian Assassin vs Italian Stallion & Claudio Montrosse

July 28, 1990
Charlotte, NC – Flea Fair
PWF
- George South vs Italian Stallion

July 28, 1990
Concord, NC – Rec Center
- George South vs. Ricky Nelson
- George South &? Vs. Manny Fernandez & Nikita Koloff

July 31, 1990
Kings Mountain, NC – Armory
PWF
- George South & Russian Assassin vs Italian Stallion & David Taylor

August 3, 1990
North Wilkesboro, NC – Armory
PWF
- George South vs David Taylor

August 4, 1990
Rocky Gap, VA – High School
PWF
- George South & Russian Assassin vs Italian Stallion & David Taylor

August 8, 1990
Concord, NC – Rec Center
- George South vs Ricky Nelson

August 11, 1990
Concord, NC – Rec Center
PWF
- George South vs. David Taylor

August 16, 1990
Monroe, NC - Armory
PWF
- George South vs. Italian Stallion

August 17, 1990
Wytheville, VA – High School
PWF
- George South vs David Taylor
- Battle Royal

August 18, 1990
Rockingham, NC – Flea Fair
PWF
- George South vs Italian Stallion

August 18, 1990
Concord, NC – Armory
• George South vs Ricky Nelson

August 23, 1990
McAdenville, NC – Community Center
PWF
• George South & Russian Assassin beat Scott & Bobby Bradley
• George South vs Italian Stallion

August 25, 1990
Elizabethtown, NC – Armory
PWF
• George South vs. Buddy Blondz

August 31, 1990
North Wilkesboro, NC – Armory
PWF
• George South vs. Scotty Bradley

September 1, 1990
Princeton, WV – Princeton High School
PWF
• George South & Russian Assassin vs Italian Stallion & Claudio Montrosse

September 8, 1990
Concord, NC – Armory
• George South vs Ricky Nelson

September 15, 1990
Rockingham, NC – Flea Fair
PWF
• George South vs Italian Stallion

September 20, 1990
Albemarle, NC – Armory
PWF
• George South & Russian Assassin vs. Italian Stallion & David Taylor

September 21, 1990
Union, WV – Union High School
PWF
• George South vs. Buddy Blondz
• Battle Royal

September 22, 1990
Bluefield, WV – Armory
PWF
• George South vs. Buddy Blondz
• George South vs. CC Hacker
• Bunkhouse Stampede

September 29, 1990
Peterstown, WV – Peterstown High School
PWF
• George South vs CC Hacker
• Bunkhouse Stampede

September 30, 1990
North Wilkesboro, NC – Armory
PWF
• George South vs Jim Gibson

October 4, 1990
Rockingham, NC – Flea Fair
PWF
- George South vs. Scotty Bradley
- Bunkhouse Stampede

October 6, 1990
Mt. Airy, NC – High School
PWF
- George South vs Scotty Bradley
- Bunkhouse Stampede

October 9, 1990
Cooleemee, NC – Elementary School
All Star Wrestling
- Jr. Heavyweight Title: Gorgeous George South* vs. Buddy Blondz

October 11, 1990
Elkin, NC – Armory
PWF
- George South vs. Scotty Bradley
- Bunkhouse Stampede

October 13, 1990
Rocky Gap, VA – High School
PWF
- George South beat CC Hacker

October 20, 1990
Union, WV – Union High School
PWF
- George South & Russian Assassin vs. Italian Stallion & Claudio Montrosse
- Bunkhouse Stampede

October 22, 1990
Gainesville, GA – Georgia Mountain Center
WCW TV Taping
- The Juicer (Art Barr) beat George South

October 26, 1990
Sophia, WV – Junior High School
PWF
- George South vs Hillbilly Willie
- George South vs Tommy Angel
- Bunkhouse Stampede

October 27, 1990
Boone, NC – Skate World - 2pm
PWF
- George South vs Chuck Coates

October 27, 1990
Montcalm, WV – High School – 8pm
PWF
- George South vs. Buddy Blondz
- Bunkhouse Stampede

October 29, 1990
Anderson, SC – Civic Center
WCW
- Tommy Rich & Ricky Morton beat George South &?

November 1, 1990
Boone, NC – ASU
WCW
- Tracey Smothers & Steve Armstrong beat George South & Bobby Eaton

November 3, 1990
Herndon, WV – High School
PWF
- George South vs. Chief
- George South vs Italian Stallion
- Bunkhouse Stampede

November 7, 1990
Beckley, WV – Civic Center
WCW
- The Juicer (Art Barr) beat George South

November 8, 1990
Kings Mountain, NC – Armory
PWF
- George South beat Scotty Bradley

November 9, 1990
War, WV – Big Creek High School
PWF
- George South beat CC Hacker
- Bunkhouse Stampede

November 10, 1990
Wytheville, WV – Cobb Co. High School
PWF
- Italian Stallion beat George South

November 13, 1990
Marietta, GA – Civic Center
WCW TV Taping
- The Nasty Boys (Jerry Sags & Brin Knobbs) beat George South & Joe Cazana
- Tommy Rich & Ricky Morton beat George South &?

November 15, 1990
Elkin, NC – Armory
PWF
- George South beat Scotty Bradley

November 17, 1990
Sophia, WV – Junior High School
PWF
- George South beat David Taylor
- Battle Royal

November 24, 1990
Fayetteville, NC – Cumberland Arena
WCW
- Brian Pillman beat George South

November 26, 1990
Albany, GA – Civic Center
WCW
- Junkyard Dog beat George South

November 27, 1990
Dothan, AL – Civic Center
WCW TV Taping
- Bobby Eaton & The Fabulous Freebirds beat George South &??

November 30, 1990
Bluefield, WV – Junior High School
PWF Two Night Tag Team Tournament
Night One
- George South & Russian Assassin vs. Italian Stallion & Claudio Montrosse

December 1, 1990
Princeton, WV – High School
PWF Two Night Tag Team Tournament
Night Two
- George South & Russian Assassin beat Wild Samoan & GQ Stratus
- George South & Russian Assassin beat CC Hacker & Brett Sawyer
- George South & Russian Assassin beat David Taylor & Ronnie Garvin
- Italian Stallion & Claudio Montrosse beat George South & Russian Assassin

December 4, 1990
Atlanta, GA – Center Stage
WCW
- Tim Horner & Allen Iron Eagle beat George South &?

December 6, 1990
East Bank, WV – High School
PWF
- George South beat Scott Bradley
- Bunkhouse Stampede

December 7, 1990
Iaeger, WV – High School
PWF
- George South beat Hillbilly Willie
- George South & Russian Assassin beat Italian Stallion & Claudio Montrosse

December 8, 1990
Mt. Airy, NC – Armory
PWF
- George South beat David Taylor

December 11, 1990
Atlanta, GA – Center Stage
WCW TV Taping
- Tim Horner beat George South (2:53)

December 13, 1990
Roanoke, VA – Civic Center
WCW
- Tim Horner beat George South

December 14, 1990
Bassett, VA – High School
PWF
- George South beat Buddy Blondz
- Bunkhouse Stampede

December 15, 1990
Fort Chiswell, VA – High School
PWF
- George South beat David Taylor
- Bunkhouse Stampede

December 21, 1990
Lewisburg, WV - High School
PWF
- George South beat David Taylor
- Bunkhouse Stampede

December 22, 1990
Richwood, WV - High School
PWF
- George South beat David Taylor
- Bunkhouse Stampede

December 26, 1990
Columbia, SC – Township Auditorium
WCW
- Dan Spivey beat George South

December 27, 1990
Charleston, SC – McAlister Field House
WCW
- Dan Spivey beat George South

December 29, 1990
Boone, NC – Skate World – 2pm
PWF
- George South beat James Clontz

December 29, 1990
Piney Creek, NC – Elementary School
PWF
- George South beat David Taylor
  - Bunkhouse Stampede

1991

January 3, 1991
Welch, WV – Mt. View High School
PWF
- George South beat David Taylor
  - Bunkhouse Stampede

January 4, 1991
Glenwood, WV – Junior High School – 2pm
PWF
- George South beat Star Ryder

January 4, 1991
Bluefield, WV – Armory – 8pm
PWF
- George South beat Star Ryder

January 5, 1991
Buchanan, WV – High School
PWF
- George South vs. Madd Maxx (Chuck Coates)
  - George South vs CC Hacker
    - Bunkhouse Stampede

January 10, 1991
Rockingham, NC – Skate Fair
PWF
- George South beat Scotty Bradley

January 12, 1991
Madison, WV – High School
PWF
- George South beat Buddy Blondz

January 17, 1991
Beckley, WV – Elementary School
PWF
- George South beat Buddy Blondz
  - Bunkhouse Stampede

January 21, 1991
Charlotte, NC – Cablevision
PWF TV Taping
- George South beat Stacey Lane
- George South beat Steve Adams

January 22, 1991
Atlanta, GA – Center Stage
WCW
- Brian Pillman beat George South
- Rick & Scott Steiner beat George South &?

January 24, 1991
Sutton, WV – High School
PWF
- George South vs. Buddy Blondz
  - Battle Royal

January 25, 1991
War, WV – Big Creek High School
PWF
- George South beat Buddy Blondz

January 31, 1991
Ronceverte, WV – High School
PWF
- George South beat Buddy Blondz

February 1, 1991
Bluefield, WV – Wade Elementary School – 2pm
PWF
- George South vs. Buddy Blondz

February 1, 1991
Bluefield, WV – Armory – 8pm
PWF
- George South vs. Italian Stallion

February 2, 1991
Glenville, WV – Elementary School
PWF
- George South beat Buddy Blondz
  - Battle Royal

February 8, 1991
Madison, WV – High School
PWF
- George South beat Buddy Blondz

February 9, 1991
Iaeger, WV - High School
PWF
- George South beat Buddy Blondz

February 12, 1991
Anderson, SC – Civic Center
WCW TV Taping
- Big Josh (Matt Borne) beat George South

February 14, 1991
Richwood, WV – High School
PWF
- George South vs Hillbilly Willie
- George South vs Italian Stallion

February 15, 1991
Clay, WV – High School
PWF
- George South vs Hillbilly Willie
- George South vs Buddy Blondz
  - Battle Royal

February 16, 1991
East Bank, WV – High School
PWF
- George South vs Hillbilly Willie
- George South vs Italian Stallion

February 22, 1991
Bluefield, WV – Wade Elementary School
PWF
- George South vs. Italian Stallion

February 23, 1991
Hillsville, VA – High School
PWF
- George South beat Buddy Blondz
  - Battle Royal

March 1, 1991
Ronceverte, WV – Armory
PWF
- George South beat Buddy Blondz
- Cage Match: Italian Stallion & Super Mario beat George South & Russian Assassin

March 2, 1991
Welch, WV – Mt. View High School
PWF
- George South vs. Buddy Blondz
- George South vs. Italian Stallion

March 6, 1991
Spencer, WV – High School
PWF
- George South beat Chuck Coates
- Battle Royal

March 7, 1991
Mountain City, TN – High School
PWF
- George South beat James Clontz

March 8, 1991
Northfork, WV – Junior High School
PWF
- George South vs Super Mario
- George South vs CC Hacker

March 9, 1991
Peterstown, WV – High School
PWF
- George South beat CC Hacker
- Battle Royal

March 14, 1991
Sutton, WV – Braxton Co. High School
PWF
- George South vs Hillbilly Willie
- George South vs Madd Maxx (Chuck Coates)

March 15, 1991
Buchannon, WV – Upshur Co. High School
PWF
- George South vs. Mark Canterbury
- George South vs. Madd Maxx

March 16, 1991
Athens, WV – High School
PWF
- George South vs Hillbilly Willie
- George South & Madd Maxx vs. Italian Stallion & CC Hacker

March 21, 1991
Naugatuck, WV – High School
PWF
- George South beat CC Hacker
- Battle Royal

March 22, 1991
Cowen, WV – Glade Elementary School
PWF
- George South vs Hillbilly Willie
- George South vs The Juicer
- Battle Royal

March 23, 1991
Fort Chiswell, VA – High School
PWF
- George South vs CC Hacker

March 28, 1991
Matoaka, WV – High School
PWF
- George South vs CC Hacker
  - Battle Royal

April 4, 1991
Glenville, WV – Glenville State College
- George South vs Ivan Koloff

April 5, 1991
Union, WV – Union High School
PWF
- George South vs CC Hacker
- George South vs Italian Stallion

April 11, 1991
Naugatuck, WV – High School – 2pm
PWF Dare School Show
- George South beat CC Hacker

April 11,1991
Ieager, WV – High School – 8pm
PWF
- George South vs Hillbilly Willie
- George South vs Italian Stallion

April 12, 1991
Pineville, WV – High School
PWF
- George South vs Hillbilly Willie
- George South vs Italian Stallion

April 13, 1991
Sparta, NC – High School
PWF
- George South vs Hillbilly Willie
- George South vs Italian Stallion
  - Battle Royal

April 18, 1991
Clay, WV – High Scholl
PWF
- George South vs Italian Stallion

April 19, 1991
Independence, VA – High School
PWF
- George South vs Italian Stallion
  - Battle Royal

April 25, 1991
East Bank, WV – High School – 2pm
PWF Dare School Show
- George South vs CC Hacker

April 25, 1990
Oak Hill, WV – High School – 8pm
PWF
- George South & Mad Maxx vs Italian Stallion & Ronnie Garvin
  - Battle Royal

April 26, 1991
Richwood, WV – High School
PWF
- George South vs Hillbilly Willie
- George South vs CC Hacker

April 27, 1991
Shinnston, WV – High School
PWF
- George South vs Italian Stallion

May 2, 1991
Shinnston, WV – Lincoln High School
PWF
- George South vs Hillbilly Willie
- George South vs CC Hacker
  - Battle Royal

May 3, 1991
War, WV – Big Creek High School
PWF
- Italian Stallion beat George South
- George South vs Hillbilly Willie

May 4, 1991
Ronceverte, WV – Armory
PWF
- George South beat Hilbilly Willie
- George South beat CC Hacker

May 8, 1991
Cowen, WV – Glade School
PWF
- George South vs. Michael McReynolds
- George South vs. CC Hacker

May 9, 1991
Pineville, WV – High School
PWF
- George South vs Hillbilly Willie
- George South vs CC Hacker

May 10, 1991
Bradshaw, WV – Junior High School
PWF
- George South vs Student
- George South vs CC Hacker

May 15, 1991
Athens, WV – High School
PWF
- George South vs Hillbilly Willie
- George South vs CC Hacker

May 17, 1991
Walton, WV – High School
PWF
- George South vs CC Hacker
- George South & Russian Assassin vs Italian Stallion & CC Hacker

May 18, 1991
Spencer, WV – High School
PWF
- George South vs Rising Sun

May 23, 1991
Sutton, WV – Braxton Co High School
PWF
- George South vs J.D.
- George South vs. CC Hacker

May 25, 1991
Peterstown, WV – High School
PWF
- George South vs. Michael McReynolds

May 30, 1990
Bradshaw, WV – Junior High School
PWF
- George South vs CC Hacker

May 31, 1991
Iaeger, WV – High School
PWF
- Italian Stallion beat George South

June 5, 1991
Weston, WV – Lewis Co. High School
PWF
- George South vs CC Hacker
- George South vs Italian Stallion

June 6, 1991
Northfork, WV – High School
PWF
- George South vs CC Hacker

June 7, 1991
Ronceverte, Wv – Armory
PWF
- George South vs CC Hacker
- George South vs Hillbilly Willie

June 13, 1991
Beckley, WV – Elementary School
PWF
- Refereed the whole show

June 14, 1991
Rockingham, NC – Crackers
PWF
- George South vs Les Parker
- Bunkhouse Battle Royal

July 1, 1991
Weston, WV – High School
PWF
- George South vs CC Hacker
- Managed Mark Canterbury
- Bunkhouse Stampede

July 2, 1991
Sutton, WV – High School
PWF
- George South vs CC Hacker
- Managed Mark Canterbury
- Bunkhouse Stampede

July 3, 1991
Princeton, WV – High School
PWF
- George South & Madd Maxx vs Italian Stallion & David Taylor

July 4, 1991
Sparta, NC – High School
PWF
- George South vs David Taylor
- Managed Mark Canterbury

July 5, 1991
Oak Hill, WV – High School
PWF
- George South vs CC Hacker
- Managed Mark Canterbury

July 6, 1991
Cowen, WV – Elementary School
PWF
- George South vs CC Hacker
- Managed Mark Canterbury
  - Battle Royal

July 11, 1991
Clay, WV – High School
PWF
- George South vs CC Hacker
- George South vs Hillbilly Willie
- Managed Mark Canterbury

July 12, 1991
Peterstown, WV – High School
PWF
- George South vs CC Hacker
- Managed Mark Canterbury

July 13, 1991
Mullens, WV – High School
PWF
- George South vs CC Hacker
- Managed Mark Canterbury
  - Battle Royal

July 20, 1991
White Sulphur, WV – Memorial Park
PWF
- George South vs CC Hacker
- George South vs Hillbilly Willie
- Managed Mark Canterbury
  - Bunkhouse Stampede

July 26, 1991
Rockingham, NC – Crackers
PWF
- George South vs Les Parker
- Managed Mark Canterbury
  - Bunkhouse Stampede

July 27, 1991
Albemarle, NC – Armory
PWF
- George South vs Benji
- Managed Mark Canterbury

August 2, 1991
Weston, WV – High School
PWF
- George South vs Mark Woods
- George South vs Chuck Woods
- Managed Mark Canterbury
  - Bunkhouse Stampede

August 16, 1991
Mountain City, TN – High School
PWF
- George South vs Southern Rocker
- George South vs CC Hacker
- Managed Mark Canterbury
- Bunkhouse Stampede

August 17, 1991
Mullens, WV – Football Field
PWF
- George South vs CC Hacker
- Managed Mark Canterbury
- Bunkhouse Stampede

August 24, 1991
Sparta, NC – High School
PWF
- George South & Mark Canterbury vs Italian Stallion & Super Mario
- George South vs Chris Hamrick
- Managed Mark Canterbury vs Italian Stallion
- George South & Mark Canterbury vs. New Wave

August 29, 1991
Jacksonville, FL – Naval Base
PWF
- George South vs Navy Seal
- Managed Mark Canterbury
- Bunkhouse Stampede

September 2, 1991
Pineville, WV – High School
PWF
- George South vs Mark Woods
- George South vs Joey Morton
- Managed Mark Canterbury
- Bunkhouse Stampede

September 18, 1991
Pineville, WV – High School
PWF
- George South vs Joey Morton
- Managed Mark Canterbury

September 19, 1991
Mountain City, TN – High School
PWF
- George South vs Joey Morton
- Battle Royal

September 26, 1991
Harrisville, WV – High School
PWF
- George South vs Joey Morton
- Managed Mark Canterbury

September 27, 1991
Belington, WV – Middle School
PWF
- George South vs Joey Morton
- Managed Mark Canterbury

October 4, 1991
McAdenville, NC – Community Center
PWF
- George South vs The Commando
- George South vs Italian Stallion
- Battle Royal

October 9, 1991
Union, WV – High School
PWF
- George South vs Hillbilly Willie
- George South vs Italian Stallion
- Managed Mark Canterbury

October 10, 1991
Alderson, WV – Junior High School
PWF
- George South vs Michael McReynolds
- Managed Mark Canterbury

October 11, 1991
Oakhill, WV – High School
PWF
- George South vs Hillbilly Willie
- George South vs Joey Morton
- Managed Mark Canterbury
- Battle Royal

October 17, 1991
Mountain City, TN – High School
PWF
- George South vs Joey Morton
- Managed Mark Canterbury
- Battle Royal

October 18, 1991
Nuttall, WV – Middle School
PWF
- George South vs Joey Morton
- Managed Mark Canterbury
- Battle Royal

October 19, 1991
Anstead, WV – Middle Scholl
PWF
- George South vs Mark Woods
- Managed Mark Canterbury

October 21, 1991
Gauley Bridge, WV – Middle School – 2pm
PWF Dare School Show
- George South vs Chuck Woods
- Managed Mark Canterbury

October 21, 1991
Montgomery, WV – Middle School – 8pm
PWF
- George South vs Chuck Woods
- Managed Mark Canterbury

October 22, 1991
Meadow Bridge, WV – High School
PWF
- PWF Junior Heavyweight Title: Gorgeous George South* beat Joey Morton

October 24, 1991
Shady Springs, WV – Junior High School – 2pm
PWF Dare School Show
- George South vs Joey Morton
- Managed Mark Canterbury

October 24, 1991
Richwood, WV – High School – 8pm
PWF
- George South vs Michael McReynolds
- Managed Mark Canterbury
- Battle Royal

October 25, 1991
Shinnston, WV – High School
PWF
- George South vs Joey Morton
- Managed Mark Canterbury

October 26, 1991
Raine, WV – Junior High School
PWF
- George South vs Hillbilly Willie
- George South vs Joey Morton
- Managed Mark Canterbury
- Bunkhouse Stampede

October 29, 1991
Ronceverte, WV – Junior High School
PWF
- George South vs Mark Woods
- Managed Mark Canterbury

October 30, 1991
Phillip Barber, WV – High School
PWF
- George South vs Italian Stallion
- Managed Mark Canterbury

November 2, 1991
Meadow Bridge, WV – High School
PWF
- George South & Mark Canterbury vs Italian Stallion & Joey Morton
- Bunkhouse Stampede

November 5, 1991
Gainesville, GA – Georgia Mountain Center
WCW TV Taping
- Kong beat George South

November 9, 1991
Weston, WV – Old Gym
PWF
- George South vs Joey Morton
- Managed Mark Canterbury
- Bunkhouse Stampede

November 11, 1991
Atlanta, GA – Center Stage
WCW TV Taping
- Van Hammer beat George South

November 14, 1991
Rupert, WV – Junior High School
PWF
- George South vs Joey Morton
- Managed Mark Canterbury

November 15, 1991
Elizabethtown, TN – High School – 2pm
PWF Dare School Show
- George South vs Charlie Peters

November 15, 1991
Elizabethtown, TN – Elementary School – 8pm
PWF
- George South vs Scotty Bradley
- Managed Mark Canterbury
- Battle Royal

November 16, 1991
Fairlea, WV - High School
PWF
- George South vs James Clontz
- Managed Mark Canterbury
- Bunkhouse Stampede

November 19, 1991
Barbersville, WV – High School
PWF
- George South vs Joey Morton
- Managed Mark Canterbury

November 20, 1991
Charmco, WV – High School
PWF
- George South vs Joey Morton
- Managed Mark Canterbury

November 21, 1991
Echo, WV – High School
PWF
- George South vs Joey Morton
- Managed Mark Canterbury

December 5, 1991
Newton, NC – Rec Center
PWF
- George South beat Scotty Bradley
  - Bunkhouse Stampede

December 6, 1991
Norfolk, VA – Naval Base
PWF
- George South vs Navy Seal
- Managed Mark Canterbury

December 7, 1991
Phillip, WV – High School
PWF
- George South vs Joey Morton
- Managed Mark Canterbury
  - Battle Royal

December 27, 1991
McAdenville, NC – Community Center
PWF
- George South vs James Clontz
- Managed Mark Canterbury
  - Bunkhouse Stampede

1992

January 3, 1992
Weston, WV – Gym
PWF
• George South vs The Juicer
• George South & Mark Canterbury vs Italian Stallion & Joey Morton
• Battle Royal

January 4, 1992
Oak Hill, WV – High School
PWF
• George South vs West Virginia Elvis
• George South & Mark Canterbury vs Italian Stallion & Joey Morton
• Battle Royal

January 17, 1992
Mt. Hope, WV – Middle School
PWF
• George South vs Joey Morton
• Managed Mark Canterbury

January 18, 1992
Point Pleasant, WV – Armory
PWF
• George South vs Joey Morton
• Managed Mark Canterbury
• Battle Royal

January 29, 1992
Ona, WV – Middle School – 2pm
PWF Dare School Show
• George South vs Joey Morton
• Managed Mark Canterbury

January 29, 192
Ona, WV – Middle School – 8pm
PWF
• George South vs Joey Morton
• Managed Mark Canterbury

January 30, 1992
Nitro, WV – High School
PWF
• George South vs Joey Morton
• Managed Mark Canterbury

January 31, 1992
Lewisburg, WV – Middle School
PWF
• George South vs Joey Morton
• Managed Mark Canterbury

February 1, 1992
Zionville, NC – Middle School
PWF
• George South vs Joey Morton
• Managed Mark Canterbury
• Battle Royal

February 7, 1992
Newton, NC – Rec Center
PWF
- George South vs Joey Morton
- Managed Mark Canterbury
- Battle Royal

February 8, 1992
McAdenville, NC – Community Center
PWF
- George South beat Joey Morton

February 12, 1992
Huntington, WV – High School
PWF
- George South vs Joey Morton
- Managed Mark Canterbury

February 15, 1992
Spencer, WV – High School
PWF
- George South vs Joey Morton
- Managed Mark Canterbury
- Battle Royal

February 17, 1992
Rock Hill, SC – College
WCW
- Marcs Bagwell beat George South

February 25, 1992
Commack, WV – Middle School
PWF
- George South vs Joey Morton
- Managed Mark Canterbury
February 26, 1992
Beverly Hills, WV – Middle School
PWF
- George South vs Joey Morton
- Managed Mark Canterbury

February 27, 1992
Locks Landing, WV – Middle School
PWF
- George South vs Joey Morton
- Managed Mark Canterbury

February 28, 1992
Salt Rock, WV – High School
PWF
- PWF Junior Heavyweight Title: Gorgeous George South* beat Joey Morton
- Managed Mark Canterbury

March 3, 1992
Atlanta, GA – Center Stage
WCW TV Taping
- Rom Simmons & Junkyard Dog beat George South & Mike Thor (3:45)

March 4, 1992
Columbus, GA – Civic Center
WCW TV Taping
- Dustin Rhodes & Barry Windham beat George South & Mark Canterbury
- Marcus Bagwell & Tom Zenk beat George South & Mark Canterbury

March 5, 1992
Norfolk, VA – Norfolk Naval Base
PWF
- PWF Junior Heavyweight Title: Gorgeous George South* beat Southern Rocker
- Managed Mark Canterbury
- 8 Man Bunkhouse Battle Royal: Gorgeous George South

March 6, 1992
Milton, WV – Milton High School
PWF
- PWF Junior Heavyweight Title: Gorgeous George South* beat Star Ryder
- Managed Mark Canterbury

March 13, 1992
Weston, WV – Gym
PWF
- George South vs Joey Morton
- Managed The Assassin
- Battle Royal

March 14, 1992
Oakdale, WV – High School
PWF
- George South vs Joey Morton
- Managed Mark Canterbury
- Battle Royal

March 19, 1992
Hurricane, WV – High School
PWF
- George South vs Joey Morton
- Managed Mark Canterbury

March 20, 1992
Norfolk, VA – Naval Base
PWF
- George South vs Joey Morton
- Managed Mark Canterbury
- Bunkhouse Stampede

March 21, 1992
Mt. Hope, WV – Middle School
PWF
- George South vs Joey Morton
- Managed Mark Canterbury

March 27, 1992
Martinsville, WV – High School
PWF
- George South vs Joey Morton
- Managed Mark Canterbury
- Bunkhouse Battle Royal

March 28, 1992
Pt. Pleasant, WV – Armory
PWF
- George South vs The Juicer
- Managed Russian Assassin vs Italian Stallion
- George South & Russian Assassin vs Italian Stallion & Super Mario
- Bunkhouse Battle Royal

March 31, 1992
Crum, WV – Middle School - 2pm
PWF Dare School Show
- George South vs Joey Morton
- Managed Mark Canterbury

March 31, 1992
Ft. Gay, WV – Middle School
PWF
• George South vs Joey Morton
• Managed Mark Canterbury

April 1, 1992
Ceredo, WV – Middle School – 2pm
PWF Dare School Show
• George South vs Joey Morton
• Managed Mark Canterbury

April 1, 1992
Ft. Gay, WV – High School – 8pm
PWF
• George South vs Joey Morton
• Managed Mark Canterbury

April 2, 1992
Kenova, WV – High School -2pm
PWF Dare School Show
• George South vs Joey Morton
• Managed Mark Canterbury

April 2, 1992
Wayne, WV – Middle School – 8pm
PWF
• George South vs Joey Morton
• Managed Mark Canterbury

April 3, 1992
Wayne, WV – Elementary School – 2pm
PWF Dare School Show
• George South vs Joey Morton
• Managed Mark Canterbury

April 3, 1992
East Lynn, WV – Elementary School – 8pm
PWF
• George South vs Joey Morton
• Managed Mark Canterbury

April 10, 1992
Rainelle, WV – Middle School
PWF
• George South vs Joey Morton
• George South, Mark Canterbury & Russian Assassin vs Italian Stallion, Joey Morton & Super Mario
• Bunkhouse Battle Royal

April 23, 1992
Jacksonville, FL – Naval Base
PWF
• George South vs Super Mario
• George South vs Southern Rocker
• Managed Mark Canterbury vs Italian Stallion
• George South & Mark Canterbury vs Italian Stallion & Super Mario

April 25, 1992
Grantsville, WV – High School
PWF
• PWF Junior Heavyweight Title: Gorgeous George South* beat Flaming Youth
• Managed Russian Assassin
• George South & Russian Assassin vs. Italian Stallion & Super Mario

April 28, 1992
Petersburg, WV – High School
PWF
- George South vs The Juicer
- Managed Mark Canterbury

April 29, 1992
Moorefield, WV – High School – 2pm
PWF Dare School Show
- George South vs The Juicer
- Managed Mark Canterbury

April 29, 1992
East Hardy, WV – High School
PWF
- PWF Junior Heavyweight Title: Gorgeous George South* beat Star Ryder
- Managed Mark Canterbury
- 8 Man Bunkhouse Battle Royal: George South

April 30, 1992
Romney, WV -Middle School – 2pm
PWF Dare School Show
- George South vs The Juicer
- Managed Mark Canterbury

April 30, 1992
Capon Bridge, WV – Middle School
PWF
- George South vs The Juicer
- Managed Mark Canterbury

May 1, 1992
Berkely Springs, WV – High School – 2pm
PWF Dare School Show
- George South vs The Juicer
- Managed Mark Canterbury

May 1, 1992
Paw Paw, WV – High School
PWF
- George South vs The Juicer
- Managed Mark Canterbury

May 2, 1992
Gauley Bridge, WV – High School
PWF
- PWF Junior Heavyweight Title: Gorgeous George South* beat Southern Rocker
- Managed Mark Canterbury
- 8 Man Bunkhouse Stampede: Cruel Connection II

May 3, 1992
Weston, WV – High School
PWF
- PWF Junior Heavyweight Title: Gorgeous George South* beat Flaming Youth
- 8 Man Bunkhouse Stampede: George South

May 4, 1992
Charles Town, WV – Middle School- 2pm
PWF Dare School Show
- George South vs The Juicer
- Managed Mark Canterbury

May 4, 1992
Harpers Ferry, WV – Junior High School
PWF
• PWF Junior Heavyweight Title: Gorgeous George South* beat Flaming Youth
• Managed Mark Canterbury
• 8 Battle Royal: Italian Stallion

May 5, 1992
Shepherdstown, WV – Middle School
PWF Dare School Show
• George South vs The Juicer
• Managed Mark Canterbury

May 23, 1992
Crum, WV – Middle School
PWF
• PWF Junior Heavyweight Title: Gorgeous George South* beat Star Ryder
• Managed Mark Canterbury
• 8 Man Battle Royal: Cruel Connection II

May 27, 1992
Anderson, SC – Civic Center
WCW TV Taping
• Johnny B. Badd beat George South

May 29, 1992
Pineville, WV – Pineville High School
• Texas Death Match - PWF Junior Heavyweight Title:
Gorgeous George South* beat Flaming Youth
• Managed Mark Canterbury

June 4, 1992
McAdenville, NC – Community Center
PWF
• George South vs Italian Stallion
• Battle Royal

June 5, 1992
North Wilkesboro, NC – Armory
PWF
• George South vs The Juicer
• Managed Mark Canterbury vs Italian Stallion
• George South & Mark Canterbury vs Italian Stallion & The Juicer

June 11, 1992
Elkin, NC – Armory
PWF
• PWF Junior Heavyweight Title: Gorgeous George South* beat Flaming Youth
• 8 Man Battle Royal: George South

June 18, 1992
Kings Mountain, NC – Armory
PWF
• Gorgeous George South & Mean Marc Canterbury beat The Star Ryders
• 8 Man Battle Royal: Flaming Youth

June 19, 1992
Lancaster, SC – Armory
PWF
• PWF Junior Heavyweight Title: Gorgeous George South* beat Austin Steele
• Battle Royal: George South

PRO WRESTLING FEDERATION
JUNE 25, 1992
PRINCETON, WV I PRINCETON HIGH SCHOOL

MAIN EVENT I PWF WORLD TITLE MATCH

CHAMPION

ITALIAN STALLION VS MEAN MARC CANTERBURY

PWF JUNIOR HEAVYWEIGHT CHAMPION

GORGEOUS GEORGE SOUTH
VS
THE FLAMING YOUTH

AUSTIN STEELE VS JOEY MORTON

PLUS 2 MORE MATCHES

PRO WRESTLING FEDERATION

June 25, 1992
Princeton, WV – High School
PWF
• PWF Junior Heavyweight Title: Gorgeous George South* beat Flaming Youth
• Managed Mark Canterbury
• Battle Royal: Italian Stallion

June 26, 1992
Tazwell, VA – Elementary School
PWF
• PWF Junior Heavyweight Title: Gorgeous George South* beat Chief Black Heart
• Battle Royal: George South

June 29, 1992
Atlanta, GA – Center Stage
WCW TV Taping
• Johnny B Badd beat George South

July 2, 1992
North Wilkesboro, NC – Armory
PWF
• George South vs The Juicer
• Managed The Harlem Knights (Men On a Mission - Mo & Mable)

July 9, 1992
McAdenville, NC – Community Center
PWF
• George South & The Harlem Knights vs Italian Stallion, Southern Rocker & American GI

July 10, 1992
Lancaster, SC – Armory
PWF
• George South vs Southern Rocker
• George South & Austin Steele vs. Italian Stallion & Star Ryder

July 11, 1992
Elkin, NC – Armory
PWF
• George South vs Southern Rocker
• Managed Kill Dozer

July 16, 1992
Augusta, GA – Augusta-Richmond Co Civic Center
WCW Great American Bash Tour
• Brian Pillman beat George South (1:35)

July 17, 1992
Kings Mountain, NC – Armory
PWF
• George South vs. Italian Stallion
• Managed Mark Canterbury

July 25, 1992
McAdenville, NC – Community Center
PWF
• George South vs Star Ryder
• Managed Kill Dozer

August 1, 1992
Ronceverte, WV – Island Park
PWF
• George South & Mark Canterbury vs Italian Stallion & Elmer Honaker

August 6, 1992
Kings Mountain, NC – Armory
PWF
• Italian Stallion & American GI beat George South & Mark Canterbury (dq)

August 7, 1992
Princeton, WV – High School
PWF
• George South & Mark Canterbury vs Italian Stallion & Scotty McKeever

August 11, 1992
Gainesville, GA – Georgia Mountain Center
WCW TV Taping
• Nikita Koloff beat George South

August 13, 1992
Hickory, NC – Armory
PWF
• George South beat Star Ryder (Chad Byrd)

August 14, 1992
Elkin, NC – Armory
PWF
• George South beat Star Ryder

August 15, 1992
North Wilkesboro, NC – Armory
PWF
• George South & Kill Dozer vs Italian Stallion & TJ Maverick

August 21, 1992
McAdenville, NC – Community Center
PWF
• George South beat Austin Steele
• Managed Kill Dozer

August 22, 1992
Mountain City, TN – High School
PWF
• George South & Kill Dozer vs Italian Stallion & TJ Maverick
• Bunkhouse Stampede: George South

August 28, 1992
Gilbert, WV – Fire House
PWF
• George South beat Star Ryder
• Managed Mark Canterbury
• Bunkhouse Battle

August 29, 1992
Oakdale, WV – High School
PWF
• George South beat Flaming Youth
• Bunkhouse Stampede: Mark Canterbury

September 11, 1992
Kings Mountain, NC – Armory
PWF
• George South & Kill Dozer vs Italian Stallion

September 12, 1992
Concord, NC – College Gym
PWF
• George South, Kill Dozer & Austin Steele vs Italian Stallion, Star Ryder & Scotty McKeever

September 13, 1992
Charlotte, NC – College Gym
PWF
• George South & Kill Dozer vs Italian Stallion & Scotty McKeever

September 15, 1992
Macon, GA -Macon Coliseum
WCW TV Taping
• Tom Zenk & Marcus Alexander Bagwell beat George South & Mark Canterbury

September 17, 1992
Hickory, NC – Armory
PWF
• George South & Austin Steele vs Terry Austin & Star Ryder

September 18, 1992
Elkin, NC – Armory
PWF
• George South vs Star Ryder
• Managed Texas Outlaw vs Italian Stallion

September 19, 1992
North Wilkesboro, NC – Armory
PWF
• George South & Kill Dozer vs Italian Stallion & Scotty McKeever

September 25, 1992
Dallas, NC – Gym
PWF
• George South, Austin Steele & Kill Dozer vs Italian Stallion, Mad Dog David Lynch & Scotty McKeever

September 26, 1992
Dallas, NC – Gym
PWF
• George South & The Harlem Knights vs Italian Stallion, Scotty McKeever & Mad Dog David Lynch

September 29, 1992
Columbus, GA – Municipal Auditorium
WCW TV Taping
• Shane Douglas beat George South

October 2, 1992
McAdenville, NC – Community Center
PWF
• George South & Kill Dozer vs Italian Stallion & Scotty McKeever

October 3, 1992
Gilbert, WV – Fire House
PWF
• George South beat Joey Morton
• Managed Mean Mark Canterbury vs Italian Stallion

October 9, 1992
Kings Mountain, NC – Armory
PWF
• George South & The Harlem Knights vs Italian Stallion, Star Ryder & Scotty McKeever
• Run-In on Harlem Knights match

October 10, 1992
Ronceverte, WV – High School
PWF
• George South vs Scotty McKeever
• Managed Mean Mark Canterbury vs Italian Stallion

October 16, 1992
Bellington, WV – Middle School
PWF
• George South beat Scotty McKeever
• Italian Stallion beat George South
• Battle Royal

October 17, 1992
Zionville, NC – Middle School
PWF
• George South beat Scotty McKeever

October 23, 1992
Belmont, NC - Armory
PWF
• George South beat Star Ryder

October 24, 1992
Elkin, NC - Armory
PWF
• George South beat Flaming Youth

October 27, 1992
Augusta, GA – Augusta-Richmond Co Civic Center
WCW TV Taping
• Tex Slazenger & Shanghai Pierce (Mark Canterbury) beat George South & Rex Cooper

October 30, 1992
Sugar Grove, NC – Old Cove Creek Gym
PWF
• George South beat Star Ryder

November 6, 1992
Fort Gay, WV – Middle School
PWF
• George South beat Star Ryder
• Managed Mad Dog David Lynch
• Italian Stallion & Star Ryder beat George South & Mad Dog David Lynch
• Battle Royal: Flaming Youth

November 7,1992
Lenoir, NC – Hibritan High School
PWF
• George South beat Scott Bradley (Hot Body)
• Managed Austin Steele vs Italian Stallion
• Battle Royal: Italian Stallion

November 13, 1992
Winston, WV - Gym
PWF
• George South beat Scotty McKeever
• Managed Austin Steele
• Battle Royal: George South

November 14, 1992
Gilbert, WV – Fire House
PWF
• George South beat Flaming Youth
• Battle Royal

November 19, 1992
McAdenville, NC – Community Center
PWF
• George South beat Star Ryder

November 20, 1992
Elkin, NC – Armory
PWF
• George South, Austin Steele & Terry Austin vs Star Ryder, Scotty McKeever & Randy Sledge
• Managed Texas Outlaw vs Italian Stallion

November 21, 1992
Lincolnton, NC – Armory
PWF
• George South beat Scotty McKeever
• Managed Austin Steele vs Italian Stallion

November 23, 1992
Atlanta, GA – Center Stage
WCW TV Taping
• Too Cold Scorpio beat George South

November 27, 1992
Kings Mountain, NC – Armory
PWF
• George South beat Star Ryder

November 28, 1992
Stanley, NC – Armory
PWF
• George South beat Scotty McKeever
• Managed Mad Dog David Lynch
• Battle Royal

November 30, 1992
Atlanta, GA – Center Stage
WCW TV Taping
• Ricky Nelson beat George South

December 1, 1992
Gainesville, GA – Georgia Mountain Center
WCW TV Taping
• Too Cold Scorpio beat George South (1:25)
• Johnny B Badd beat George South (1:58)

December 5, 1992
Gastonia, NC – Armory
PWF
• George South beat Flaming Youth
• Battle Royal: George South

December 11, 1992
North Wilkesboro, NC – Armory att. 100
PWF
• George South beat Star Ryder
• Managed Texas Outlaw vs Italian Stallion

December 12, 1992
Charlotte, NC – Northside Church Gym att. 2,050
PWF
• George South beat Cruel Connection II
• Battle Royal

December 18, 1992
Elkin, NC – Armory
PWF
• George South beat Star Ryder
• Managed Texas Outlaw

December 19, 1992
Gilbert, WV – Fire House
PWF
• George South beat Scotty McKeever
• Battle Royal: George South

December 22, 1992
St. Mary, WV – High School
PWF
- George South beat Star Ryder
- Managed Mad Dog David Lynch vs Italian Stallion

December 25, 1992
Belmont, NC – Armory
PWF
- Barbed Wire Match: George South beat Star Ryder
- Managed Terry Austin
- Managed The Harlem Knights (Nelson Knight & Bobby Knight aka Men on a Mission)

December 26, 1992
Lincolnton, NC – Armory
PWF
- George South beat Star Ryder
- Managed Terry Austin vs Italian Stallion
- Managed The Harlem Knights

1993

January 1, 1993
Kings Mountain, NC – Armory
PWF
• Barbed Wire Match: Gorgeous George South beat Star Ryder
• Managed The Harlem Knights vs American GI & Italian Stallion

January 2, 1993
North Wilkesboro, NC – Armory
PWF
• Gorgeous George South, Nelson Knight & Bobby Knight (Men on a Mission)
beat Star Ryder, Italian Stallion & American GI

January 8, 1993
Belmont, NC – Armory
PWF
• PWF Junior Heavyweight Title: Gorgeous George South* beat Star Ryder

January 9, 1993
Lincolnton, NC – Armory
PWF
• PWF Junior Heavyweight Title: Gorgeous George South* beat Star Ryder

January 15, 1993
Ghent, WV
PWF
• Gorgeous George South vs Italian Stallion
• Bunkhouse Stampede:

January 16, 1993
Rockford, WV
PWF
• PWF Junior Heavyweight Title: Gorgeous George South* beat Scotty McKeever
• Lethal Lottery

January 22, 1993
Elkin, NC
PWF
• George South & Austin Steele vs Italian Stallion & The Juicer
• Lethal Lottery

January 23, 1993
Gilbert, WV
PWF
• Gorgeous George South vs Italian Stallion

January 29, 1993
Taylorsville, NC – Armory
PWF
• PWF Junior Heavyweight Title: Gorgeous George South* beat Flaming Youth
• Managed Austin Steele vs Italian Stallion
• Lethal Lottery

January 30, 1993
Taylorsville, NC – Church Show
PWF
• George South vs Tony Smith

February 5, 1993
Norfolk, VA – Naval Base
PWF
• PWF Junior Heavyweight Title: Gorgeous George South* beat Flaming Youth
• Managed Austin Steele vs Italian Stallion
• Battle Royal

February 6, 1993
Kings Mountain, NC – Armory
PWF
• PWF Junior Heavyweight Title: Gorgeous George South* beat Star Ryder
• Managed The Harlem Knights

February 12, 1993
Belmont, NC – Armory
PWF
• PWF Junior Heavyweight Title: Gorgeous George South* beat Juicer

February 13, 1993
North Wilkesboro, NC – Armory
PWF
• PWF Junior Heavyweight Title: Gorgeous George South* beat Star Ryder
• Managed The Harlem Knights

February 19, 1993
Elkin, NC - Armory
PWF
• PWF Junior Heavyweight Title: Gorgeous George South* beat Flaming Youth
• Bunkhouse Battle Royal

February 20, 1993
Gilbert, WV
PWF
• PWF Junior Heavyweight Title: Gorgeous George South* beat Flaming Youth
• Managed Austin Steele

February 27, 1993
Point Pleasant, WV – High School
PWF
• PWF Junior Heavyweight Title: Gorgeous George South* beat Scotty McKeever
• Managed Austin Steele vs Italian Stallion
• Lethal Lottery

March 5, 1993
Spencer, WV
PWF
• PWF Junior Heavyweight Title: Gorgeous George South* beat Joey Morton
• Managed The Russian vs Italian Stallion
• Lethal Lottery

March 6, 1993
Cowen, WV – Elementary School
PWF
• Barbed Wire Match: Gorgeous George South beat Scotty McKeever
• Managed The Russian vs Italian Stallion
• Lethal Lottery

March 7, 1993
Fayetteville, NC -Civic Center
WWF TV Taping
• Tatanka beat George South
• Rick & Scott Steiner beat George South &?

March 11, 1993
North Wilkesboro, NC – Armory
PWF
• PWF Junior Heavyweight Title: Gorgeous George South* beat Southern Rocker
• Managed Austin Steele vs Italian Stallion

March 12, 1993
Elkin, NC – Armory
PWF

- PWF Junior Heavyweight Title: Gorgeous George South* beat Southern Rocker
  - Managed Texas Outlaw
  - Managed Austin Steele

March 19, 1993
Kings Mountain, NC – Armory
PWF

- PWF Junior Heavyweight Title: Gorgeous George South* beat Southern Rocker
  - Managed The Russian

March 20, 1993
Taylorsville, NC – Armory
PWF

- First Blood Match: Gorgeous George South beat Southern Rocker
  - Managed Austin Steele vs Italian Stallion
  - Battle Royal

March 25, 1993
Pine Grove, WV – High School
PWF

- Barbed Wire Match: Gorgeous George South beat Southern Rocker
  - Managed The Russian

March 27, 1993
Ripley, WV
PWF

- Barbed Wire Match: Gorgeous George South beat Southern Rocker
  - Managed The Russian
  - Battle Royal

April 2, 1993
Gilbert, WV – Firehouse
PWF

- PWF Junior Heavyweight Title: Gorgeous George South* beat Southern Rocker
  - Managed The Russian

April 3, 1993
Rockingham, NC – Armory
PWF

- PWF Junior Heavyweight Title: Gorgeous George South* beat Southern Rocker

April 9, 1993
Belmont, NC – Armory
PWF

- PWF Junior Heavyweight Title: Gorgeous George South* beat Scotty McKeever
  - Managed The Russian

April 10, 1993
Taylorsville, NC – Armory
PWF

- PWF Junior Heavyweight Title: Gorgeous George South* beat Scotty McKeever
  - Managed Kill Dozer
  - Battle Royal

April 16, 1993
Kings Mountain, NC -Armory
PWF

- 4 Team Elimination: Italian Stallion & American GI beat George South & Terry Austin, Scotty McKeever & Mad Dog David Lynch and Texas Outlaw & Jeff Victory

April 17, 1993
Elkin, NC – Armory
PWF

- PWF Junior Heavyweight Title: Gorgeous George South* beat Cruel Connection II

April 23, 1993
Lincolnton, NC – Armory
PWF
- PWF Junior Heavyweight Title: Gorgeous George South* beat Cruel Connection II

April 24, 1993
Parkersburg, WV
PWF
- PWF Junior Heavyweight Title: Gorgeous George South* beat Star Ryder

April 30, 1993
Wallace, NC
PWF
- PWF Junior Heavyweight Title: Gorgeous George South* beat Cruel Connection II

May 1, 1993
Sugar Grove, NC – Old Cove Creek Gym
PWF
- PWF Junior Heavyweight Title: Gorgeous George South* beat Star Ryder

May 8, 1993
Norfolk, VA – Naval Base
PWF
- PWF Junior Heavyweight Title: Gorgeous George South* beat Scotty McKeever
- George South & Terry Austin vs Dozer & Randy Sledge
- Battle Royal

May 14, 1993
Kings Mountain, NC – Armory
PWF
- PWF Junior Heavyweight Title: Gorgeous George South* beat Scotty McKeever
- Lethal Lottery

May 15, 1993
Taylorsville, NC – Armory
PWF
- PWF Junior Heavyweight Title: Gorgeous George South* beat Cruel Connection II

May 20, 1993
Mayport, FL – Naval Base
PWF
- PWF Junior Heavyweight Title: Gorgeous George South* beat Scotty McKeever
- Managed Terry Austin vs Italian Stallion
- Battle Royal

May 22, 1993
Belmont, NC – Armory
PWF
- PWF Junior Heavyweight Title: Gorgeous George South* beat Scotty McKeever
- Managed Terry Austin vs Italian Stallion
- Battle Royal

May 28, 1993
Iaegar, WV
PWF
- PWF Junior Heavyweight Title: Gorgeous George South* beat Joey Morton
- Managed Terry Austin
- Battle Royal

May 29, 1993
Kings Mountain, NC – Armory
PWF
- PWF Junior Heavyweight Title: Gorgeous George South* beat Scotty McKeever
- Managed Terry Austin
- Battle Royal

June 5, 1993
Rockingham, NC – Armory
PWF
• PWF Junior Heavyweight Title: Gorgeous George South* beat Scotty McKeever

June 11, 1993
Elkin, NC – Armory
PWF
• PWF Junior Heavyweight Title: Gorgeous George South* beat Flaming Youth
• Battle Royal

June 12, 1993
Taylorsville, NC – Armory
• George South & Black Scorpion beat Flaming Youth & Cruel Connection II (dq)
• Managed Austin Steele & Terry Austin vs Italian Stallion & American GI
• Battle Royal

June 18, 1993
Belmont, NC – Armory
PWF
• PWF Junior Heavyweight Title: Gorgeous George South* beat Scotty McKeever
• Battle Royal

June 19, 1993
Lincolnton, NC – Armory
PWF
• PWF Junior Heavyweight Title: Gorgeous George South* beat Flaming Youth
• Managed Terry Austin & Austin Steele vs Italian Stallion & American GI
• Battle Royal

June 20, 1993
Rocky Gap, VA
PWF
• PWF Junior Heavyweight Title: Gorgeous George South* beat Rocky Gap Mascot

June 25, 1993
Kings Mountain, NC – Armory
PWF
• PWF Junior Heavyweight Title: Gorgeous George South* beat Ric Starr
• Managed Terry Austin & Austin Steele vs Italian Stallion & American GI

June 26, 1993
Princeton, WV – High School
PWF
• PWF Junior Heavyweight Title: Gorgeous George South* beat Flaming Youth

July 3, 1993
Morganton, NC – I-40 Flea Market
PWF
• PWF Junior Heavyweight Title: Gorgeous George South* beat Scotty McKeever
• Managed Austin Steele vs Italian Stallion
• Battle Royal

July 9, 1993
Morganton, NC – I-40 Flea Market
PWF
• PWF Junior Heavyweight Title: Gorgeous George South* beat Scotty McKeever
• Managed Terry Austin & Austin Steele vs Italian Stallion & American GI
• Battle Royal

July 10, 1993
Elkin, NC – Armory
PWF
• George South & Terry Austin beat The Heartbreakers (Scotty Hot Body & Scotty McKeever)
• Battle Royal

PRO WRESTLING FEDERATION
JULY 16, 1993
KINGS MOUNTAIN, NC I NATIONAL GUARD ARMORY

MAIN EVENT I PWF WORLD TITLE MATCH

CHAMPION
AUSTIN STEELE vs ITALIAN STALLION

SEMI-MAIN EVENT I PWF TAG TEAM CHAMPIONS
GORGEOUS GEORGE SOUTH & TERRY AUSTIN
VS
THE HEARTBREAKERS

AMERICAN GI vs JEFF VICTORY
MAD DOG LYNCH vs KILLDOZER
RAVISHING RANDY SLEDGE
VS
RAY HUDSON
PLUS MANY MORE MATCHES
PRO WRESTLING FEDERATION

July 16, 1993
Kings Mountain, NC – Armory
PWF
• George South & Terry Austin beat The Heartbreakers (Scotty Hot Body & Scotty McKeever)
• Battle Royal

July 17, 1993
Albemarle, NC – Armory
PWF
• George South & Terry Austin beat The Heartbreakers
• Managed Austin Steele vs Italian Stallion
• Battle Royal

July 23, 1993
North Wilkesboro, NC – Armory
PWF
• PWF Junior Heavyweight Title: Gorgeous George South* beat Flaming Youth (Ray Hudson)
• Battle Royal

July 24, 1993
Taylorsville, NC – Armory
PWF
• PWF Junior Heavyweight Title: Gorgeous George South* beat Star Ryder
• Battle Royal

July 30, 1993
Belmont, NC – Armory
PWF
• PWF Junior Heavyweight Title: Gorgeous George South* beat Ray Hudson
• Battle Royal

July 31, 1993
Lincolnton, NC – Armory
PWF
• PWF Junior Heavyweight Title: Gorgeous George South* beat Star Ryder
• Battle Royal

August 4, 1993
Charlotte, NC – Latter Park
PWF
• Italian Stallion beat George South

August 6, 1993
Elkin, NC – Armory
PWF
• PWF Junior Heavyweight Title: Gorgeous George South* beat Star Ryder
• Managed Austin Steele
• Battle Royal

August 7, 1993
Morganton, NC – I—40 Flea Market
PWF
• PWF Junior Heavyweight Title: Gorgeous George South* beat Star Ryder
• Manage Austin Steele
• Battle Royal

August 13, 1993
Kings Mountain, NC – Armory
• PWF Junior Heavyweight Title: Gorgeous George South* beat Ray Hudson
• Managed Terry Austin & Austin Steele vs Italian Stallion & American GI
• Battle Royal

August 14, 1993
Taylorsville, NC – Armory
PWF
• George South beat Ray Hudson
• Managed Austin Steele
• Battle Royal

August 20, 1993
Bluefield, WV – Armory
WCW
• Keith & Kent Cole beat George South & Italian Stallion

August 21, 1993
Albemarle, NC – Armory
PWF
- George South beat Benji
- Managed Terry Austin
- Battle Royal

August 27, 1993
Kings Mountain, NC – Armory
PWF
- George South beat Ray Hudson
- Managed Austin Steele
- Battle Royal

August 28, 1993
Kings Mountain, NC – Armory
PWF
- George South beat Star Ryder (Ray Hudson)
- Managed Austin Steele
- Managed Terry Austin
- Battle Royal

September 3, 1993
Elkin, NC -Armory
PWF
- George South vs Texas Outlaw
- George South & Terry Austin vs Jeff Victory & Randy Sledge
- Managed Austin Steele vs Italian Stallion

September 4, 1993
Morganton, NC – I-40 Flea Market
PWF
- George South vs Star Ryder (Ray Hudson)
- George South & Austin Steele vs Jeff Victory & Randy Sledge
- Battle Royal

September 10, 1993
Belmont, NC – Armory
PWF
- George South beat Star Ryder
- Managed Terry Austin & Austin Steele vs Italian Stallion & Jeff Victory

September 11, 1993
Lincolnton, NC – Armory
PWF
- George South beat Star Ryder
- Managed Terry Austin & Austin Steele vs Italian Stallion & Jeff Victory
- Battle Royal

September 17, 1993
Kings Mountain, NC – Armory
PWF
- George South & Terry Austin beat Star Ryder & Randy Sledge
- Managed Austin Steele vs Italian Stallion

September 18, 1993
Albemarle, NC – Armory
PWF
- George South, Austin Steele & Terry Austin vs Italian Stallion, Star Ryder & Randy Sledge

September 25, 1993
Taylorsville, NC – Armory
PWF
- George South beat Midnight Rider
- Managed Austin Steele vs Italian Stallion

October 1, 1993
Belmont, NC – Armory
PWF
• George South & Terry Austin beat Star Ryder & Emillo Ulacia
• Managed Austin Steele

October 2, 1993
Norfolk, VA – Naval Base
PWF
• George South beat Star Ryder
• Managed Austin Steele

October 8, 1993
Elkin, NC – Armory
PWF
• George South & Terry Austin beat Texas Outlaw & Randy Sledge
• Managed Austin Steele
• Battle Royal

October 9, 1993
Morganton, NC – I-40 Flea Market
PWF
• George South beat Star Ryder
• Managed Austin Steele

October 15, 1993
Marion, NC – Armory
PWF
• George South & Terry Austin beat Flaming Youth & Cruel Connection II
• George South & Black Scorpion beat Jeff Victory & Star Ryder
• Battle Royal

October 16, 1993
Hamlet, NC – Armory
PWF
• PWF Junior Heavyweight Title: Gorgeous George South* beat Flaming Youth
• Managed Austin Steele
• Battle Royal

October 22, 1993
Albemarle, NC – Armory
PWF
• PWF Junior Heavyweight Title: Gorgeous George South* beat Star Ryder
• Managed Austin Steele
• Battle Royal

October 23, 1993
Taylorsville, NC – Armory
PWF
• George South & Terry Austin beat Flaming Youth & Cruel Connection II
• Italian Stallion beat George South
• Battle Royal

October 29, 1993
Elizabethtown, NC
PWF
• George South & Terry Austin beat Flaming Youth & Cruel Connection II

October 30, 1993
Kings Mountain, NC – Armory
PWF
• PWF Junior Heavyweight Title: Star Ryder beat Gorgeous George South* (dq)
• Managed Black Scorpion vs Italian Stallion
• Battle Royal:

November 5, 1993
Elkin, NC – Armory
PWF
- George South & Terry Austin beat Tim Woody & Star Ryder
- Battle Royal

November 6, 1993
Morganton, NC – I-40 Flea Market
PWF
- George South & Terry Austin beat Flaming Youth & Randy Sledge
- Managed Black Scorpion vs Italian Stallion
- Battle Royal

November 12, 1993
Hamlet, NC – Armory
PWF
- George South & Terry Austin beat The Southern Rockers
- Battle Royal

November 12, 1993
Rockingham, NC – High School – 1pm
PWF Dare School Show
- George South beat Star Ryder
- Managed Black Scorpion vs Italian Stallion

November 12, 1993
Hamlet, NC – Armory – 8pm
PWF
- George South beat Tim Woody
- Managed Black Scorpion vs Italian Stallion
- Battle Royal

November 13, 1993
Belmont, NC – Armory
PWF
- George South & Terry Austin double count out Flaming Youth & Star Ryder
- Managed Austin Steele
- Battle Royal

November 19, 1993
Dallas, NC
PWF
- George South & Terry Austin beat Southern Rockers

November 20, 1993
Albemarle, NC – Breakers
PWF
- George South & Terry Austin beat Tyrone Knox & Benji Beechum
- Battle Royal

November 24, 1993
Burlington, NC - Armory
PWF
- George South & Terry Austin beat Flaming Youth & Star Ryder
- Managed Austin Steele vs Italian Stallion
- Battle Royal

November 25, 1993
Taylorsville, NC – Armory
PWF
- George South & Terry Austin beat Flaming Youth & Star Ryder
- Bunkhouse Stampede

November 26, 1993
Kings Mountain, NC – Armory
PWF
• Italian Stallion beat George South (dq)
• Battle Royal

November 27, 1993
Lincolnton, NC – Armory
PWF
• Italian Stallion, Star Ryder & Randy Sledge beat George South, Terry Austin & Russian Assassin
• Bunkhouse Battle Royal

December 3, 1993
Belmont, NC – Armory
PWF
• Italian Stallion beat George South
• Battle Royal

December 4, 1993
Morganton, NC – I-40 Flea Market att. 61
PWF
• Scott Powers, Italian Stallion & Star Ryder beat George South, Terry Austin & Austin Steele
• Battle Royal

December 10, 1993
Charlotte, NC- Charlotte Coliseum att. 4,500
PWF
• George South & Italian Stallion beat Austin Steele & Black Scorpion
• Battle Royal: George South & Italian Stallion

December 11, 1993
Kings Mountain, NC – Armory att. 58
PWF
• George South & Terry Austin beat Mike Maverick & David Taylor
• Managed Chris Hamrick vs Italian Stallion
• Battle Royal

December 18, 1993
Hamlet, NC – Armory
PWF
• Italian Stallion beat George South
• Battle Royal

December 19, 1993
Elkin, NC – Armory
PWF
• George South beat Star Ryder
• Managed Austin Steele

December 25, 1993
Taylorsville, NC – Armory
PWF
• George South beat Star Ryder
• Managed Randy Sledge
• Battle Royal

1994

January 1, 1994
Belmont, NC – Armory
PWF
• George South & Terry Austin beat Italian Stallion & Star Ryder
• Battle Royal

January 7, 1994
Elkin, NC – Armory
PWF
• Italian Stallion & Star Ryder beat George South & Terry Austin
• Battle Royal

January 8, 1994
Morganton, NC – I-40 Flea Market
PWF
• Italian Stallion, Star Ryder & Scott Powers beat George South, Austin Steele & Terry Austin

January 10, 1994
Richmond, VA – Richmond Coliseum
WWF TV Taping
• Tananka beat George South

January 11, 1994
Florence, SC – Civic Center
WWF TV Taping
The Bushwackers (Butch Miller & Luke Williams) beat George South & Brooklyn Brawler

January 12, 1994
Fayetteville, NC – Cumberland Co. Memorial Auditorium
WWF TV Taping
• Doink the Clown beat George South

January 14, 1994
Hamlet, NC – Armory
PWF
• George South & Terry Austin beat Italian Stallion & Star Ryder
• Battle Royal

January 15, 1994
Kings Mountain, NC – Armory
PWF
• George South beat Tryone Knox
• Battle Royal

January 22, 1994
Taylorsville, NC – Armory
PWF
• George South & Russian Assassin beat Randy Sledge & Flaming Youth
• Managed Austin Steele

January 28, 1994
Forest City, NC – Armory
PWF
• George South beat Star Ryder
• Managed The Russian
• Battle Royal

January 29, 1994
Inman, SC- Armory
PWF
• Italian Stallion & Sta Ryder beat George South & Chris Hamrick
• Battle Royal

February 4, 1994
Elkin, NC – Armory att.87
PWF
• George South beat Super Ninja (Brian Lee)

February 5, 1994
Morganton, NC – I-40 Flea Market att. 61
PWF
• George South beat Super Ninja
• Battle Royal

February 12, 1994
Pt. Pleasant, WV – Central Gym
PWF
• George South beat Super Ninja
• Battle Royal

February 17, 1994
Belmont, NC – Armory
PWF
• George South beat Super Ninja
• Battle Royal

February 18, 1994
Kings Mountain, NC – Armory att. 65
PWF
• George South beat Super Ninja
• Battle Royal

February 19, 1994
Hamlet, NC – Armory
PWF
• George South beat Super Ninja
• Battle Royal

February 25, 1994
York, SC – Armory
PWF
• George South beat American Ninja (Brian Lee)
• Battle Royal

February 26, 1994
Taylorsville, NC – Armory
PWF
• George South beat Super Ninja
• Managed Austin Steele & Terry Austin

March 4, 1994
Forest City, NC – Armory
PWF
• George South beat Super Ninja
• Managed Austin Steele & Terry Austin

March 5, 1994
Inman, SC – Armory
PWF
• George South beat American Ninja
• Managed Austin Steele & Terry Austin

March 11, 1994
Elkin, NC – Armory
PWF
• George South beat American Ninja
• Battle Royal

March 12, 1994
Morganton, NC – I-40 Flea Market
PWF
• George South beat American Ninja
• Battle Royal

March 17, 1994
Belmont, NC – Armory
PWF
• George South beat American Ninja
• Battle Royal

March 18, 1994
Taylorsville, NC – Armory
PWF
• George South beat American Ninja
• Battle Royal
• Managed Austin Steele

March 19, 1994
North Wilkesboro, NC – Armory
PWF
• George South beat American Ninja
• Battle Royal
• Managed Austin Steele

March 22, 1994
Lowell, MA – Memorial Auditorium att. 3,200
WWF TV Taping
• Lex Luger beat George South

March 23, 1994
White Plains, NY – Civic Center
WWF TV Taping
• The Smoking Guns (Billy & Bart Gunn) beat George South & Terry Austin

March 25, 1994
Kings Mountain, NC – Armory
PWF
• George South & Terry Austin vs Italian Stallion & American Ninja

March 26, 1994
Hamlet, NC - Armory
PWF
• George South vs American Ninja
• Managed Austin Steele vs Italian Stallion

March 31, 1994
York, SC - Armory
PWF
• George South vs American Ninja
• Battle Royal

April 1, 1994
Forest City, NC - Armory
PWF
• George South vs American Ninja
• George South, Austin Steele & Terry Austin vs Italian Stallion, Chris Hamrick & Star Ryder

April 8, 1994
Inman, SC - Armory
PWF
• George South, Austin Steele & Terry Austin vs Italian Stallion, American Ninja & Black Eagle

April 9, 1994
Morganton, NC – I-40 Flea Market
PWF
• George South vs Italian Stallion

April 15, 1994
Elkin, NC - Armory
PWF
• George South, Austin Steele & Terry Austin vs Italian Stallion, Chris Hamrick & Star Ryder
• Battle Royal

April 16, 1994
Cowen, WV – High School
PWF
• George South Scott Powers
• Battle Royal

April 22, 1994
Hamlet, NC - Armory
PWF
• George South vs American Ninja
• Battle Royal

April 23, 1994
Taylorsville, NC - Armory
PWF
• George South vs American Ninja
• Battle Royal

April 28, 1994
Belmont, NC - Armory
PWF
• George South vs Italian Stallion

April 29, 1994
Kings Mountain, NC – Armory
PWF
• Brian Lee beat George South

April 30, 1994
Forest City, NC Armory
PWF
• George South & Terry Austin vs Krazy Kane Adams & Star Ryder
• Bunkhouse Battle Royal

May 6, 1994
Red Springs, NC - Armory
PWF
• George South vs American Ninja

May 7, 1994
Reidsville, NC - Armory
PWF
• George South vs American Ninja
• Battle Royal

May 13, 1994
Inman, SC - Armory
PWF
• Chief Black Eagle beat George South
• Battle Royal

May 14, 1994
Siler City, NC - Armory
PWF
• George South vs Star Ryder
• George South, Austin Steele & Terry Austin vs Italian Stallion, American Ninja & Star Ryder

May 20, 1994
Elkin, NC - Armory
PWF
• George South vs Wolverine
• Battle Royal

May 21, 1994
North Wilkesboro, NC - Armory
PWF
• George South vs Star Ryder

May 23, 1994
Struthers, OH – Struthers Field House att. 1,500
WWF TV Taping
• 123 Kid beat George South

May 24, 1994
Canton, OH – Civic Center att. 1,800
WWF TV Taping
• Tatanka beat George South

May 25, 1994
Erie, PA – Civic Center att. 3,500
WWF TV Taping
• Sparky Plug bet George South (2:47)

May 27, 1994
Taylorsville, NC - Armory
PWF
• George South vs American Ninja
• Managed Austin Steele

May 28, 1994
Hamlet, NC - Armory
PWF
• PWF Tag Team Title: Austin Steele & Terry Austin* beat George South & Italian Stallion

June 3, 1994
Kings Mountain, NC - Armory
PWF
• PWF Tag Team Title: Austin Steele & Terry Austin* beat George South & Italian Stallion

June 4, 1994
Reidsville, NC - Armory
PWF
• George South& Italian Stallion beat Randy Sledge & Chris Hamrick
• Battle Royal

June 11, 1994
Inman, SC – Armory att. 70
PWF
• Brian Lee beat George South

June 17, 1994
Elkin, NC – Armory
PWF
• George South beat The Inferno
• PWF Tag Team Title: Austin Steele & Terry Austin* beat George South & Italian Stallion

June 18, 1994
Forest City, NC – Armory att. 60
PWF
• PWF Tag Team Title: George South & Italian Stallion beat Austin Steele & Terry Austin* to win the titles
• Battle Royal

June 24, 1994
Taylorsville, NC – Baseball Field
PWF
• George South beat The Wildcat

June 25, 1994
Hamlet, NC – Armory
PWF
• PWF Tag Team Titles: George South & Italian Stallion* beat Austin Steele & Terry Austin

July 1, 1994
Bushkill, PA – Fernwood Resort Center att. 1,600 sell out
WWF TV Taping
• Thurman Plugg (Bob Holly) beat George South (2:37)

July 2, 1994
Bethlehem, PA - Stabler Arena att. 3,000
WWF TV Taping
• The Bushwackers beat George South & Tyrone Knox

July 8, 1994
Belmont, NC – Armory
PWF
• George South beat Scotty McKeever
• Battle Royal

July 9, 1994
Inman, SC – Armory att.60
PWF
• George South beat Greg Collins
• George South beat Scotty McKeever

July 15, 1994
Elkin, NC - - Armory
PWF
• George South vs Scotty McKeever
• Battle Royal

July 16, 1994
Hamlet, NC – Armory
PWF
• George South vs Scotty McKeever

July 22, 1994
Taylorsville, NC - Armory
PWF
• George South beat Troy Conyers
• Battle Royal

July 23, 1994
Forest City, NC - Armory
PWF
• George South & Italian Stallion beat Black Scorpion & Texas Outlaw
• Battle Royal

July 29, 1994
Belmont, NC - Armory
PWF
• George South & Italian Stallion beat Austin Steel & Terry Austin
• Battle Royal

July 30, 1994
Concord, NC – Church
PWF
• George South beat David Woodland

Highway Run into the Midnight Sun

August 5, 1994
Morganton, NC – I-40 Flea Market
PWF
• George South vs Terry Austin
• Lethal Lottery

August 6, 1994
Inman, SC - Armory
PWF
• George South & Italian Stallion beat Terry Austin & Chris Hamrick
• Lethal Lottery

August 12, 1994
Belmont, NC- Armory
PWF
• George South & Italian Stallion beat Terry Austin & Troy Conyers
• Battle Royal

August 18, 1994
Elkin, NC - Armory
PWF
• George South & Italian Stallion beat Scotty McKeever & Star Ryder
• Lethal Lottery

August 19, 1994
Elkin, NC - Armory
PWF
• George South beat Scotty McKeever
• George South & Italian Stallion beat Scott Powers & Texas Outlaw
• Lethal Lottery

August 20, 1994
Forest City, NC - Armory
PWF
• George South & Italian Stallion beat Scotty McKeever & Russian Assassin
• Battle Royal

August 26, 1994
Taylorsville, NC - Armory
PWF
• George South & Italian Stallion vs Austin Steele & Terry Austin
• Battle Royal

August 27, 1994
Reidsville, NC - Armory
PWF
• George South beat Scotty McKeever

September 2, 1994
Belmont, NC - Armory
PWF
• George South beat Scotty McKeever

September 3, 1994
Morganton, NC – I-40 Flea Market
PWF
• George South & Italian Stallion beat The Panther & Russian Assassin

September 9, 1994
Elkin, NC - Armory
PWF
• George South & Italian Stallion beat Terry Austin & Scotty McKeever
• Battle Royal

September 10, 1994
Hamlet, NC - Armory
PWF
• George South & Italian Stallion vs Terry Austin & Scotty McKeever
• Battle Royal

September 17, 1994
Forest City, NC - Armory
PWF
• George South & Italian Stallion beat Scotty McKeever & Troy Conyers
• Battle Royal

September 24, 1994
Taylorsville, NC - Armory
PWF
• George South & Italian Stallion beat Scotty McKeever & Scotty Hot Body
• Battle Royal

October 3, 1994
Morganton, NC – Collett Street Rec Center att. 450
Smoky Mountain Wrestling (Jim Cornette)
TV Taping
• Tracey Smothers beat George South (3:33)
• Brian Lee & Lance Storm beat George South & Steve Skyfire (1:58)
• Pull Apart: Ricky Morton vs. New Jack

October 22, 1994
Kings Mountain, NC - Armory
NAWA (Buddy Porter)
• George South vs Flaming Youth
• Battle Royal

October 24, 1994
Atlanta, GA – Center Stage
WCW TV Taping
• Hacksaw Jim Duggan beat George South

October 25, 1994
Atlanta, GA – Center Stage
WCW TV Taping
Kevin Sullivan & The Shark (John Tenta) beat George South &?

October 27, 1994
Charlotte, NC – Bing Hall
• George South &? Vs. Mad Maxx & Mexican Twin Devil

November 7, 1994
Oakwood, VA – Garden High School att. 400
SMW TV Taping
• SMW Beat the Champ TV Title: Bryant Anderson* beat George South via submission (2:38)
• Boo Bradley beat George South (2:27)
• George South beat Bruiser Bedlem w/ Jim Cornette (2:25 dq)

November 8, 1994
Atlanta, GA – Center Stage
WCW TV Taping
• The Shark beat George South
• Dustin Rhodes beat George South

November 9, 1994
Atlanta, GA – Center Stage
WCW TV Taping
• Dave Sullivan beat George South

November 12, 1994
Morristown, TN – Rec Center
SMW
• Killer Kyle beat George South

November 24, 1994
Kings Mountain, NC - Armory
NAWA (Buddy Porter)
• George South beat Flaming Youth James Clontz

November 28, 194
Atlanta, GA – Center Stage
WCW TV Taping
• Alex Wright beat George South

November 29, 1994
Macon, GA – Civic Center
WCW TV Taping
• The Nasty Boys beat George South &?

December 6, 1994
Dalton, GA – Civic Center
WCW
• The Nasty Boys beat George South &?

December 31, 1994
Kings Mountain, NC – Armory
NAWA (Buddy Porter)
• George South beat Flaming Youth James Clontz
• Managed The Texas Outlaws
• George South vs. Flaming Youth

1995

January 2, 1995
Sevierville, TN – Catan's Chapel Elementary School att. 400
SMW TV Taping
• SMW Beat the Champ TV Title" Buddy Landel* beat George South via submission (2:42)
• Smoky Mountain Rumble Battle Royal
• Pull Apart: Bob Armstrong – The Gangstas

January 8, 1995
Atlanta, GA – Center Stage
WCW V Taping
• Hacksaw Jim Duggan beat George South

January 9, 1995
Columbus, GA – Auditorium
WCW TV Taping
• Dustin Rhodes beat George South

January 11, 1995
Atlanta, GA – Center Stage
WCW V Taping
• Brian Pillman beat George South

January 14, 1995
Atkinson, NC – Old School Gym
ICW (Marc Watkins)
• George South beat Dark Star
• George South & Mean Marc Ash vs. Dark Star & The Real Deal

February 6, 1995
Lenoir, NC – Mulberry Street Rec Center att. 375
SMW TV Taping
• Al Snow beat George South (2:50)
• Al Snow beat George South
Note: Match was re-taped
• Billy Black beat George South (3:30)
• Al Snow & Unabom (Kane) beat George South & Anthony Michaels (2:23)

February 11, 1995
Kings Mountain, NC – Armory
NAWA (Buddy Porter)
• George South & Jeff Victory vs. American GI & Dozer

February 21, 1995
Gainesville, GA – GA Mountain Center
WCW TV Taping
• Nasty Boys beat George South &?

February 22, 1995
Atlanta, GA – Center Stage
WCW TV Taping
• Stars & Stripes (Del Wilks & Buff Bagwell) beat George South &?

February 25, 1995
Wilmington, NC – Armory
ICW (Marc Watkins)
• George South beat Dark Star
• Battle Royal

March 11, 1995
Kings Mountain, NC – Armory
NAWA (Buddy Porter)
George South vs. Jeff Victory

March 18, 1995
Jonesville, SC – Armory
• George South vs. Michael Idol
• Battle Royal

March 24, 1995
Atkinson, NC – Old School Gym
ICW (Marc Watkins)
• George South & Mean Marc Ash beat Chief Wahoo McDaniel & Dark Star

March 31, 1995
Loris, SC – High School
• George South vs. Masters
• George South vs. Super Mario

April 1, 1995
Kings Mountain, NC – Middle School
• George South vs. Bobby Storm
• Run In

April 5, 1995
Atlanta, GA – Center Stage
WCW TV Taping
• Stars & Stripes beat George South &?

April 13, 1995
Waynesville, NC – High School att. 350
SMW TV Taping
• Bobby Fulton beat George South
• Al Snow & Unabom beat George South & Mike Mason (dq)
• Boo Bradley beat George South

April 15, 1995
Morristown, TN – East High School att. 450
SMW
• Unabom beat George South

Match # 2000
April 22, 1995
Lenoir, NC – Mulberry Street Rec Center att. 305
SMW
• Unabom beat George South

April 24, 1995
Dothan, AL – Civic Center
WCW
• Dave Sullivan beat George South

April 25, 1995
Atlanta, GA – Center Stage
WCW TV Taping
• Johnny B. Badd beat George South

May 3, 1995
Lenoir, NC – Fairgrounds
FPWF (Kandy Ryan)
• George South vs. Jay Eagle

May 4, 1995
Sugar Grove, NC – Bethel School
Pro Atlantic Championship Wrestling (George South)
• George South beat Dozer

May 5, 1995
Mt. Holly, NC
Pro Atlantic Championship Wrestling (George South)
• Managed: Mark Henderson vs. Jeff Victory
• George South vs. Jay Eagle

May 6, 1995
Johnson City, TN – Freedom Hall att. 650
SMW
• Bobby Blaze beat George South

May 11, 1995
Kings Mountain, NC – Armory
Pro Atlantic Championship Wrestling (George South)
• George South & Scotty McKeever beat Bobby Fulton & Dozer
• Bunkhouse Stampede: Dozer

May 13, 1995
Hildebran, NC – Gym
Pro Atlantic Championship Wrestling (George South)
• Jay Eagle beat George South (dq)
• Battle Royal:

May 20, 1995
Atkinson, NC – Old Gym
ICW (Marc Watkins)
• George South beat Student

May 27, 1995
Charlotte, NC -Corner of Trade & Tryon
WCW Saturday Night Live on TBS
• WCW World Tag Team Title: Nasty Boys* beat George South & Scotty McKeever (2:20)

June 15, 1995
Charlotte, NC – Training Center
PWF
• PWF Heavyweight Title: Star Ryder* beat George South

June 22, 1995
Charlotte, NC – Training Center
PWF
• George South & Terry Austin vs. Italian Stallion & Randy Sledge

June 23, 1995
Hideebran, NC – Community Center
PWF
• PWF Heavyweight Title: Star Ryder* beat George South
• Battle Royal

June 24, 1995
Mooresville, NC – Armory
PWF
• PWF Heavyweight Title: Star Ryder* beat George South
• Battle Royal

June 29, 1995
Charlotte, NC – Training Center
PWF
• George South beat Southern Rocker
• Managed X
• Battle Royal

June 30, 1995
Inman, SC – Armory
PWF
• PWF Heavyweight Title: Star Ryder* beat George South
• Battle Royal

July 1, 1995
Marion, NC – Rec Center
PWF
• PWF Heavyweight Title: Star Ryder* beat George South
• Battle Royal

July 6, 1995
Charlotte, NC – Training Center
PWF
• George South beat Flaming Youth

July 7, 1995
Hamlet, NC – Armory
PWF
• George South beat Southern Rocker
• Battle Royal

July 8, 1995
Forest City, NC – Armory
PWF
• George South beat Southern Rocker
• Battle Royal

July 13, 1995
Charlotte, NC – Training Center
PWF
• George south vs Italian Stallion
• Battle Royal

July 14, 1995
Taylorsville, NC – Armory
PWF
• George South beat Southern Rocker
• Battle Royal

July 15, 1995
Lincolnton, NC – Armory
PWF
• George South beat Randy Sledge

July 20, 1995
Charlotte, NC – Training Center
PWF
• George South beat Southern Rocker

July 21, 1995
Thomasville, NC – Armory
PWF
• George South beat Star Ryder

July 22, 1995
Mooresville, NC – Armory
PWF
• George South beat Southern Rocker

July 27, 1995
Charlotte, NC – Training Center
PWF
• George South beat Star Ryder
• Managed Terminator X

July 28, 1995
Inman, SC – Armory
PWF
• George South beat Star Ryder

July 29, 1995
Kings Mountain, NC – Armory
PWF
• George South bet Star Ryder
• Battle Royal

August 3, 1995
Charlotte, NC – Training Center
PWF
• George South beat Carolina Dreamer
• Battle Royal

August 4, 1995
Elkin, NC – Armory
PWF
• George South beat Star Ryder
• Battle Royal

August 5, 1995
Marion, NC – Rec Center
PWF
• George South beat Carolina Dreamer
• Battle Royal

August 10, 1995
Charlotte, NC – Training Center
PWF
• George South & Austin Steele vs Italian Stallion & Carolina Dreamer
• Battle Royal

August 11, 1995
Hildebran, NC – Community Center
PWF
• George South & Austin Steele beat Star Ryder & Southern Rocker
• Battle Royal

August 12, 1995
Forest City, NC - Armory
PWF
• George South beat Hillbilly Pete
• Battle Royal

August 17, 1995
Charlotte, NC – Training Center
PWF
• George South beat Star Ryder
• Battle Royal

August 18, 1995
Taylorsville, NC – Armory
PWF
• George South beat Star Ryder

August 19, 1995
Mooresville, NC - Armory
PWF
• George South beat Star Ryder
• Battle Royal

August 24, 1995
Charlotte, NC – Training Center
PWF
• George South beat Star Ryder
• Battle Royal

August 25, 1995
Marion, NC – Rec Center
PWF
• George South beat Star Ryder

August 26, 1995
Kings Mountain, NC – Armory
PWF
• George South beat Star Ryder
• George South &? Vs Austin Steele & Terry Austin

August 30, 1995
Atlanta, GA – Center Stage
WCW TV Taping
• The Renegade w/ Jimmy Hart beat George South

August 31, 1995
Charlotte, NC – Training Center
PWF
• George South beat Southern Rocker

September 1, 1995
Hildebran, NC – Community Center
PWF
• George South beat Southern Rocker
• Battle Royal

September 2, 1995
Marion, NC – Rec Center
PWF
• George South beat Southern Rocker

September 8, 1995
Elkin, NC – Armory
PWF
• George South beat Randy Sledge

September 9, 1995
Hamlet, NC – Armory
PWF
• George South beat Southern Rocker
• Battle Royal

September 14, 1995
Charlotte, NC – Training Center
PWF
• George South vs Italian Stallion
• Battle Royal

September 15, 1995
Inman, SC – Armory
PWF
• George South beat Sweet Brown Sugar

September 16, 1995
Forest City, NC - Armory
PWF
• George South beat Southern Rocker
• George South & Scotty McKeever vs Austin Steele & Terry Austin

September 21, 1995
Charlotte, NC – Training Center
PWF
• George South & Scotty McKeever vs Austin Steele & Terry Austin

September 22, 1995
Taylorsville, NC – Armory
PWF
• George South & Scotty McKeever vs Austin Steele & Terry Austin

September 23, 1995
Mooresville, NC – Armory
PWF
• George South & Scotty McKeever vs Austin Steele & Terry Austin

September 28, 1995
Charlotte, NC – Training Center
PWF
• George South & Scotty McKeever vs Austin Steele & Terry Austin

September 29, 1995
Kings Mountain, NC – Armory
PWF
• George South & Scotty McKeever vs Austin Steele & Terry Austin
• Battle Royal

September 30, 1995
Lincolnton, NC – Armory
PWF
• George South beat Southern Rocker
• Battle Royal

October 5, 1995
Charlotte, NC – Church
PWF
• George South & Scotty McKeever vs Austin Steele & Terry Austin

October 7, 1995
Charlotte, NC – Training Center
PWF
• George South & Scotty McKeever vs Italian Stallion & Southern Rocker

October 14, 1995
Charlotte, NC – Training Center
PWF
• Managed The Barbarian
• Managed The Equalizer

October 15, 1995
Hildebran, NC – Old Gym
PWF
• George South, Terry Austin & Scotty McKeever vs.
Italian Stallion, Carolina Dreamer & Sweet Brown Sugar

October 16, 1995
Albemarle, NC – Armory
PWF
• George South beat Carolina Dreamer

October 21, 1995
Charlotte, NC – Training Center
PWF
• George South vs Randy Sledge
• Managed The Equalizer
• Battle Royal

October 22, 1995
Kings Mountain, NC – Armory
PWF
• George South vs Randy Sledge
• Managed The Equalizer

October 23, 1995
Forest City, NC – Armory
PWF
• George South beat Carolina Dreamer

October 26, 1995
Charlotte, NC – Training Center
PWF
• George South vs Italian Stallion

October 28, 1995
Charlotte, NC – Training Center
PWF
• George South vs Italian Stallion

October 29, 1995
Taylorsville, NC – Armory
PWF
• George South vs Italian Stallion

October 30, 1995
Mooresville, NC – Armory
PWF
• George South beat Tyrone Knox

November 2, 1995
Charlotte, NC – Training Center
PWF
• George South vs Star Ryder

November 7, 1995
Charlotte, NC – Training Center
PWF
• George South & Terry Austin vs Italian Stallion & Hillbilly

November 9, 1995
Charlotte, NC – Training Center
PWF
• George South & The Equalizer vs Randy Sledge & Carolina Dreamer

November 11,1995
Hamlet, NC – Armory
PWF
• George South & The Equalizer vs Italian Stallion & Carolina Dreamer

November 14, 1995
Charlotte, NC – Training Center
PWF
• George South & The Equalizer vs Randy Sledge & Carolina Dreamer

November 18, 1995
Lincolnton, NC – Armory
PWF
• Managed Samoan Tai vs Italian Stallion
• Bunkhouse Battle Royal

November 21, 1995
Charlotte, NC – Training Center
PWF
• George South beat Carolina Dreamer

November 23, 1995
Mooresville, NC – Armory
PWF
• George South & The Equalizer beat Randy Sledge & Carolina Dreamer
• Battle Royal

November 24, 1995
Forest City, NC - Armory
PWF
• George South & The Equalizer beat Randy Sledge & Carolina Dreamer
• Managed The Barbarian vs Italian Stallion
• Battle Royal

November 25, 1995
Inman, SC - Armory
PWF
• George South & The Equalizer beat Randy Sledge & Italian Stallion

November 28, 1995
Charlotte, NC – Training Center
PWF
• George South beat Sweet Brown Sugar

November 30, 1995
Charlotte, NC – Training Center
PWF
• George South & The Equalizer beat Terry Austin & Carolina Dreamer

December 2, 1995
Concord, NC – High School
PWF
• George South & The Equalizer beat Randy Sledge & Carolina Dreamer
• Managed The Barbarian vs Italian Stallion

December 7, 1995
Charlotte, NC – Training Center
PWF
• George South beat Sweet Brown Sugar
• George South, The Equalizer & Scotty McKeever vs Italian Stallion, Terry Austin & Randy Sledge

December 9, 1995
Gaffney, SC – Armory
PWF
• George South & Scotty McKeever beat Randy Sledge & Carolina Dreamer

December 14, 1995
Mooresville, NC – Armory
PWF
• George South & Scotty McKeever vs Italian Stallion & Tyrone Knox

December 15, 1995
Kings Mountain, NC – Armory
PWF
• George South, Scotty McKeever & The Equalizer vs Italian Stallion, Randy Sledge & Star Ryder

December 17, 1995
Charlotte, NC – Old Coliseum
PWF Christmas Show
• George South & Scotty McKeever vs The Rock & Roll Express

December 21, 1995
Charlotte, NC – Training Center
PWF
• George South beat Sweet Brown Sugar

December 26, 1998
Charlotte, NC – Training Center
PWF
• George South beat Star Ryder

December 28, 1995
Charlotte, NC – Training Center
PWF
• George South vs. Star Ryder
• Battle Royal

December 29, 1995
Forest City, NC – Armory
PWF
• George South, Scotty McKeever, Austin Steele & Terry Austin beat Italian Stallion, Chris Hamrick,
Randy Sledge & Star Ryder

December 20, 1995
Lincolnton, NC – Armory
PWF
• George South & Scotty McKeever vs Italian Stallion & Star Ryder

1996

January 2, 1996
Charlotte, NC – Training Center
PWF
• George South vs. Star Ryder
• Managed Scotty McKeever vs Italian Stallion
• George South & Scotty McKeever vs. Italian Stallion & Star Ryder
• Battle Royal

January 4, 1996
Charlotte, NC – Training Center
PWF
• George South vs. Italian Stallion

January 5, 1996
Elkin, NC – Armory
PWF
• George South & Scotty McKeever vs Austin Steele & Terry Austin
• George South & Scotty McKeever vs Italian Stallion & Star Ryder

January 9, 1996
Charlotte, NC – Training Center
PWF
• George South vs. The Assassin
• Managed Scotty McKeever
• George South & Scotty McKeever vs Italian Stallion & Carolina Dreamer

January 11, 1996
Charlotte, NC – Training Center
PWF
• George South vs. Sweet Brown Sugar
• George South, Scotty McKeever & The Russian vs Italian Stallion, Sweet Brown Sugar & Carolina Dreamer
• Battle Royal

January 13, 196
Gaffney, SC – Armory
PWF
• George South & Scotty McKeever beat Italian Stallion & Chris Hamrick (dq)
• Battle Royal

January 16, 1996
Charlotte, NC – Training Center
PWF
• George South, Scotty McKeever & The Equalizer vs. Italian Stallion, Star Ryder & Carolina Dreamer
• Battle Royal

January 18, 1996
Charlotte, NC – Training Center
PWF
• George South vs. Sweet Brown Sugar
• George South & Scotty McKeever beat Star Ryder & Randy Sledge
• Battle Royal

January 19, 1996
Kings Mountain, NC – Armory
PWF
• George South & Scotty McKeever vs Italian Stallion & Star Ryder
• War Games

January 20, 1996
Mooresville, NC - Armory
PWF
- George South & Scotty McKeever vs Star Ryder & Italian Stallion
- War Games

January 23, 1996
Charlotte, NC – Training Center
PWF
- George South vs. Blue Diamond
- Battle Royal

January 25, 1996
Charlotte, NC – Training Center
PWF
- George South & Scotty McKeever vs. Italian Stallion & Sweet Brown Sugar
- Battle Royal

January 26, 1996
Inman, SC – Armory
PWF
- George South & Equalizer beat Italian Stallion & Sweet Brown Sugar
- Battle Royal

January 27, 1996
Forest City, NC – Armory
PWF
- George South & The Equalizer vs Italian Stallion & Star Ryder
- Battle Royal

February 1, 1996
Charlotte, NC – Training Center
PWF
- George South vs. Italian Stallion

February 2, 1996
Hamlet, NC – Armory
PWF
- George South & Scotty McKeever vs Italian Stallion & Sweet Brown Sugar
- Battle Royal

February 8, 1996
Charlotte, NC – Training Center
PWF
- George South & Scotty McKeever vs. Italian Stallion & Baby Huey

February 9, 1996
North Wilkesboro, NC – Armory
PWF
- George South vs Black Angel
- Battle Royal

February 10, 1996
Charlotte, NC – Training Center
PWF
- George South vs. Italian Stallion
- George South vs. Black Angel
- Battle Royal

February 15, 1996
Charlotte, NC – Training Center
PWF
- George South vs. Black Angel

February 16, 1996
Kings Mountain, NC – Armory
PWF
• George South vs David Jericho
• Battle Royal

February 17, 1996
Gaffney, SC – Armory
PWF
• George South & Scotty McKeever vs. Italian Stallion & Baby Huey
• Battle Royal

February 18, 1996
Charlotte, NC – Training Center
PWF
• George South beat Sweet Brown Sugar
• George South, Scotty McKeever & Jeff Victory beat Emilo Ulacia, Carolina Dreamer & Sweet Brown Sugar

February 22, 1996
Charlotte, NC – Training Center
PWF
• George South & Scotty McKeever beat Carolina dreamer & Sweet Brown Sugar
• Battle Royal

February 24, 1996
Forest City, NC – Armory
PWF
• George South & Scotty McKeever vs Star Ryder & Italian Stallion

February 25, 1996
Charlotte, NC – Training Center
PWF
• George South vs. Baby Huey
• Battle Royal

February 28, 1996
Cramerton, NC – Middle School
PWF
• George South & Scotty McKeever vs Austin Steele & Terry Austin

February 29, 1996
Charlotte, NC – Training Center
PWF
• George South vs. Sweet Brown Baby
• Battle Royal

March 1, 1996
Monroe, NC – Armory
PWF
• George South & Scotty McKeever vs Italian Stallion & Star Ryder
• Battle Royal

March 2, 1996
Mooresville, NC – Armory
PWF
• George South vs Ricky Morton
• Battle Royal

March 3, 1996
Charlotte, NC – Training Center
PWF
• George South vs. Black Angel
• George South & Scotty McKeever vs Italian Stallion & Black Angel

March 7, 1996
Charlotte, NC – Training Center
PWF
• George South vs. Carolina Dreamer

March 8, 1996
Hamlet, NC – Armory
PWF
• George South beat Carolina Dreamer
• Italian Stallion & Ricky Morton beat George South & Scotty McKeever

March 9, 1996
Morganton, NC - Armory
PWF
• George South & Scotty McKeever vs Italian Stallion & Star Ryder
• Battle Royal

March 10, 1996
Charlotte, NC – Training Center
PWF
• George South vs. Black Angel
• George South vs Italian Stallion

March 14, 1996
Charlotte, NC – Training Center
PWF
• George South & Scotty McKeever vs. Star Ryder & Tyrone Knox

March 15, 1996
Inman, SC – Armory
PWF
• George South beat Billy the Kid
• Italian Stallion beat George South (dq)
• Battle Royal

March 17, 1996
Charlotte, NC – Training Center
PWF
• George South vs. The Russian

March 21, 1996
Charlotte, NC – Training Center
PWF
• George South, Scotty McKeever & Jeff Victory vs. Baby Huey, Star Ryder & Sweet Brown Sugar

March 22, 1996
Kings Mountain, NC – Armory
PWF
• George South beat Brian Williams
• Managed The Assassin vs Italian Stallion
• Battle Royal

March 23, 1996
Forest City, NC – Armory
PWF
• George South beat Carolina Dreamer
• War Games

March 24, 1996
Charlotte, NC – Training Center
PWF
• George South vs. Italian Stallion

March 28, 1996
Charlotte, NC – Training Center
PWF
• George South vs. Carolina Dreamer
• Battle Royal

March 29, 1996
Lincolnton, NC – Armory
PWF
• George South & Scotty McKeever vs Italian Stallion & David Jericho
• Barbed Wire War Games

March 30, 1996
Greer, SC – Armory
PWF
• George South vs Baby Huey
• George South vs Italian Stallion

April 4, 1996
Charlotte, NC – Training Center
PWF
• George South & Scotty McKeever vs. Sweet Brown Sugar & Baby Huey

April 5, 1996
Hamlet, NC – Armory
PWF
• George South & Scotty McKeever vs. Italian Stallion & Carolina Dreamer

April 6, 1996
Gaffney, SC – Armory
PWF
• George South vs Carolina Dreamer

April 11, 1996
Charlotte, NC – Training Center
PWF
• George South vs. Italian Stallion
• Battle Royal

April 12, 1996
Monroe, NC – Armory
PWF
• George South vs Sweet Brown Sugar
• Barbed Wire Match: George South vs Italian Stallion

April 13, 1996
Mooresville, NC – Amory
PWF
• George South beat Carolina Dreamer

April 18, 1996
Charlotte, NC – Training Center
PWF
• George South vs. The Juicer
• Battle Royal

April 19, 1996
Kings Mountain, NC – Armory
PWF
• George South beat Carolina Dreamer
• Battle Royal

April 20, 1996
Forest City, NC – Armory
PWF
• George South vs Italian Stallion

PRO WRESTLING FEDERATION

MAY 4, 1996

GAFFENY, SC I NATIONAL GUARD ARMORY

MAIN EVENT I PWF WORLD TITLE MATCH

CHAMPION GORGEOUS
GEORGE SOUTH VS **CAROLINA DREAMER**

PWF TAG TEAM CHAMPIONS

AUSTIN STEELE & TERRY AUSTIN
VS
ITALIAN STALLION & STAR RYDER

PWF EASTERN STATES CHAMPION
CHRIS HAMRICK VS GLADIATOR II

PLUS 2 MORE BIG MATCHES

PRO WRESTLING FEDERATION

April 25, 1996
Charlotte, NC – Training Center
PWF
• George South vs. Italian Stallion

April 26, 1996
Inman, SC – Armory
PWF
• George South beat Carolina Dreamer
• Battle Royal

April 27, 1996
Morganton, NC – Armory
PWF
• George South beat Carolina Dreamer
• Battle Royal

May 2, 1996
Charlotte, NC – Training Center
PWF
• George South & Scotty McKeever vs. Italian Stallion & Baby Huey
• Battle Royal

May 3, 1996
Lincolnton, NC – Armory
PWF
• George South beat Carolina Dreamer
• Battle Royal

May 4, 1996
Gaffney, SC – Armory
PWF
• George South beat Carolina Dreamer
• Battle Royal

May 9, 1996
Charlotte, NC – Training Center
PWF
• George South & Scotty McKeever beat Star Ryder & Carolina Dreamer
• Battle Royal

May 10, 1996
Hamlet, NC – Armory
PWF
• George South beat Carolina Dreamer
• George South & Scotty McKeever vs Italian Stallion & Carolina Dreamer

May 11, 1996
• George South & Scotty McKeever vs Italian Stallion & Star Ryder
• Battle Royal

May 16, 1996
Charlotte, NC – Training Center
PWF
• George South & Scotty McKeever vs Italian Stallion & Dr. Fellgood
• Battle Royal

May 17, 1996
Kings Mountain, NC – Armory
PWF
• George South & Scotty McKeever vs Italian Stallion & Star Ryder
• Managed Austin Steele
• Battle Royal

May 18, 1996
Forest City, NC – Armory
PWF
• George south vs Italian Stallion
• Managed Austin Steele
• Battle Royal

May 23, 1996
Charlotte, NC – Training Center
PWF
• George South & Austin Steele beat Dr. Feelgood & Sweet Brown Sugar
• Battle Royal

May 24, 1996
Inman, SC – Armory
PWF
• George South & Austin Steele vs Italian Stallion & Chris Hamrick
• Battle Royal

May 25, 1996
Morganton, NC – Armory
PWF
• George South beat Black Angel

May 28, 1996
North Charleston, SC – Coliseum att. 4,500
WWF TV Taping
• Jake The Snake Roberts beat George South

May 30, 1996
Charlotte, NC – Training Center
PWF
• George South & Austin Steele beat Carolina Dreamer & Sweet Brown Sugar

May 31, 1996
Charlotte, NC – Training Center
PWF
• George South & Austin Steele beat The Juicer & Carolina Dreamer
• Battle Royal

June 1, 1996
Mooresville, NC – Armory
PWF
• George South beat Carolina Dreamer
• George South & Austin Steele beat The Juicer & Sweet Brown Sugar
• Battle Royal

June 6, 1996
Charlotte, NC – Training Center
PWF
• George South beat Carolina Dreamer
• Battle Royal

June 8, 19966
Gaffney, SC - Armory
PWF
• George South beat Carolina Dreamer
• Battle Royal

June 13, 1996
Charlotte, NC – Training Center
PWF
• George South beat Baby Huey
• Battle Royal

June 14, 1996
Kings Mountain, NC – Armory
PWF
• George South & Scotty McKeever beat Sweet Brown Sugar & The Juicer
• War Games

June 15, 1996
Greer, SC – Armory
PWF
• George South beat Carolina Dreamer
• Battle Royal

June 20, 1996
Charlotte, NC – Training Center
PWF
• George South & Scotty McKeever beat The Juicer & Sweet Brown Sugar
• Battle Royal

June 21, 1996
Rockingham, NC – Armory
PWF
• George South vs Carolina Dreamer
• Barbed Wire Match: George South vs Italian Stallion

June 22, 1996
Forest City, NC – Armory
PWF
• George South vs Carolina Dreamer
• Barbed Wire War Games

June 27, 1996
Charlotte, NC – Training Center
PWF
• George South beat Dr. Feelgood
• Battle Royal

June 28, 1996
Inman, SC – Armory
PWF
• George South beat Billy Jack
• Battle Royal

June 29, 1996
Mooresville, NC – Armory – 2pm
PWF
• George South beat Billy Jack
• Managed Terry Austin vs Italian Stallion

June 29, 1996
Lincolnton, NC – Armory – 8pm
PWF
• Italian Stallion beat George South
• War Games

July 3, 1996
Gaffney, SC – Armory
PWF
• George South beat Black Angel
• Battle Royal

July 4, 1996
Charlotte, NC – Training Center
PWF
• George South beat Black Angel
• Battle Royal

July 5, 1996
Rockingham, NC – Armory
PWF
• George South beat Black Angel
• Battle Royal

July 6, 1996
Gastonia, NC – Armory
PWF
• George South beat Black Angel
• Battle Royal

July 11,1996
Charlotte, NC – Training Center
PWF
• George South beat Dr Feelgood
• Battle Royal

July 12, 1996
Monroe, NC – Armory
PWF
• George South beat Star Ryder
• Battle Royal

July 13, 1996
Greer, SC – Armory
PWF
• George South beat Star Ryder
• Battle Royal

July 18, 1996
Charlotte, NC – Training Center
PWF
• George South beat Carolina Dreamer
• Battle Royal

July 19, 1996
Kings Mountain, NC – Armory
PWF
• George South & Terry Austin beat Billy Jack & David Jericho
• Battle Royal

July 20, 1996
Forest City, NC – Armory
PWF
• George South beat Carolina Dreamer

July 25, 1996
Charlotte, NC – Training Center
PWF
• George South & Terry Austin beat Flaming Youth & Carolina Dreamer
• Battle Royal

July 26, 1996
Taylorsville, NC – Armory
PWF
• George South beat Carolina Dreamer
• War Games

July 27, 1996
Lincolnton, NC – Armory
PWF
• George South beat Flaming Youth
• Battle Royal

August 1, 1996
Charlotte, NC – Training Center
PWF
- George South vs Italian Stallion
- Battle Royal

August 2, 1996
Rockingham, NC – Armory
PWF
- George South beat Carolina Dreamer
- Battle Royal

August 3, 1996
Mooresville, NC – Armory
PWF
- George South beat Carolina Dreamer
- Battle Royal

August 8, 1996
Charlotte, NC – Training Center
PWF
- George South, Austin Steele & Terry Austin beat Baby Huey, Flaming Youth & Carolina Dreamer

August 9, 1996
Monroe, NC – Armory
PWF
- George South beat Carolina Dreamer
- Battle Royal

August 10, 1996
Gaffney, SC – Armory
PWF
- George South beat Quantez
- Battle Royal

August 15, 1996
Charlotte, NC – Training Center
PWF
- Managed The Secret Weapon vs Italian Stallion

August 16, 1996
Inman, SC – Armory
PWF
- George South beat Carolina Dreamer
- Battle Royal

August 17, 1996
Gastonia, NC – Armory
PWF
- George South beat Carolina Dreamer
- Battle Royal

August 22, 1996
Charlotte, NC – Training Center
PWF
- George South beat Iceman
- Battle Royal

August 24, 1996
Forest City, NC – Armory
PWF
- George South beat Billy Jack
- Battle Royal

August 29, 1996
Charlotte, NC – Training Center
PWF
• George South beat Carolina Dreamer
• Battle Royal

August 30, 1996
Taylorsville, NC – Armory
PWF
• George South beat Carolina Dreamer
• Battle Royal

August 31, 1996
Kings Mountain, NC – Armory
PWF
• George South & Austin Steele beat Chris Hamrick & Carolina Dreamer
• Battle Royal

September 5, 1996
Charlotte, NC – Training Center
PWF
• George South vs Italian Stallion
• Battle Royal

September 6, 1996
Rockingham, NC – Armory
PWF
• George South beat Carolina Dreamer
• George South & Terry Austin vs Italian Stallion & Carolina Dreamer
• Battle Royal

September 7, 1996
Gaffney, SC – Armory
PWF
• George South vs Italian Stallion
• Battle Royal

September 12, 1996
Charlotte, NC – Training Center
PWF
• George South beat Carolina Dreamer
• Italian Stallion, Black Angel & Sweet Brown Sugar beat George South, Austin Steele & Terry Austin
• Battle Royal

September 14, 1996
Inman, SC – Amory
PWF
• George South vs Black Angel
• Battle Royal

September 15, 1996
Mooresville, NC – Armory
PWF
• George South vs JC Dililon
• Battle Royal

September 17, 1996
Jacksonville, FL – Naval Base
PWF
• George South vs Ricky Morton
• Battle Royal

September 21, 1996
PWF
Gastonia, NC – Armory
• George South vs Italian Stallion & Carolina Dreamer
• Battle Royal

September 26, 1996
Charlotte, NC – Training Center
PWF
• George South vs Carolina Dreamer
• Battle Royal

September 28, 1996
Forest City, NC – Armory
PWF
• George South & Austin Steele vs Italian Stallion & Chris Hamrick
• Battle Royal

October 3, 1996
Charlotte, NC – Training Center
PWF
• George South vs Black Angel
• Battle Royal

October 4, 1996
Kings Mountain, NC – Armory
PWF
• George South & Austin Steele vs Chris Hamrick & Carolina Dreamer
• Weapons Match
• Battle Royal

October 5, 1996
Gaffney, SC – Armory
PWF
• George South vs JC Dillion
• Battle Royal

October 10, 1996
Charlotte, NC – Training Center
PWF
• George South vs Wasted Youth & Carolina Dreamer
• Battle Royal

October 11, 1996
Rockingham, NC – Armory
PWF
• George South vs Carolina Dreamer
• George South, Austin Steele & Terry Austin vs Wasted Youth, Italian Stallion & Carolina Dreamer
• Battle Royal

October 12, 1996
Inman, NC – Armory
PWF
• George South vs Carolina Dreamer
• Lumberjack Match
• Battle Royal

October 17, 1996
Charlotte, NC – Training Center
PWF
• George South vs The Breeze
• Battle Royal

October 19, 1996
Lincolnton, NC – Armory
PWF
• George South vs Billy Jack
• Battle Royal

October 25, 1996
Charlotte, NC – Training Center
PWF
• George South & Austin Steele vs Black Angel & Carolina Dreamer

October 26, 1996
Mooresville, NC – Armory
PWF
• George South vs Chris Hamrick
• Battle Royal

November 1, 1996
Kings Mountain, NC – Armory
PWF
• George South & Austin Steele vs Chris Hamrick & Carolina Dreamer
• Battle Royal

November 2, 1996
Gaffney, NC – Armory
PWF
• George South & Austin Steele vs Billy Jack & Italian Stallion
• Battle Royal

November 6, 1996
Charlotte, NC – Training Center
PWF
• George South & Austin Steele vs Black Angel & Carolina Dreamer
• Battle Royal

November 8, 1996
Gastonia, NC – Armory
PWF
• George South vs Billy Jack
• Lumberjack Match
• Battle Royal

November 14, 1996
Charlotte, NC – Training Center
PWF
• George South vs Carolina Dreamer
• Battle Royal

November 16, 1996
Lake Waccamaw, NC – High School
PWF
• George South vs Carolina Dreamer
• Battle Royal

November 21, 1996
Panama City, FL – Naval Base
PWF
• George South vs Italian Stallion
• Battle Royal

November 22, 1996
Inman, SC – Armory
PWF
• George South vs Lethal Lottery

November 23, 1996
Thomasville, NC – NAPA Store
PWF
• George South vs Carolina Dreamer
• Battle Royal

November 26, 1996
Charlotte, NC – Training Center
PWF
• George South vs Billy Jack
• Battle Royal

November 28, 1996
Gastonia, NC – Armory
PWF
• George South vs Italian Stallion
• Battle Royal

November 29, 1996
Forest City, NC – Armory
PWF
• George South vs Italian Stallion
• Battle Royal

November 30, 1996
Gaffney, NC – Armory
PWF
• George South & Austin Steele vs Chris Hamrick & Carolina Dreamer
• Battle Royal

December 6, 1996
Kings Mountain, NC – Armory
PWF
• George South vs Chief White Owl
• Battle Royal

December 7, 1996
Wellford, SC – Armory
PWF
• George South & Austin Steele vs Chris Hamrick & Carolina Dreamer

December 13, 1996
Inman, SC – Armory
PWF
• George South & Austin Steele vs Chris Hamrick & Italian Stallion

December 14, 1996
Mooresville, NC – Armory
PWF
• George South & Austin Steele vs Italian Stallion & Chris Hamrick
• Battle Royal

December 15, 1996
Charlotte, NC – Grady Cole
PWF
• George South vs Italian Stallion

December 19, 1996
Charlotte, NC – Training Center
PWF
• George South & Austin Steele vs Lucky & Black Angel

December 20, 1996
Charlotte, NC – Training Center
PWF
• George South vs Chief Crazy Horse
• 3-Way Match…George South vs Italian Stallion vs. Chief Crazy Horse

December 25, 1996
Kings Mountain, NC – Armory
PWF
• George South vs Italian Stallion
• Battle Royal

December 26, 1996
Charlotte, NC – Training Center
PWF
• George South vs. Italian Stallion
• Battle Royal

December 27, 1996
Forest City, NC – Armory
PWF
• George South & Austin Steele vs Wasted Youth & Italian Stallion
• Leather Strap Match
• Battle Royal

December 28, 1996
Gaffney, SC – Armory
PWF
• George South & Austin Steele vs Italian Stallion & Chief Crazy Horse
• Lumberjack Match
• Battle Royal

1997

January 2, 1997
Charlotte, NC – Training Center
PWF
• George South & Austin Steele vs Italian Stallion & Carolina Dreamer
• Battle Royal

January 3, 1997
Greer, SC – Armory
PWF
• George South vs Italian Stallion
• Battle Royal

January 4, 1997
Hamlet, NC – Armory
PWF
• George South vs Italian Stallion
• Battle Royal

January 9, 1997
Charlotte, NC – Training Center
PWF
• George South vs Troy Conyers

January 10, 1997
Kings Mountain, NC – Armory
PWF
• George South & Terry Austin vs Italian Stallion & Chris Hamrick

January 11, 1997
Gaffney, SC - Armory
PWF
• George South vs Italian Stallion

January 16, 1997
Charlotte, NC – Training Center
PWF
• George South & Austin Steele beat Black Angel & Wasted Youth
• Battle Royal

January 18, 1997
Gastonia, NC - Armory
PWF
• George South & Austin Steele vs Italian Stallion & Troy Conyers

January 19, 1997
Mooresville, NC – Armory
PWF
• George South beat Body Adonis

January 23, 1997
Charlotte, NC – Training Center
PWF
• George South & Austin Steele beat Black Angel & Wasted Youth
• Battle Royal

January 24, 1997
Inman, SC - Armory
PWF
• George South vs Italian Stallion
• George South & Austin Steele beat Chris Hamrick & Body Adonis
• Battle Royal

January 25, 1997
Forest City, NC – Armory
PWF
• Lethal Lottery

January 30, 1997
Charlotte, NC – Training Center
PWF
• George South & Austin Steele vs Black Angel & Texas Outlaw
• George South vs Italian Stallion

January 31, 1997
Hamlet, NC - Armory
PWF
• George South vs Italian Stallion

February 1, 1997
Gaffney, SC - Armory
PWF
• George South vs Italian Stallion

February 6, 1997
Charlotte, NC – Training Center
PWF
• George South vs Italian Stallion

February 7, 1997
Greer, SC - Armory
PWF
• George South vs Italian Stallion
• Lethal Lottery

February 8, 1997
Gastonia, NC - Armory
PWF
• George South beat Rock Bottom
• Battle Royal

February 9, 1997
PWF
Mooresville, NC - Armory
• George South vs Italian Stallion

February 14, 1997
Kings Mountain, NC - Armory
PWF
• George South vs Italian Stallion
• Battle Royal

February 15, 1997
Forest City, NC - Armory
PWF
• George South beat Black Angel
• Battle Royal

February 20, 1997
Charlotte, NC – Training Center
PWF
• George South beat Texas Outlaw

February 21, 1997
Taylorsville, NC - Armory
PWF
• George South vs Italian Stallion

February 22, 1997
Morganton, NC - Armory
PWF
• George South vs Italian Stallion

February 28, 1997
Inman, SC – Armory
PWF
• George South beat Black Angel
• Battle Royal

March 1, 1997
Greer, SC- Armory
PWF
• George South vs Italian Stallion
• Battle Royal

March 6, 1997
Charlotte, NC – Training Center
PWF
• George South vs Italian Stallion

March 7, 1997
Lincolnton, NC - Armory
PWF
• George South vs Italian Stallion

March 8, 1997
Gaffney, SC - Armory
PWF
• George South vs Italian Stallion
• Battle Royal

March 9, 1997
Hamlet, NC - Armory
PWF
• George South vs Italian Stallion

March 14, 1997
Kings Mountain, NC - Armory
PWF
• George South vs Italian Stallion

March 15, 1997
Forest City, NC - Armory
PWF
• George South vs Italian Stallion

March 20, 1997
Charlotte, NC – Training Center
PWF
• George South beat Rock Bottom
• Battle Royal

March 21, 1997
Morganton, NC - Armory
PWF
• George South vs Italian Stallion

March 22, 1997
Gastonia, NC – Armory
PWF
• George South vs Italian Stallion
• Battle Royal

March 26, 1997
Charlotte, NC – Training Center
PWF
• George South & Austin Steele beat Black Angel & Rock Bottom
• George South beat Texas Outlaw
• Battle Royal

March 27, 1997
Inman, SC – Armory
PWF
• George South beat Wasted Youth
• Battle Royal

March 28, 1997
Greer, SC – Armory
PWF
• George South beat Wasted Youth
• Battle Royal

April 1, 1997
Hamlet, NC - Armory
PWF
• George South beat Italian Stallion
• Battle Royal

Match # 4000
April 3, 1997
Taylorsville, NC - Armory
PWF
• George South beat Italian Stallion
• Battle Royal

April 4, 1997
Kings Mountain, NC - Armory
PWF
• George South beat Italian Stallion
• Battle Royal

April 5, 1997
Panama City, FL – Naval Base
PWF
• George South beat Naval Seal
• Battle Royal

April 10, 1997
Charlotte, NC – Training Center
PWF
• George South & Austin Steele beat Colt Justice & Chad Jordon
• Battle Royal

April 11, 1997
Lincolnton, NC – Armory
PWF
• George South beat Italian Stallion
• Battle Royal

April 12, 1997
Mooresville, NC – Armory
PWF
• George South beat Italian Stallion
• Battle Royal

April 17, 1997
Charlotte, NC – Training Center
PWF
• George South beat Wasted Youth
• Battle Royal

April 18, 1997
Morganton, NC – Armory
PWF
• George South beat Italian Stallion
• Battle Royal

April 19, 1997
Forest City, NC – Armory
PWF
• George South beat Italian Stallion
• Battle Royal

April 24, 1997
Charlotte, NC – Training Center
PWF
• Battle Royal

April 25, 1997
Taylorsville, NC – Armory
PWF
• George South beat Italian Stallion
• Battle Royal

April 26, 1997
Gastonia, NC – Armory
PWF
• George South beat Italian Stallion

May 1, 1997
Hamlet, NC – Armory
PWF
• George South beat Italian Stallion
• Battle Royal

May 2, 1997
Inman, SC – Armory
PWF
• George South beat Chad Jordon
• Battle Royal

May 3, 1997
Mooresville, NC – Armory
PWF
• George South beat Italian Stallion
• Battle Royal

May 8, 1997
Charlotte, NC – Training Center
PWF
• George South beat Chad Jordon
• Battle Royal

May 10, 1997
Forest City, NC – Armory
PWF
• George South beat Italian Stallion
• Battle Royal

May 15, 1997
Charlotte, NC – Training Center
PWF
• George South & Austin Steele beat Black Angel & Avenger

May 16, 1997
Morganton, NC – Armory
PWF
• George South vs Italian Stallion
• Battle Royal

May 17, 1997
Taylorsville, NC – Armory
PWF
• George South & Peggy Lee vs Italian Stallion & Mad Maxine
• Lethal Lottery

May 22, 1997
Charlotte, NC – Training Center
PWF
• George South & Austin Steele beat Rock Jordon & Chris Hamrick
• Battle Royal

May 23, 1997
Gaffney, SC – Armory
PWF
• George South vs Italian Stallion
• Battle Royal

May 24, 1997
Gastonia, NC – Armory
PWF
• George South beat Italian Stallion
• Battle Royal

May 29, 1997
Charlotte, NC – Training Center
PWF
• George South & Austin Steele vs Black Angel & Chris Hamrick

May 31, 1997
Mooresville, NC - Armory
PWF
• George South vs Jeff Hart
• Battle Royal

June 6, 1997
Kings Mountain, NC - Armory
PWF
• George South & Austin Steele vs Black Angel & Italian Stallion
• Battle Royal

June 7, 1997
Lincolnton, NC - Armory
PWF
• George South vs Italian Stallion
• Battle Royal

June 12, 1997
Taylorsville, NC - Armory
PWF
• George South vs Italian Stallion

June 13, 1997
Inman, SC - Armory
PWF
• George South vs Italian Stallion
• Battle Royal

June 14, 1997
Forest City, NC - Armory
PWF
- George South vs Italian Stallion
- Battle Royal

June 20, 1997
Morganton, NC - Armory
PWF
- George South vs Italian Stallion
- Battle Royal

June 21, 1997
James Island, SC - Armory
PWF
- George South vs Italian Stallion

June 26, 1997
Hamlet, NC - Armory
PWF
- George South vs Italian Stallion
- Battle Royal

June 27, 1997
Gaffney, SC - Armory
PWF
- George South vs Italian Stallion
- Battle Royal

June 28, 1997
Gastonia, NC - Armory
PWF
- George South vs Italian Stallion
- Battle Royal

July 1, 1997
Charlotte, NC – Training Center
PWF
- George South vs Wasted Youth
- Battle Royal

July 3, 1997
Morganton, NC - Armory
PWF
- George South vs Italian Stallion
- Battle Royal

July 5, 1997
Mooresville, NC - Armory
PWF
- George South vs Italian Stallion
- Battle Royal

July 8, 1997
Charlotte, NC – Training Center
PWF
- George South vs Wasted Youth
- Battle Royal

July 11, 1997
Inman, Sc - Armory
PWF
- George South vs Italian Stallion
- Battle Royal

July 12, 1997
Gaffney, SC - Armory
PWF
• George South vs Italian Stallion
• Battle Royal

July 15, 1997
Charlotte, NC – Training Center
PWF
• George South vs Cyclone
• Battle Royal

July 18, 1997
Kings Mountain, NC - Armory
PWF
• George South vs Italian Stallion
• Battle Royal

July 19, 1997
Mooresville, NC - Armory
PWF
• George South & Dr. Feelgood vs Black Angel & Terry Austin
• Battle Royal

July 22, 1997
Charlotte, NC – Training Center
PWF
• George South vs Scotty McKeever
• Battle Royal

July 25, 1997
Gastonia, NC - Armory
PWF
• George South vs Italian Stallion
• Battle Royal

July 26, 1997
Forest City, NC - Armory
PWF
• George South vs Italian Stallion
• Battle Royal

July 29, 1997
Charlotte, NC – Training Center
PWF
• George South & Austin Steele beat Gladiators
• Battle Royal

July 31, 1997
Charlotte, NC – Training Center
PWF
• George South vs Black Angel
• Battle Royal

August 1, 1997
Inman, SC - Armory
PWF
• George South vs Italian Stallion
• Battle Royal

August 2, 1997
Mooresville, NC – Armory
PWF
• George South vs Italian Stallion
• Battle Royal

August 5, 1997
Charlotte, NC – Training Center
PWF
• George South beat Rock Bottom

August 8, 1997
Gaffney, SC - Armory
PWF
• George South vs Italian Stallion
• Battle Royal

August 9, 1997
Kings Mountain, NC - Armory
PWF
• George South Italian Stallion
• Battle Royal

August 12, 1997
Charlotte, NC – Training Center
PWF
• George South vs Tim Jackson

August 14, 1997
Taylorsville, NC - Armory
PWF
• George South vs Italian Stallion
• Battle Royal

August 15, 1997
Morganton, NC - Armory
PWF
• George South vs Italian Stallion

August 16, 1997
Sugar Grove, NC -Old Cove Creek Gym
PWF
• George South vs Italian Stallion
• Battle Royal

August 19, 1997
Charlotte, NC – Training Center
PWF
• George South vs Wasted Youth
• George South vs The Breeze

August 22, 1997
Gastonia, NC - Armory
PWF
• George South vs Italian Stallion
• Battle Royal

August 23, 1997
Forest City, NC - Armory
PWF
• George South vs Colt Justice

August 26, 1997
Charlotte, NC – Training Center
PWF
• George South vs Scotty McKeever

August 29, 1997
Sugar Grove, NC – Old Cove Creek Gym
PWF
• George South vs Italian Stallion

August 30,1997
Gaffney, SC - Armory
PWF
- George South vs Italian Stallion

September 4, 1997
Kings Mountain, NC - Armory
PWF
- George South vs Ricky Morton

September 5, 1997
Inman, SC - Armory
PWF
- George South vs Ricky Morton
- Battle Royal

September 6, 1997
Lincolnton, NC - Armory
PWF
- George South vs Italian Stallion

September 9, 1997
Charlotte, NC – Training Center
PWF
- George South beat Texas Outlaw
- Battle Royal

September 11, 1997
Gastonia, NC - Armory
PWF
- George South vs Ricky Morton

September 12, 1997
Morganton, NC - Armory
PWF
- George South vs Ricky Morton

September 13, 1997
Rockingham, NC - Armory
PWF
- George South vs Carolina Dreamer
- Battle Royal

September 18, 1997
Mooresville, NC - Armory
PWF
- George South vs Italian Stallion

September 20, 1997
Charleston, SC – High School
- PWF
George South vs Italian Stallion

September 25, 1997
Charlotte, NC – Training Center
PWF
- George South vs Scotty McKeever
- Battle Royal

September 27, 1997
Forest City, NC - Armory
PWF
- George South vs Italian Stallion

October 1, 1997
Concord, NC – 1st Assembly
PWF
• George South & Scotty McKeever beat Nikita Koloff & Big Al

October 2, 1997
Inman, SC - Armory
PWF
• George South vs Italian Stallion

October 4, 1997
Gaffney, SC - Armory
PWF
• George South vs Italian Stallion

October 7, 1997
Charlotte, NC – Training Center
PWF
• George South vs Blue Demon

October 9, 1997
Mooresville, NC - Armory
PWF
• George South & Scotty McKeever vs Italian Stallion & Ricky Morton

October 10, 1997
Morganton, NC - Armory
PWF
• George South vs Italian Stallion
• Battle Royal

October 11, 1997
Kings Mountain, NC - Armory
PWF
• George South vs Italian Stallion
• Battle Royal

October 17, 1997
Charlotte, NC – Training Center
PWF
• George South vs Ricky Morton

October 18, 1997
Forest City, NC - Armory
PWF
• George South vs Italian Stallion
• Battle Royal

October 25, 1997
Gastonia, NC - Armory
PWF
• George South vs Italian Stallion

October 31, 1997
Kings Mountain, NC - Armory
PWF
• George South & Scotty McKeever vs Italian Stallion & Ricky Morton
• Battle Royal

November 1, 1997
Gaffney, SC - Armory
PWF
• George South vs Italian Stallion
• Battle Royal

Highway Run into the Midnight Sun

November 7, 1997
Morganton, NC - Armory
PWF
• George South vs Max Cortez
• Battle Royal

November 8, 1997
Lincolnton, NC – Armory
PWF
• George South vs Italian Stallion
• Managed The Bodyguard

177

November 15, 1997
Forest Coty, NC - Armory
PWF
• George South & Austin Steele vs Italian Stallion & The Breeze

November 22, 1997
Gastonia, NC – Armory
PWF
• George South vs Italian Stallion
• Battle Royal

November 27, 1997
Kings Mountain, NC -Armory
PWF
• George South vs Italian Stallion

November 28, 1997
Morganton, NC – Armory
PWF
• George South vs Italian Stallion
• Battle Royal

November 29, 1997
Kings Mountain, NC – Armory
PWF
• George South vs Italian Stallion
• Battle Royal

December 6, 1997
Kings Mountain, NC - Armory
PWF
• George South vs Mustafa Saed

December 12, 1997
Jefferson, NC - Armory
PWF
• George South vs Italian Stallion
• George South & Austin Steele vs Italian Stallion & Black Angel

December 14, 1997
Charlotte, NC – Grady Cole Center
PWF
• George South vs Italian Stallion
• Battle Royal

December 25, 1997
Kings Mountain, NC - Armory
PWF
• George South vs Italian Stallion
• Battle Royal

December 26, 1997
Forest City, NC - Armory
PWF
• George South vs Italian Stallion
• Battle Royal

December 27, 1997
Gastonia, NC - Armory
PWF
• George South vs Italian Stallion
• Battle Royal

1998

January 1, 1998
Mooresville, NC - Armory
PWF
• George South & Scotty McKeever vs Krush & Italian Stallion
• Battle Royal

January 2, 1998
Jefferson, NC - Armory
PWF
• George South vs Italian Stallion
• Battle Royal

January 3, 1998
Kings Mountain, NC - Armory
PWF
• George South vs Italian Stallion
• Battle Royal

January 9, 1998
Forest City, NC - Armory
PWF
• George South vs Italian Stallion
• Lethal Lottery

January 10, 1998
Lincolnton, NC - Armory
PWF
• George South vs Italian Stallion
• Battle Royal

January 17, 1998
Monroe, NC - Armory
PWF
• George South vs Italian Stallion
• Battle Royal

January 18, 1998
Mooresville, NC - Armory
PWF
• George South vs Italian Stallion
• Battle Royal

January 22, 1998
Albemarle, NC - Armory
PWF
• George South vs Italian Stallion
• Battle Royal

January 24, 1998
Gastonia, NC - Armory
PWF
• George South vs Italian Stallion
• Battle Royal

January 30, 1998
Inman, SC - Armory
PWF
• George South vs Star Ryder
• Battle Royal

January 31, 1998
Gaffney, SC - Armory
PWF
• George South vs Star Ryder
• Weapons Battle Royal

February 6, 1998
Jefferson, NC - Armory
PWF
• George South vs Italian Stallion
• Battle Royal

February 7, 1998
Kings Mountain, NC - Armory
PWF
• George South vs Italian Stallion
• Battle Royal

February 12, 1998
Albemarle, NC - Armory
PWF
• George South vs Italian Stallion
• Lethal Lottery

February 14, 1998
Gastonia, NC - Armory
PWF
• George South vs Italian Stallion
• Battle Royal

February 15, 1998
Mooresville, NC - Armory
PWF
• George South vs Italian Stallion
• Battle Royal

February 20, 1998
Kings Mountain, NC - Armory
PWF
• George South vs Italian Stallion
• Battle Royal

February 21, 1998
Forest City, NC - Armory
PWF
• George South vs Italian Stallion
• Battle Royal

February 27, 1998
Inman, SC - Armory
PWF
• George South vs Italian Stallion
• Battle Royal

February 28, 1998
Gaffney, SC - Armory
PWF
• George South vs Italian Stallion
• Battle Royal

March 5, 1998
Albemarle, NC - Armory
PWF
• George South vs Italian Stallion
• Battle Royal

March 6, 1998
Jefferson, NC - Armory
PWF
• George South vs Italian Stallion
• George South & Scotty McKeever vs Super Brat & Overlord
• Battle Royal

March 7, 1998
Kings Mountain, NC - Armory
PWF
• George South & Scotty McKeever vs Italian Stallion & Black Angel

March 13, 1998
Forest City, NC - Armory
PWF
• George South vs Italian Stallion
• Battle Royal

March 14, 1998
Monroe, NC - Armory
PWF
• George South vs Italian Stallion
• Battle Royal

March 20, 1998
Gaffney, SC - Armory
PWF
• George South & Scotty McKeever vs
Italian Stallion & Black Angel
• Battle Royal

March 21, 1998
Gastonia, NC - Armory
PWF
• George South vs Italian Stallion
• Battle Royal

March 27, 1998
Demision, OH – Middle School
PWF
• Italian Stallion beat George South
• Battle Royal

March 28, 1998
Kings Mountain, NC - Armory
PWF
• George South vs Italian Stallion

April 3, 1998
Kings Mountain, NC - Armory
PWF
• George South vs Italian Stallion
• Tag Team Battle Royal

April 4, 1998
Mooresville, NC - Armory
PWF
• George South vs Italian Stallion

April 10, 1998
Inman, SC - Armory
PWF
• George South vs Italian Stallion
• Battle Royal

April 11, 1998
Gastonia, NC - Armory
PWF
• George South vs Italian Stallion
• Bunkhouse Battle Royal

April 15, 1998
Forest City, NC - Armory
PWF
• George South vs Italian Stallion
• Lethal Lottery

April 17, 1998
Weirton, WV – Community Center
PWF
• George South vs Italian Stallion

April 18, 1998
Kings Mountain, NC - Armory
PWF
• George South vs Italian Stallion
• Battle Royal

April 30, 1998
Kings Mountain, NC - Armory
PWF
• George South vs Black Angel
• Battle Royal

May 1, 1998
Jefferson, NC - Armory
PWF
• George South vs Black Angel
• Battle Royal

May 2, 1998
Mooresville, NC - Armory
PWF
• George South vs Star Ryder
• Battle Royal

May 8, 1998
Lincolnton, NC - Armory
PWF
• George South vs Italian Stallion
• Battle Royal

May 9, 1998
Jefferson, NC - Armory
PWF
• George South vs Black Angel
• George South & Scotty McKeever vs Italian Stallion & Black Angel
• Battle Royal

May 15, 1998
Forest City, NC - NC - Armory
PWF
• George South vs Black Angel
• Battle Royal

May 16, 1998
Kings Mountain, NC - Armory
PWF
• George South vs Black Angel
• Battle Royal

May 18, 1998
Charlotte, NC – Church
PWF
• George South vs Italian Stallion

May 22,1998
Wheeling, WV – Civic Center
PWF
• George South vs Italian Stallion

May 24, 1998
Gaffney, SC - Armory
PWF
• George South vs Italian Stallion

May 29, 1998
Inman, SC - Armory
PWF
• George South vs Italian Stallion
• Battle Royal

May 30, 1998
Charleston, SC – County Hall
PWF
• George South vs Bubba Smith

June 5, 1998
Jefferson, NC - Armory
PWF
• George South vs Italian Stallion
• Battle Royal

June 6, 1998
Mooresville, NC - Armory
PWF
• George South vs Super Ninja

June 13, 1998
Gastonia, NC - Armory
PWF
• George South vs Italian Stallion
• Battle Royal

June 19, 1998
Forest City, NC - Armory
PWF
• George South vs Black Angel

June 20, 1998
Kings Mountain, NC - Armory
PWF
• George South vs Black Angel
• Battle Royal

June 26, 1998
Inman, SC - Armory
PWF
• George South vs Italian Stallion
• Lethal Lottery

June 27, 1998
Gaffney, SC - Armory
PWF
• George South vs Italian Stallion
• Battle Royal

July 3, 1998
Lincolnton, NC - Armory
PWF
• George South vs Italian Stallion
• Battle Royal

July 10, 1998
Jefferson, NC - Armory
PWF
• George South vs Italian Stallion
• Battle Royal

July 11, 1998
Mooresville, NC - Armory
PWF
• George South vs Black Angel

July 14, 1998
Charlotte, NC – Training Center
PWF
• George South beat Black Angel
• Battle Royal

July 17, 1998
Kings Mountain, NC - Armory
PWF
• George South vs Italian Stallion
• Battle Royal

July 18, 1998
Gaffney, SC - Armory
PWF
• George South vs Italian Stallion
• Battle Royal

July 21, 1998
Charlotte, NC – Training Center
PWF
• George South vs Rock Jordon
• Battle Royal

July 24, 1998
Forest City, NC - Armory
PWF
• George South vs Italian Stallion
• Battle Royal

July 25, 1998
Charlotte, NC – Gordon Church
PWF
• George South vs Italian Stallion
• Battle Royal

July 25, 1998
Gastonia, NC - Armory
PWF
• George South vs Italian Stallion
• Battle Royal

July 28, 1998
Charlotte, NC – Training Center
PWF
• George South vs Super Ninja
• Battle Royal

July 31, 1998
Inman, SC - Armory
PWF
- George South vs Italian Stallion
- Battle Royal

August 1, 1998
Lincolnton, NC - Armory
PWF
- George South vs Italian Stallion
- Battle Royal

August 4, 1998
Charlotte, NC – Training Center
PWF
- George South vs The Juicer
- Lethal Lottery

August 7, 1998
Jefferson, NC - Armory
PWF
- George South vs Italian Stallion
- Battle Royal

August 8, 1998
Gastonia, NC - Armory
PWF
- George South vs Italian Stallion
- Battle Royal

August 11, 1998
Petal, MS - Church
PWF
- George South vs Italian Stallion

August 13, 1998
Kosciusko, MS – Church
PWF
- George South vs Italian Stallion
- Battle Royal

August 14, 1998
Kings Mountain, NC - Armory
PWF
- George South vs The Juicer
- Battle Royal

August 15, 1998
NC - Armory
PWF
- George South vs The Juicer
- Lethal Lottery

August 18, 1998
Charlotte, NC – Training Center
PWF
- George South vs Super Ninja
- Battle Royal

August 21, 1998
Forest City, NC - Armory
PWF
- George South vs Italian Stallion
- Battle Royal

August 22, 1998
Lincolnton, NC - Armory
PWF
• George South vs Italian Stallion

August 28,1998
Inman, SC - Armory
PWF
• George South vs Italian Stallion
• Battle Royal

August 29, 1998
Gaffney, SC - Armory
PWF
• George South vs Italian Stallion

September 11, 1998
Forest City, NC - Armory
PWF
• George South vs Italian Stallion

September 12, 1998
Mooresville, NC - Armory
PWF
• George South vs The Breeze
• Battle Royal

September 18,1998
Inman, SC - Armory
PWF
• George South vs Italian Stallion
• Battle Royal

September 19, 1998
Gaffney, SC - Armory
PWF
• George South vs Italian Stallion
• Battle Royal

September 22, 1998
Charlotte, NC – Training Center
PWF
• George South vs Super Ninja
• Battle Royal

September 26, 1998
Gastonia, NC - Armory
PWF
• George South vs Italian Stallion
• Battle Royal

September 27, 1998
Webster, NC – Church
PWF
• George South vs Italian Stallion

October 2, 1998
Lilian, GA – Church
PWF
• George South vs Italian Stallion

October 3, 1998
Lincolnton, NC - Armory
PWF
• George South & Scotty McKeever vs
Italian Stallion & The Breeze

October 9, 1998
North Wilkesboro, NC - Armory
PWF
- George South vs Italian Stallion
- Battle Royal

October 10, 1998
Baltimore, MD – Colonial Church
PWF
- George South vs Italian Stallion

October 15, 1998
Kings Mountain, NC - Armory
PWF
- George South vs Italian Stallion

October 16, 1998
Sumpter, SC - Armory
PWF
- George South vs Italian Stallion
- Battle Royal

October 17, 1998
Jefferson, NC - Armory
PWF
- George South vs Italian Stallion
- Battle Royal

October 24, 1998
Gastonia, NC - Armory
PWF
- George South vs Italian Stallion

October 29, 1998
Kings Mountain, NC - Armory
PWF
- George South vs Italian Stallion
- Battle Royal

October 30, 1998
Inman, SC - Armory
PWF
- George South vs Italian Stallion
- Battle Royal

November 6, 1998
Jefferson, NC - Armory
PWF
- George South vs Italian Stallion
- Battle Royal

November 13, 1998
Forest City, NC - Armory
PWF
- George South vs Italian Stallion
- Battle Royal

November 14, 1998
Mooresville, NC - Armory
PWF
- George South vs Italian Stallion
- Battle Royal

November 21, 1998
Lincolnton, NC - Armory
PWF
- George South vs Italian Stallion

November 26, 1998
Gastonia, NC - Armory
PWF
• George South vs Italian Stallion
• Battle Royal

December 5, 1998
Jefferson, NC - Armory
PWF
• George South vs Italian Stallion
• Battle Royal

December 6, 1998
Forest City, NC - Armory
PWF
• George South vs Italian Stallion
• Battle Royal

December 11, 1998
North Wilkesboro, NC - Armory
PWF
• George South vs Italian Stallion
• Battle Royal

December 18, 1998
Fallston, NC – Middle School
PWF
• George South vs Italian Stallion

December 20, 1998
Mooresville, NC - Armory
PWF
• George South vs Italian Stallion
• Battle Royal

December 25, 1998
Gastonia, NC - Armory
PWF
• George South vs Italian Stallion
• Battle Royal

December 26, 1998
Gaffney, SC - Armory
PWF
• George South vs Italian Stallion
• Battle Royal

December 29, 1998
Inman, SC - Armory
PWF
• George South vs American GI
• Lethal Lottery

1999

January 1, 1999
Mooresville, NC – Armory
PWF
• Italian Stallion beat George South
• Battle Royal

January 9, 1999
Kings Mountain, NC – Armory
PWF
• George South vs Italian Stallion
• Battle Royal

January 17, 1999
North Wilkesboro, NC – Armory
PWF
• George South vs Italian Stallion
• Battle Royal

January 22, 1999
Taylorsville, NC – Armory
PWF
• George South vs Italian Stallion
• Battle Royal

January 23, 1999
Gastonia, NC – Armory
PWF
• George South vs Italian Stallion
• Battle Royal

February 12, 1999
Duluth, GA – Church
• George South beat Black Angel

February 27, 1999
Chesnee, SC – Shamrock Café
American Pro Wrestling (Jerry Bragg)
APW TV Taping
• George South vs Lee Strom
• George South vs Sonny Stone

March 5, 1999
Sugar Grove, NC – Old Cove Creek Gym
NAWA (Mark Henderson)
• George South beat Kenny Varner

March 6, 1999
Charlotte, NC – Gym
• George South beat The Flame

March 13, 1999
Columbia, SC – YMCA
• George South vs Black Angel

March 19, 1999
Chesnee, SC – Shamrock Café
APW
• George South vs Terry Austin
• George South vs Jay Eagle

March 20, 1999
Charleston, SC – College of Charleston
• George South vs Thunderfoot

March 27, 1999
Chesnee, SC – Shamrock Café
APW
• George South vs Terry Austin

April 3, 1999
Sugar Grove, NC – Old Cove Creek Gym
NAWA
• George South vs Able Adams

April 10, 1999
Charleston, SC – CSU
• George South & Peggy Lee vs Thunderfoot & Judy Martin

April 16, 1999
Chesnee, SC – Shamrock Café
APW
• George South vs Jesse Magnum
• George South vs Henry Eagle
• Battle Royal

April 17,1999
Gastonia, NC – High School
• George South vs Krazy Kane Adams

April 23, 1999
Concord, NC – Rec Center
• George South vs Terry Austin

April 30, 1999
Chesnee, SC – Shamrock Café
APW
• George South vs Hillbilly
• George South vs Twisted Sister
• George South vs Jay Eagle

May 1, 1999
Monroe, NC – High School
• George South vs Scotty Youngblood

May 7, 1999
Lincolnton, NC – High School
• George South vs Sgt. Craig Pittman

May 15, 1999
Lincolnton, NC – New Vision
• George South vs American GI

May 21, 1999
Jena, LA – High School
• George South vs The Mascot

May 22, 1999
Hickory, NC – Rec Center
• George South vs Terry Austin

June 4, 1999
Cowen, WV – Elementary School
• George South vs Anthony Perdue
• George South vs Joey Morton
• Battle Royal

June 8, 1999
Baton Rouge, LA – Church
• George South vs Anthony Perdue

June 9, 1999
Panama City, FL – Laguna Beach
• George South vs Anthony Perdue

June 15, 1999
Beckley, WV – Bargain Park
• George South vs Ryan Wild

June 17, 1999
Birmingham, AL – Ranger Camp
• George South vs Scotty McKeever
• George South vs Scotty McKeever

June 23, 1999
Brownwood, TX - College
• George South vs Scotty McKeever

July 1, 1999
Jacksonville, FL – 1st Baptist Church
• George South vs Scotty McKeever
• Battle Royal

July 15, 1999
Concord, NC – EWA Arena
EWA
• George South vs Scotty McKeever
• George South vs The Bodyguard

July 22, 1999
Concord, NC – EWA Arena
EWA
• George South vs The Bodyguard
• George South vs Scotty McKeever

July 23, 1999
Sommerville, SC – Church
• George South vs Bubba
• Battle Royal

July 29, 1999
Concord, NC – EWA Arena
EWA
• George South vs Scotty McKeever

July 30, 1999
Sommerville, SC – Church
EWA
• George South vs Scotty McKeever
• George South vs Youth Pastor

August 5, 1999
Concord, NC – EWA Arena
EWA
• George South vs Scotty McKeever
• George South vs The Bodyguard

August 7, 1999
Hickory, NC – Brookford Gym
EWA
• George South vs Scotty McKeever
• George South &? vs Scotty McKeever & Ryan Wild

August 12, 1999
Concord, NC – EWA Arena
EWA
• George South vs The Bodyguard
• George South vs. Scotty McKeever

August 14, 1999
Hickory, NC – Brookford Gym
EWA
• George South vs Scotty McKeever
• Battle Royal

August 19, 1999
Concord, NC – EWA Arena
EWA
• George South vs Badstreet
• George South vs The Bodyguard

August 21, 1999
Charlotte, NC – Oasis Temple
• George South vs Colt Steele

August 26, 1999
Concord, NC – EWA Arena
EWA
• George South vs The Bodyguard
• George South &? vs Flaming Youth & The Bodyguard

August 28, 1999
Hickory, NC – Brookford Gym
EWA
• George South vs The Bodyguard

September 2, 1999
Concord, NC – EWA Arena
EWA
• George South vs The Bodyguard

September 3, 1999
Statesville, NC – Karate School
EWA
• George South vs The Bodyguard

September 4, 1999
Hickory, NC – Brookford Gym
EWA
• George South vs Scotty McKeever
• George South vs The Bodyguard

September 9, 1999
Concord, NC – EWA Arena
EWA
• George South vs The Bodyguard

September 10, 1999
Statesville, NC – Karate School
EWA
• George South & Masked Superstar vs
Sweet Dreams & The Bodyguard

September 11, 1999
Hickory, NC – Brookford Gym
EWA
• George South vs The Bodyguard

September 16, 1999
Concord, NC – EWA Arena
EWA
• George South vs Scotty McKeever

September 17, 1999
Statesville, NC – Karate School
EWA
• George South vs Scotty McKeever
• George South vs The Bodyguard

September 18, 1999
Hickory, NC – Brookford Gym
EWA
• George South vs Badstreet
• George South vs The Bodyguard

September 23, 1999
Concord, NC – EWA Arena
EWA
• George South vs Scotty McKeever
• George South vs Sweet Dreams

September 24, 1999
Statesville, NC – Karate School
EWA
• George South vs Sweet Dreams
• George South & Masked Superstar vs
Sweet Dreams & The Bodyguard

September 25, 1999
Hickory, NC – Brookford Gym
EWA
• George South vs The Bodyguard

September 30, 1999
Concord, NC – EWA Arena
EWA
• George South vs Scotty McKeever

October 2, 1999
Hickory, NC – Brookford Gym
EWA
• George South vs Scotty McKeever

October 7, 1999
Concord, NC – EWA Arena
EWA
• George South vs The Bodyguard

October 9, 1999
Hickory, NC – Rec Center
EWA
• George South vs Black Angel

October 14, 1999
Concord, NC – EWA Arena
EWA
• George South vs Scotty McKeever
• George South vs The Bodyguard

October 16, 1999
Hickory, NC – Brookford Gym
EWA
• George South vs Scotty McKeever

October 21, 1999
Concord, NC – EWA Arena
EWA
• George South vs Scotty McKeever
• George South vs The Bodyguard

October 22, 1999
Hickory, NC – Brookford Gym
EWA
- George South vs Scotty McKeever
- George South vs The Bodyguard

October 23, 1999
Delaware, OH – Gym
- George South vs Scotty McKeever

October 28, 1999
Concord, NC – EWA Arena
EWA
- George South vs Scotty McKeever

October 29, 1999
Hickory, NC – Brookford Gym
EWA
- George South vs Scotty McKeever

October 30, 1999
Hildebran, NC – Gym
EWA
- George South vs Scotty McKeever

October 31, 1999
Lincolnton, NC – New Vision
- George South vs Scotty McKeever

November 4, 1999
Concord, NC – EWA Arena
EWA
- George South beat The Bodyguard

November 5, 1999
Hickory, NC – Brookford Gym
EWA
- George South beat Scotty McKeever
- George South Sr & Jr vs Scotty McKeever & The Bodyguard

November 6, 1999
Concord, NC – Fun Park
EWA
- George South beat Scotty McKeever

November 11, 1999
Concord, NC – EWA Arena
EWA
- George South beat Scotty McKeever

November 12, 1999
Hickory, NC – Brookford Gym
EWA
- George South vs Ricky Morton

November 13, 1999
Sugar Grove, NC – Old Cove Creek Gym
EWA
- George South vs Scotty McKeever
- George South Sr & Jr beat Scotty McKeever & The Bodyguard

November 15, 1999
Concord, NC – EWA Arena
EWA
- George South beat Carolina Dreamer

November 18, 1999
Concord, NC – EWA Arena
EWA
• George South beat The Bodyguard

November 20, 1999
Hickory, NC – Brookford Gym
EWA
• George South beat Scotty McKeever

November 21, 1999
Charlotte, NC – Tato Bill's
EWA
• George South beat Scotty McKeever

November 25, 1999
Concord, NC – EWA Arena
EWA
• George South beat Scotty McKeever
• George South Sr & Jr beat Scotty McKeever & Tim Jackson

November 26, 1999
Sugar Grove, NC – Old Cove Creek Gym
EWA
• George South beat Scotty McKeever
• George South Sr & Jr beat Scotty McKeever & Joe Brody

November 27, 1999
Hickory, NC – Brookford Gym
EWA
• George South beat Scotty McKeever

December 2, 1999
Concord, NC – EWA Arena
EWA
• George South beat The Bodyguard

December 4, 1999
Hickory, NC – Brookford Gym
EWA
• George South beat Scotty McKeever

December 6, 1999
Concord, NC – EWA Arena
EWA
• George South beat Scotty McKeever
• George South Sr & Jr beat Scotty McKeever & Black Dragon

December 9, 1999
Hickory, NC – Brookford Gym
EWA
• George South beat Scotty McKeever

December 14, 1999
Sugar Grove, NC – Old Cove Creek Gym
EWA
• George South vs Ricky Morton

December 15, 1999
Concord, NC – EWA Arena
EWA
• George South beat Scotty McKeever

December 18, 1999
Sumpter, SC – 1st Assembly
EWA
• George South beat Scotty McKeever

December 19, 1999
Hickory, NC – Brookford Gym
EWA
• George South beat Scotty McKeever

December 23, 1999
Concord, NC – EWA Arena
EWA
• George South beat Scotty McKeever

December 25, 1999
Hickory, NC – Brookford Gym
EWA
• George South vs Tommy Rich

December 30, 1999
Concord, NC – EWA Arena
EWA
• George South beat Scotty McKeever

2000

January 1, 2000
Hickory, NC – Brookford Gym
EWA
• George South vs Scotty McKeever
• Battle Royal

January 6, 2000
Concord, NC – EWA Arena
EWA
• George South vs Scotty McKeever

January 8, 2000
Hickory, NC – Brookford Gym
EWA
• George South vs Scotty McKeever
• Battle Royal

January 13, 2000
Concord, NC – EWA Arena
EWA
• George South vs Scotty McKeever

January 14, 2000
Hickory, NC – Brookford Gym
EWA
• George South vs Showcase
• George South vs Scotty McKeever

January 15, 2000
Greensboro, NC – Conv. Center
• George South vs Scotty McKeever
• George South vs Percy

January 20, 2000
Concord, NC – EWA Arena
EWA
• George South vs Scotty McKeever

January 21, 2000
Wentworth, NC – Rec Center
EWA
• George South vs Robert Roma

January 27, 2000
Concord, NC – EWA Arena
EWA
• George South vs Scotty McKeever

February 3, 2000
Concord, NC – EWA Arena
EWA
• George South vs Scotty McKeever
• George South vs The Ninja

February 4, 2000
Wentworth, NC – Rec Center
EWA
• George South vs Robert Roma

February 5, 2000
Hickory, NC – Brookford Gym
EWA
• George South vs Scotty McKeever

February 6, 2000
Concord, NC – EWA Arena
EWA
• George South vs Scotty McKeever

February 10, 2000
Concord, NC – EWA Arena
EWA
• George South vs Scotty McKeever

February 11, 2000
Hickory, NC – Brookford Gym
EWA
• George South vs Scotty McKeever
• Battle Royal

February 12, 2000
Wentworth, NC – Rec Center
EWA
• George South vs Scotty McKeever

February 19, 2000
Hickory, NC – Brokford Gym
EWA
• George South vs Scotty McKeever

February 24, 2000
Concord, NC – EWA Arena
EWA
• George South vs The Ninja

February 26, 2000
Aiken, SC – Crown Center
• George South vs Scotty McKeever

February 27, 2000
Hickory, NC – Brookford Gym
EWA
• Royal Rumble

March 2, 2000
Concord, NC – EWA Arena
EWA
• George South vs Scotty McKeever

March 3, 2000
Wentworth, NC – Rec Center
EWA
• George South vs Jimmy Valiant

March 4, 2000
Hickory, NC – Brookford Gym
EWA
• George South vs Scotty McKeever

March 9, 2000
Concord, NC – EWA Arena
EWA
• George South vs Scotty McKeever

March 10, 2000
Wentworth, NC – Rec Center
EWA
• George South vs The Conceited Kid

March 11, 2000
Hickory, NC – Brookford Gym
EWA
• George South vs Scotty McKeever
• George South vs The Bodyguard

March 17, 2000
Hickory, NC – Brookford Gym
EWA
• George South Sr & Jr vs Scotty McKeever & The Bodyguard

March 18, 2000
Cowen, WV – Elementary School
• George South vs Scotty McKeever
• George South vs Badstreet

March 23, 2000
Concord, NC – EWA Arena
EWA
• George South vs Scotty McKeever

March 24, 2000
Wentworth, NC – Rec Center
EWA
• George South vs The Conceited Kid

March 25, 2000
Wentworth, NC – Rec Center
• George South vs Scotty McKeever

March 26, 2000
Hickory, NC – Brookford Gym
EWA
• George South vs Badstreet

March 30, 2000
Concord, NC – EWA Arena
EWA
• George South vs Badstreet

March 31, 2000
Wentworth, NC – Rec Center
EWA
• George South vs Scotty McKeever

April 1, 2000
Wentworth, NC – Rec Center
EWA
• George South vs Scotty McKeever

April 2, 2000
Hickory, NC – Brookford Gym
EWA
• George South vs Scotty McKeever

April 5, 2000
Augusta, GA – Fairgrounds
• George South vs Scotty McKeever
• George South & Masked Superstar vs Scotty McKeever & Jorge Estrade

April 6, 2000
Concord, NC – EWA Arena
EWA
• George South vs Badstreet

April 7, 2000
Atlanta, GA - Tabernacle
- George South vs Scotty McKeever

April 8, 2000
Wentworth, NC – Rec Center
- George South vs Sweet Daddy

April 12, 2000
Petal, MS - Fairgrounds
- George South vs Scotty McKeever
- George South & Masked Superstar vs Scotty McKeever & El Granada

April 13, 2000
Petal, MS – Fairgrounds
- George South vs Scotty McKeever

April 14, 2000
Wentworth, NC – Rec Center
EWA
- George South beat Cyclone

April 15, 2000
Troutman, NC – High School
EWA
- George South beat Badstreet

April 20, 2000
Concord, NC – EWA Arena
EWA
- George South & Masked Superstar beat Badstreet & The Ninja

April 22, 2000
Wentworth, NC – Rec Center
- George South vs Tommy Rich

April 27, 2000
Concord, NC – EWA Arena
EWA
- George South beat Scotty McKeever

April 28, 2000
Wentworth, NC – Rec Center
EWA
- George South & Masked Superstar vs Sweet Daddy & Chris Nelson

April 29, 2000
Elizabethtown, KY – High School
SSW
- George South vs Scotty McKeever
- George South & Masked Superstar vs Scotty McKeever & Badstreet

May 4, 2000
Concord, NC – EWA Arena
EWA
- George South vs Scotty McKeever

May 5, 2000
Wentworth, NC – Rec Center
EWA
- George South vs Enigma

May 6, 2000
Wentworth, NC – Rec Center
EWA
- George South vs Blizzard

May 11, 2000
Concord, NC – EWA Arena
EWA
- George South beat Scotty McKeever
- George South & Masked Superstar beat Scotty McKeever & Badstreet

May 12, 2000
Wentworth, NC – Rec Center
EWA
- George South vs The Bodyguard

May 13, 2000
Fayetteville, GA – Church
- George South vs Coach Bailey
- Battle Royal

May 18, 2000
Concord, NC – EWA Arena
EWA
- George South vs Scotty McKeever

May 19, 2000
Wentworth, NC – Rec Center
EWA
- George South beat Iron Horse

May 20, 2000
Wentworth, NC – Rec Center
EWA
- George South beat Badstreet

May 25, 2000
Concord, NC – EWA Arena
EWA
- George South vs Badsteet
- George South & Masked Superstar vs Badstreet & Carolina Dreamer

May 27, 2000
Charlotte, NC – Church – 2pm
EWA
- George South vs. Scotty McKeever

May 27, 2000
Shelby, NC – Fairgrounds – 8pm
- George South vs Scotty McKeever

June 1, 2000
Concord, NC – EWA Arena
EWA
- George South vs Badstreet

June 2, 2000
Wentworth, NC – Rec Center
EWA
- George South vs Badstreet

June 3, 2000
Wentworth, NC – Rec Center
EWA
- George South vs Scott Wilner
- George South vs Conceited Kid

June 8, 2000
Concord, NC – EWA Arena
EWA
• George South vs JasonKing

June 10, 2000
Wentworth, NC – Rec Center
EWA
• George South vs Jason King

June 15, 2000
Concord, NC – EWA Arena
EWA
• George South vs Ninja

June 17, 2000
Concord, NC – EWA Arena
EWA
• George South vs Carolina Dreamer

June 19, 2000
Vale, NC – Auction Barn
• George South vs Carolina Dreamer
• Battle Royal

June 22, 2000
Concord, NC – EWA Arena
EWA
• George South vs Carolina Dreamer

June 23, 2000
Wentworth, NC – Rec Center
EWA
• George South vs Mo Money

June 24, 2000
Wentworth, NC – Rec Center
EWA
• George South vs Butch Steele

June 29, 2000
Concord, NC – EWA Arena
EWA
• George South vs Badstreet

June 30, 2000
Sommerville, SC – Mills River Church
• George South vs Ricky Morton
• George South vs Youth Pastor

June 31, 2000
Hickory, NC – Brookford Gym
EWA
• George South vs The Barbarian

July 3, 2000
Vale, NC – Auction World
• George South vs Ricky Morton

July 8, 2000
Concord, NC – EWA Arena
EWA
• George South vs Badstreet

July 13, 2000
Concord, NC – EWA Arena
EWA
• George South vs Carolina Dreamer

July 14, 2000
Concord, NC – EWA Arena
EWA
• George South vs Badstreet

July 22, 2000
Wentworth, NC – Rec Center
EWA
• George South vs Scotty McKeever

July 29, 2000
Wentworth, NC – Rec Center
EWA
• George South vs Scotty McKeever

August 4, 2000
Wentworth, NC – Rec Center
EWA
• George South vs Butch Steele

August 5, 2000
Wentworth, NC – Rec Center
EWA
• George South vs Scotty McKeever

August 7, 2000
Vale, NC – Auction World
• George South vs Ricky Morton

August 12, 2000
Wentworth, NC – Rec Center
EWA
• George South vs Dalton Steele

August 19, 2000
Wentworth, NC – Rec Center
EWA
• George South vs Butch Steele
• Battle Royal

August 25, 2000
Wentworth, NC – Rec Center
EWA
• George South vs. Butch Steele

August 26, 2000
Troutman, NC – American Legion
EWA
• George South vs Badstreet

September 1, 2000
Newton, NC – Armory
• George South vs Scotty McKeever

September 2, 2000
Wentworth, NC – Rec Center
EWA
• George South vs Nerdy Boy

September 4, 2000
Vale, NC – Auction World
• George South vs Ricky Morton

September 8, 2000
Chesnee, SC – Shamrock Café
• George South vs Nick Foley
• George South vs Ricky Noble

September 9, 2000
Yanceyville, NC – American Legion
• George South vs Frank Dalton

September 16, 2000
Hickory, NC – Armory
• George South vs Ryan Wild

September 18, 2000
Sawmills, NC – Auction Barn
• George South vs Carolina Dreamer

September 20, 2000
Morganton, NC - Fairgrounds
BCW
• George South vs Scotty McKeever

September 22, 2000
Wentworth, NC – Rec Center
EWA
• George South vs The Bodyguard

September 23, 2000
Kings Mountain, NC - Armory
EWA
• George South vs Carolina Dreamer
• Battle Royal

September 30, 2000
Dumphries, VA – Wal Mart
• George South vs Scotty McKeever

October 2, 2000
Vale, NC – Auction World
• George South vs Ricky Morton

October 4, 2000
Shelby, NC – Fairgrounds
• George South vs Ricky Morton

October 7, 2000
Randallstown, MD – Church
• George South vs Masked Superstar

October 13, 2000
Pelham, NC – Comm. Building
• George South vs Jimmy Love

October 14, 2000
Wentworth, NC – Rec Center
EWA
• George South vs Scott Whiner

October 27, 2000
Wentworth, NC – Rec Center
EWA
• George South vs Butch Steele

October 28, 2000
Ceasar, NC – Park
• George South vs Ryan Wild

October 29, 2000
Lincolnton, NC – New Vision
• George South vs Ricky Morton

November 3, 2000
Pelham, NC – Comm Building
• George South vs Scotty McKeever

November 6, 2000
Vale, NC – Auction World
• George South vs Scotty McKeever

November 11, 2000
Hickory, NC – Brookford Gym
EWA
• George South vs Scotty McKeever

November 17, 2000
Pelham, NC – Comm Building
• George South vs Ricky Morton

November 18, 2000
Savannah, GA – Ft. Stewart
• George South vs Ricky Morton

November 24, 2000
Wentworth, NC – Rec Center
EWA
• George South vs Beautiful Bobby Eaton

December 4, 2000
Vale, NC – Auction World
• George South vs Ricky Morton

December 9, 2000
Yanceyville, NC – High School
• George South vs Chris Nelson

December 15, 2000
Wentworth, NC – Rec Center
EWA
• George South vs Chuck Jones

December 30, 2000
Wentworth, NC – Rec Center
EWA
• George South vs Badstreet

2001

January 8, 2001
Vale, NC – Auction World
EWA
• George South & The Superstar vs Bobby Eaton & Carolina Dreamer

January 13, 2001
Newton, NC – Armory
EWA
• George South & The Superstar vs Bobby Eaton & Carolina Dreamer

January 27, 2001
Kings Mountain, NC – Armory
EWA
• George South vs Scotty McKeever
• George South vs Badstreet

February 3, 2001
Hickory, NC – Brookford Gym
EWA
• George South vs Badstreet
• George South vs Cruel Connection II

February 4, 2001
Bluefield, WV – Community Center
EWA
• George South vs Badstreet

February 6, 2001
Vale, NC – Auction World
EWA
• George South & The Superstar vs Scotty McKeever & Badstreet

February 9, 2001
Ocean City, MD – Convection Center
• George South vs The Superstar

February 10, 2001
Ocean City, MD – Convection Center
• George South vs The Superstar

February 16, 2001
Maiden, NC – Rec Center
EWA
• George South vs Scotty McKeever

February 17, 2001
Yanceyville, NC – High School
• George South & Scotty McKeever vs Coach & Chris Nelson

February 23, 2001
Arcadia, NC – VFW Building
• George South vs Scotty McKeever

February 24, 2001
Aiken, SC – Crown Center
• George South vs Scotty McKeever

March 4, 2001
Hickory, NC – Brookford Gym
EWA
• George South beat Badstreet

March 9, 2001
Maiden, NC – Rec Center
EWA
• George South vs Scotty McKeever

March 11, 2001
Greensboro, GA – Church
• George South vs Badstreet

March 16, 2001
Kings Mountain, NC – Armory
EWA
• George South vs Badstreet
• George South vs The Hardcore Kid (George South Jr)
• George South vs Badstreet

March 24, 2001
Kings Mountain, NC – Armory
EWA
• George South vs Badstreet

March 31, 2001
Harrisburg, NC – Body Shop
• George South vs Badstreet
• George South vs Scotty McKeever

April 7, 2001
Winnsboro, LA – Town Festival
EWA
• George South vs Badstreet
• George South vs Badstreet
• George South vs Badstreet

April 14, 2001
Harrisburg, NC – Body Shop
EWA
• George South vs Badstreet
• George South vs Scotty McKeever

April 17, 2001
Newport News, VA – Church
EWA
• George South vs Scotty McKeever

April 19, 2001
Kings Mountain, NC – Armory
EWA
• George South vs Ryan Joseph
• George South vs Scotty McKeever

April 20, 2001
Savannah, Ga – Ball Park
George South vs Madd Maxx

April 26, 2001
Athens, WV – Concord College
• George South vs Ricky Morton

April 28, 2001
Harrisburg, NC – Body Shop
EWA
• George South vs Badstreet

May 12, 2001
Kings Mountain, NC – Armory
EWA
- George South vs Badstreet
- George South vs Badstreet

May 13, 2001
Florence, KY – High School
- George South vs Badstreet
- George South vs Hector Guerrero

May 18, 2001
Wagner, SC – High School
- George South vs Badstreet

May 19, 2001
Goldsboro, NC – Air Force Base
- George South vs Doink the Clown

May 25, 2001
Maiden, NC – Rec Center
EWA
- George South vs Badstreet
- George South & The Superstar vs Scotty McKeever & Badstreet

May 26, 2001
Sugar Grove, NC – Old Cove Creek Gym
EWA
- George South & The Superstar vs Scotty McKeever & The Hardcore Kid

June 2, 2001
Harrisburg, NC – Body Shop
EWA
- George South vs Badstreet
- George South vs Scotty McKeever

June 9, 2001
Kings Mountain, NC – Armory
EWA
- George South vs Badstreet
- George South vs Badstreet

June 16, 2001
Shelby, NC – Rec Center
CCW
- George South beat Jay Eagle

June 17, 2001
Princeton, WV – Rec Center
EWA
- Ricky Morton beat George South

June 21, 2001
Sommerville, SC – Prison Camp
EWA
- Ricky Morton beat George South

June 22, 2001
Kings Mountain, NC – Armory
EWA
- George South vs Badstreet

June 23, 2001
Gastonia, NC – Armory
EWA
- George South vs Badstreet
- George South vs Scotty McKeever

June 29, 2001
Harrisburg, SC – Body Shop
EWA
• George South vs Scotty McKever
• George South vs The Hardcore Kid

June 30, 2001
Aiken, SC – Crown Center
• George South vs Badstreet

July 4, 2001
Scottsburg, VA – Fairgrounds
• George South vs Badstreet

July 6, 2001
Kings Mountain, NC – Armory
EWA
• George South vs Badstreet

July 7, 2001
Coward, SC – Ballpark
• George South vs Ricky Morton

July 13, 2001
Rock Hill, SC – Coliseum
George South & Scotty McKeever vs Jason King & Hector Guerrero

July 14, 2001
Harrisburg, SC – Body Shop
EWA
• George South vs Jason King

July 27, 2001
Lincolnton, NC – Prison Camp
EWA
• Ricky Morton beat George South

July 28, 2001
Kings Mountain, NC – Armory
EWA
• George South vs Scotty McKeever

July 29, 2001
Harrisburg, NC – Body Shop
EWA
• George South vs Scotty McKeever

August 2, 2001
Rock Hill, SC – YMCA
EWA
George South vs Jason King

August 3, 2001
Sommerville, SC – Church
EWA
• George South &? Vs S&S Express

August 4, 2001
Sommerville, SC – Church – 1pm
EWA
• George South vs Madd Maxx

August 4, 2001
Elkin, NC – Armory – 8pm
• George South & Scotty McKeever vs.
Sgt. Buddy Lee Parker & Sacro Jr

August 10, 2001
King Mountain, NC – Armory
EWA
- George South vs Jason King
- George South vs Ricky Morton

August 11, 2001
Jacksonville, NC – Camp Lejune
- George South vs Jason King
- Battle Royal

August 19, 2001
Charlotte, NC – Revolution Park
EWA
- George South vs Scotty McKeever

August 20, 2001
Harrisburg, NC – Body Shop
EWA
- George South vs Scotty McKeever
- George South vs George South Jr

August 31, 2001
Harrisburg, NC – Body Shop
EWA
- George South vs Jason King

September 3, 2001
Harrisburg, NC – Body Shop
EWA
- George South vs Jason King
- George South vs Jason King

September 5, 2001
Athens, WV – Concord College
- George South vs Jimmy Valiant

September 8, 2001
Kings Mountain, NC – Armory
EWA
- George South vs Scotty McKeever

September 15, 2001
Kannapolis, NC – Fieldcrest Cannon Stadium
- George South & Scotty McKeever vs Jason King & Hector Guerrero

September 21, 2001
Taylorsville, NC – Fairgrounds
- George South vs Chris Hefner
- George South & Scotty McKeever vs Chris Hefner & Kid Konga
- Battle Royal

September 22, 2001
Harrisburg, NC – Body Shop
EWA
- George South vs Jason King
- George South vs Jason King

September 28, 2001
Charlotte, NC – WPEG - 2pm
- George South vs Scotty McKeever

September 28, 2001
Chesnee, SC – Arena – 8pm
- George South vs Jason King

October 6, 2001
Big Spring, TX - Coliseum
• George South vs Jason King

October 12, 2001
Harrisburg, NC – Body Shop
EWA
• George South vs Scotty McKeever
• George South vs Jason King

October 13, 2001
High Schools, NC – Ball Field
• George South vs Scotty McKeever

October 20, 2001
Harrisburg, NC – Body Shop
EWA
• George South vs Scotty McKeever

October 25, 2001
Morganton, NC – Fairgrounds
BCW (Jeff Patton)
• George South vs Scotty McKeever

October 26, 2001
Harrisburg, NC – Body Shop
EWA
• George South vs Scotty McKeever
• George South vs Scotty McKeever

October 27, 2001
Concord, NC – Hartsville Gym
EWA
• George South &? vs Scotty McKeever & Jason King

2002

January 9, 2002
Conover, NC – 1st Baptist Church
EWA
• George South beat The Gladiator

January 12, 2002
Lenoir, NC – American Legion Hall
UWA (Roger Knight)
• George South vs James Brody

January 18, 2002
Yanceyville, NC – VFW
• George South vs Chris Nelson

January 19, 2002
Pleasant Grove, NC – Rec Center
• George South vs Badstreet

January 25, 2002
Kings Mountain, NC – Armory
EWA
• George South vs Ray Hudson

January 26, 2002
Lenoir, NC – American Legion Hall
UWA
• George South vs James Brody

February 2, 2002
Reidsville, NC – YMCA
• George South beat Chris Nelson

February 5, 2002
Attended Nelson Royals Funeral in Mooresville, NC with Paul Jones

February 9, 2002
Hartville, AL – Praise Assembly of God
• George South beat Scotty McKeever w/ Ted DiBaise

February 16, 2002
Lenoir, NC – American Legion Hall
UWA
• George South w/ Paul Jones beat Bruiser Graham

February 20, 2002
Preached at Pitts Baptist in Concord, NC

February 23, 2002
Fayetteville, NC – YMCA
• George South beat Scotty McKeever

February 28, 2002
Kings Mountain, NC – Armory
EWA
• George South vs Ray Hudson

March 1, 2002
Greenville, WV – Old Gym
EWA
• George South vs Scotty McKeever

March 2, 2002
Lenoir, NC – American Legion Hall
UWA
• George South beat Assassin

March 8, 2002
Taylorsville, NC – Fairgrounds
• George South vs Raggin Bull Manny Fernandez

March 9, 2002
Lenoir, NC - American Legion Hall
UWA
• George South vs The Barbarian

March 16, 2002
Taylorsville, NC – John Boy Chevy – 2pm
• George South vs Local

March 16, 2002
Lenoir, NC - American Legion Hall - 8pm
UWA
• George South vs Local

March 17, 2002
Shelby, NC – Solid Rock Church
EWA
• George South beat Gladiator

March 20, 2002
Lenoir, NC – 1st Baptist Church
EWA
• George South vs Gladiator

March 22, 2002
Mooresville, NC- Armory
EWA
• George South beat Badstreet

March 23, 2002
Hinesville, GA – Rec Center
EWA
• George South vs Ricky Morton

March 24, 2002
Douglas, GA – Rec Center
EWA
• George South vs Ricky Morton

March 25, 2002
Preached in Spindale, NC

March 27, 2002
Gastonia, NC – Church
EWA
• George South vs Preacher Dave

March 28, 2002
Sugar Grove, NC – Old Cove Creek Gym
• EWA
George South beat Scotty McKeever

March 29, 2002
Pelham, NC – Community Center
• George South beat Chris Nelson

March 30, 2002
Lenoir, NC – American Legion Hall
UWA
• George South vs James Brody

April 3, 2002
Columbia, MS – Mt. Zion Baptist Church
• George South vs Scotty McKeever

April 5, 2002
Dunmore, WV – High School
• George South vs Scotty McKeever

April 6, 2002
Cowan, WV – Elementary School
• George South beat Ninja

April 7, 2002
Shelby, NC – Solid Rock Church
EWA
• George South vs Local

April 11, 2002
Sugar Grove, NC – Old Cove Creek Gym
EWA
• George South beat Scotty Hot Body

April 12, 2002
Murphy, NC – Armory
• Jimmy Valiant beat George South

April 13, 2002
Gap Mills, WV - Old Gym
EWA
• George South vs Scotty McKeever

April 20, 2002
Indianapolis, IN – RCA Dome
• With Sting, Nikita Koloff, & Ted Bibaise

April 23, 2002
Bluefield, WV – Concord College
• George South vs Eric Lester

April 26, 2002
Virgie, KY – Middle School
SSW
• George South beat John Noble

April 27, 2002
Taylorsville, NC – Fairgrounds – 2pm
• George South vs Scotty McKeever

April 27, 2002
Lenoir, NC - American Legion Hall – 8pm
UWA
• George South vs Jimmy Valiant

June 1, 2002
Lenoir, NC - American Legion Hall
UWA
• George South vs Gladiator

June 6, 2002
Sugar Grove, NC – Old Cove Creek Gym
EWA
• George South vs Scotty McKeever

June 7, 2002
Sugar Grove, NC – Old Cove Creek Gym
EWA
• George South vs Scotty Hot Body

June 8, 2002
Pine Flats, TN – Church
SSW
• George South vs Beau James

June 14, 2002
Gap Mills, WV - Gym
• George South vs Scotty McKeever

June 15, 2002
Lenoir, NC – American Legion Hall
UWA
• George South vs Bruiser Graham

June 20, 2002
Sugar Grove, NC – Old Cove Creek Gym
EWA
• George South vs Scotty McKeever

June 21, 2002
Fall Branch, TN – Church
SSW
• George South vs Beau James

June 22, 2002
Taylorsville, NC – Fairgrounds
• George South vs Scotty McKeever

June 29, 2002
Yanceyville, NC – High School
• George South vs Chris Nelson

July 2, 2002
Beaver, WV – Fire Dept
EWA
• George South vs Scotty McKeever

July 3, 2002
Harrisburg, NC – Park
EWA
George South vs Badstreet

July 4, 2002
Harrisburg, NC – Park
EWA
George South vs Badstreet

July 5, 2002
Silva, NC – Uncle Bill's Flea Market
• George South vs Buddy Landel

July 6, 2002
Silva, NC – Uncle Bill's Flea Market
• George South vs Buddy Landel

July 12, 2002
Greenville, WV – Old Gym
EWA
• George South vs Scotty McKeever

July 13, 2002
Morganton, NC – Fairgrounds
BCW
• George South beat James Brody

July 14, 2002
Orange, VA – Mt. Zion Baptist Church
• George South vs Local

July 16, 2002
Morganton, NC – Western Carolina Center
EWA
• George South vs Big Donnie Webb

July 18, 2002
Sugar Grove, NC – Old Cove Creek Gym
EWA
• George South vs Scotty McKeever

July 19, 2002
Mountain City, TN – Forge Creek Community Center
• George South vs Scotty McKeever

July 20, 2002
Dublin, WV – Rec Center
• George South vs Scotty McKeever

July 26, 2002
Memphis, TN – Mid-South Coliseum
• Mood Dog Rex beat George South

July 27, 2002
Hardee, AK – Rhodes Arena
• George South vs Scotty McKeever

August 1, 2002
Sugar Grove, NC – Old Cove Creek Gym
EWA
• George South vs James Clontz

August 3, 2002
Charlotte, NC – Freedom Center
EWA
• George South vs Badstreet

August 9, 2002
Middleburg, IN - Fairgrounds
• George South vs. Scotty McKeever w/ Ted DiBasie

August 10, 2002
Middleburg, IN - Fairgrounds
• George South vs. Scotty McKeever w/Ted DiBasie

August 23, 2002
Greenville, Wv – Old Gym
• George South vs. Scotty McKeever

August 24, 2002
Silva, NC – Uncle Bill's Flea Market
• Iron Sheik beat George South

August 31, 2002
Lorain, OH – Rec Center
• George South vs. Scotty McKeever

September 2, 2002
Greenville, WV – Old Gym
• George South vs. Scotty McKeever

September 3, 2002
Beaver, WV – Fire Dept
• George South vs. Scotty McKeever

September 6, 2002
Sugar Grove, NC – Old Cove Creek Gym
EWA
• George South vs. Scotty McKeever

September 14, 2002
Plymouth, MI – United Church
• Road Warriors w/ Ted DiBasie beat George South & Scotty McKeever

September 15, 2002
Plymouth, MI – United Church
• Road Warriors w/ Ted DiBasie beat George South & Scotty McKeever

September 21, 2002
Wadesboro, NC – Harvest Church
• George South beat Local

September 28, 2002
Newton Grove, NC – Weeks Park
• George South beat Badstreet

October 11, 2002
Albemarle, NC – Extreme fitness
EWA
• George South vs Jason King

October 12, 2002
Spindale, NC – Men's Prison
EWA
• George South vs Local

October 17, 2002
Morganton, NC - Fairgrounds
BCW
• George South vs Big Donnie Webb

October 18, 2002
Williamsburg, VA – Rec Center
• George South beat Shane Austin

October 22, 2002
Wells, TX – Calvary Church
• George South vs Scotty McKeever w/ Ted DiBasie

October 23, 2002
Wells, TX – Calvary Church
• George South vs Scotty McKeever w/ Ted DiBasie

October 26, 2002
Charlotte, NC – North Park Mall
EWA
• George South vs Jason King

November 8, 2002
Greenville, WV – Old Gym
EWA
• George South vs Scotty McKeever

November 16, 2002
Cleveland, OH – Convention Center
• Preached w/ Sting, Nikita Koloff & Ted DiBasie

November 22, 2002
Pelham, NC – Community Center
• George South vs Chris Nelson

November 27, 2002
Breakfast with Paul Jones

November 30, 2002
Lenoir, NC – Armory
• George South beat Jason King

December 4, 2002
Breakfast with Paul Jones

December 12, 2002
Supper with Paul Jones

December 25, 2002
Albemarle, NC – Extreme Fitness
EWA
• George South vs Jason King

2003

January 3, 2003
La Fayette, GA – High School
EWA
• George South vs Jim Powers

January 4, 2003
Greenville, GA – High School
EWA
• George South vs Jim Powers

January 5, 2002
Greenville, GA – Free Chapel Worship Center
• With Sting, Road Warriors & Ted DiBasie

January 10, 2003
Albemarle, NC – Extreme fitness
EWA
• George South beat Jason King

January 21, 2003
Morganton, NC – Western Carolina Center
EWA
• George South vs Big Donnie Webb

January 25, 2003
Statesville, NC – High School
• Road Warrior Hawk beat George South

January 24, 2002
White Sulphur Springs, WV – Cobra Club
• George South vs Scotty McKeever

January 31, 2003
Albemarle, NC – Extreme fitness
EWA
• George South beat Badstreet

February 8, 2003
Minneapolis, MN – Target Center
• With Sting, Nikita Koloff, & Ted Bibaise

February 11, 2003
Concord, NC – Training Center
EWA
• George South vs Scotty McKeever

February 14, 2003
Albemarle, NC – Extreme fitness
EWA
• George South vs Jason King

February 15, 2002
Mt. Holly, NC – Optimist Park – 2pm
• George South vs Local

February 15, 2003
Spartanburg, SC – Shamrock Club – 8pm
APW
• George South vs Jay Eagle

February 18, 2003
Concord, NC – Training Center
EWA
• George South beat Badstreet

February 20, 2003
Indian Head, MD – Naval Base
• George South vs Local

February 22, 2003
Tampa, FL – St. Pete Times Arena
• With Sting, Nikita Koloff, & Ted Bibaise
February 25, 2002
Concord, NC – Training Center
EWA
• George South vs Gladiator

March 7, 2003
Albemarle, NC – Extreme fitness
EWA
• Jimmy Valiant beat George South

March 21, 2003
Gastonia, NC – East Gaston High School
• George South &? Vs Craig Pittman & Scotty McKeever

March 22, 2003
Greensboro, NC – Coliseum
• With Sting & Ted DiBasie

March 24, 2003
Left for California with Little George

March 27, 2003
San Francisco, CA
Toured to World Famous Cow Palace

March 29, 2003
Sacramento, CA – Capital Center
• With Sting & Ted DiBasie

March 30, 2003
Modesto, CA – Gym
• George South vs Scotty McKeever

April 4, 2003
Albemarle, NC – Extreme fitness
EWA
• George South beat Local

April 5, 2003
Mt. Holly, NC – Gym
• George South vs Local

April 7, 2003
Greenville, SC – Washington Baptist Church
EWA
• George South beat Jason King

April 10, 2003
Quantites, VA – Marine Base
• George South vs The Hardcore Kid (George South Jr)

April 12, 2003
Concord, NC – Toy Show
EWA
• George South vs Scotty McKeever

April 25, 2003
Albemarle, NC – Extreme fitness
EWA
• George South vs Jason King

April 26, 2003
Shelby, NC – Men's Prison – 2pm
EWA
• George South vs Scotty McKeever

April 26, 2003
Concord, NC – Training Center
EWA
• George South vs Scotty McKeever

May 9, 2003
Albemarle, NC – Extreme Fitness
EWA
• George South vs Jason King

May 10, 2003
Charlotte, NC – Freedom Christian Center
• EWA
George South beat Jimmy Jack Funk Jr

May 16, 2003
Ate Breakfast with Paul Jones

May 17, 2003
Concord, NC – Training Center
EWA
• George South vs Badstreet

May 24, 2003
Concord, NC – Training Center
EWA
• George South vs Jason King

May 30, 2003
Concord, NC – Training Center
EWA
• George South vs Gladiator

May 31, 2003
Hartwell, GA – Middle School
EWA
• George South vs Jason King

June 1, 2003
Hartsville, GA – Baptist Church
EWA
• George South vs Pastor Ronald

June 7, 2003
Concord, NC – Training Center
EWA
• George South vs Beautiful Bobby Eaton

June 10, 2003
Ate lunch with Paul Jones & Tommy Young

June 12, 2003
Richmond, VA – Bottom Line Club
• George South vs Badstreet

June 13, 2003
Sugar Grove, NC – Old Cove Creek Gym
• EWA
George South vs Scotty McKeever

June 14, 2003
Concord, NC – Training Center
EWA
• George South vs Jason King

June 19, 2003
Lincolnton, NC – Men's Prison
EWA
• George South vs Ricky Morton

June 21, 2003
Concord, NC – Training Center
EWA
• George South vs Badstreet

June 26, 2003
Concord, NC – Training Center
EWA
• George South vs Student

June 27, 2003
Summerville, SC – Men's Prison
EWA
• George South vs Ricky Morton

June 28, 2003
Summerville, SC – Miles Road Baptist Church
EWA
• George South vs Ricky Morton

June 29, 2003
Kernersville, NC – End Zone Club
EWA
• George South vs Gladiator

July 3, 2003
Harrisburg, VA – Park Club
EWA
• George South vs Jason King

July 4, 2003
Scottsboro, VA – Fairgrounds
EWA
• George South vs Badstreet

July 5, 2003
Concord, NC – Training Center
EWA
• George South vs Scotty McKeever

July 12, 2003
Marlingon, WV – Fairgrounds
EWA
• George South vs Scotty McKeever

July 13, 2003
Orange, VA – Zion Baptist Church
EWA
• George South vs Assassin

Highway Run into the Midnight Sun

July 14, 2003
Morganton, NC – Western Carolina Center
EWA
- George South vs Big Donnie Webb

July 17, 2003
Valdosta, GA – Civic Center
- George South vs Brad Armstrong

July 18, 2003
Pelzer, SC – Washington Baptist Church
EWA
- George South vs Pastor Ronald

July 19, 2003
Augusta, GA – Rec Center
- George South vs Gladiator

July 20, 2003
Concord, NC – Training Center
EWA
- George South vs Badstreet

July 25, 2003
Concord, NC – Training Center
EWA
- George South vs Student

July 26, 2003
Gastonia, NC – Armory
EWA
- George South vs Ray Hudson

August 2, 2003
Concord, NC – Training Center
EWA
- George South vs Jason King

August 8, 2003
Roswell, NM – Church on Main
- George South &? Vs The Road Warriors w/ Ted DiBasie

August 9, 2003
Rowell, NM – Church on Main
- George South Sr & Jr vs The Road Warriors

August 15, 2003
Concord, NC – Training Center
EWA
- George South vs George South Jr

August 16, 2003
Concord, NC – Training Center
EWA
- George South vs Jason King

August 22, 2003
Concord, NC – Training Center
EWA
- George South vs Gladiator

August 28, 2003
Concord, NC – Training Center
EWA
- George South vs Badstreet

August 29, 2003
Denver, NC – Campground
EWA
• George South vs Badstreet

September 2, 2003
Spartanburg, SC – Memorial Auditorium
CCW
• George South vs David Isley w/ Dusty Rhodes

September 5, 2003
Union, SC – Baptist Church
EWA
• George South vs Jason King

September 6, 2003
Kingston, NC – Minor League Baseball Stadium
• George South vs Scotty McKeever

September 13, 2003
Concord, NC – Training Center
EWA
• George South vs Jason King

September 19, 2003
Concord, NC – Training Center
EWA
• George South vs Gladiator

September 20, 2003
Concord, NC – Training Center
EWA
• George South vs Jason King

September 26, 2003
Concord, NC – Training Center
EWA
• George South vs Jason King

September 27, 2003
Concord, NC – Training Center
EWA
• George South vs Tony Polk

October 2, 2003
Morganton, NC - Fairgrounds
BCW
• George South vs Jeff Patton

October 3, 2003
Hartwell, GA – High School
EWA
• George South vs Ricky Morton

October 4, 2003
Hartwell, GA – High School
EWA
EWA World Title: George South* beat Masked Superstar

October 5, 2003
Lincolnton, NC - New Vision Church
EWA
• George South vs Body Guard

October 10, 2003
Concord, NC – Training Center
EWA
• George South vs Jason King

October 11, 2003
High Point, NC – Boys & Girls Club
EWA
• George South vs Jason King

October 13, 2003
Lincolnton, NC – Oak Grove Baptist Church
EWA
• George South vs Local

October 18, 2003
Nacogdoches, TX – Civic Center
• George South vs Scotty McKeever

October 19, 2003
Nacogdoches, TX – Civic Center
• George South vs Jason King

October 25, 2003
Scottsburg, IN – High School
• George South vs Scotty McKeever

October 31, 2003
St. Stephan, SC – Rec Center
EWA
• George South vs Scotty McKeever

November 1, 2003
Concord, NC – Training Center
EWA
• George South vs Jason King

November 6, 2003
Greer, SC – Corner St. Gym
• George South vs Jay Eagle

November 8, 2003
Charlotte, NC – North Park Mall – 12pm
EWA
• George South vs Jason King

November 8, 2003
Concord, NC – Training Center – 8pm
EWA
• George South vs Tony Polk

November 14, 2003
Concord, NC – Training Center
EWA
• George South vs Body Guard

November 15, 2003
Concord, NC – Training Center
EWA
• George South vs Jason King

November 27, 2003
Concord, NC – Training Center
EWA
• George South vs Jason King

November 28, 2003
Kings Mountain, NC – Armory
EWA
• George South vs Ray Hudson

November 29, 2003
Gastonia, NC – Armory
EWA
• George South vs Scotty McKeever

November 30, 2003
Sawmills, NC – Auction Barn
EWA
• George South vs Ricky Morton

December 6, 2003
Lenoir, NC – Mulberry Rec Center
CCW
• George South vs Masked Superstar

December 11, 2003
Concord, NC – Training Center
EWA
• George South vs Jimmy Valiant

December 12, 2003
Lavoria, VA – Elementary School
SSW
• George South vs Jason King

December 13, 2003
Pikeville, KY – Elementary School
SSW
• George South vs Jason King

December 25, 2003
Kings Mountain, NC – Armory
EWA
• George South vs Ray Hudson

December 26, 2003
Concord, NC – Training Center
EWA
• George South vs Jason King

December 27, 2003
Greenville, SC – Wade Hampton High School
• George South vs Ricky Morton

2004

January 14, 2004
Greer, SC – Franklin Baptist Church
EWA
• George South vs Scotty McKeever

January 17, 2004
Concord, NC – Training Center
EWA
• George South vs Jimmy Jack Funk Jr

January 21, 2004
Morganton, NC – Western Carolina Center
EWA
• George South vs Big Donnie Webb

January 22, 2004
Spartanburg, SC – Memorial Auditorium
• George South vs Jimmy Valiant

January 24, 2004
Kings Mountain, NC – Armory
EWA
• George South vs Ray Hudson

January 25, 2004
Union, SC – Baptist Church
EWA
• George South vs Local

January 31, 2004
Charlotte, NC – Mid-Atlantic Fan Fest
• George South vs Scotty McKeever

February 1, 2004
Charlotte, NC – Mid-Atlantic Fan Fest
• George South vs Scotty McKeever

February 14, 2004
Anderson, SC – Civic Center
• George South vs Ronnie Gossett

February 15, 2004
Kings Mountain, NC – Armory
EWA
• George South vs Ray Hudson

February 21, 2004
Spartanburg, SC – Memorial Auditorium
• George South vs Scotty McKeever

March 4, 2004
Logan, WV – Earl Ray Convention Center
• George South & Scotty McKeever vs The Rock & Roll Express

March 5, 2004
Lancaster, SC – Middle School
EWA
• George South vs Scotty McKeever

March 6, 2004
Lenoir, NC – Mulberry Rec
• George South vs Masked Superstar

March 7, 2004
Cross, NC – Olive Baptist Church
EWA
• George South vs Local

March 12, 2004
Concord, NC – Training Center
EWA
• George South vs Ray Hudson

March 13, 2004
Concord, NC – Training Center
EWA
• George South vs Scrappy

March 19, 2004
Concord, NC – Training Center
EWA
• George South vs Scrappy

March 20, 2004
Alexander, MD – Rec Center
• George South vs Scotty McKeever

March 26, 2004
Orlando, FL – New Image Church
• George South vs Eric Darkstorm

March 27, 2004
Danville, FL – Old Gym
• George South vs Local

April 2, 2004
Lancaster, SC – Middle School
EWA
• George South vs Jimmy Jack Funk Jr

April 3, 2004
Lenoir, NC – Mulberry Rec Center
• George South vs Brad Armstrong

April 10, 2004
Gastonia, NC – Armory
EWA
• George South vs Ray Hudson

April 17, 2004
Gastonia, NC - Midway Baptist Church – 2pm
EWA
• George South vs David Flair

April 17, 2004
Gastonia, NC – Middle School – 8pm
EWA
• George South vs Ray Hudson

April 18, 2004
Concord, NC – Training Center
EWA
• George South vs Jimmy Jack Funk Jr

April 20, 2004
Charleston, SC – Minor League Baseball Stadium
• Refereed Midget Wrestling

Highway Run into the Midnight Sun

April 23, 2004
Gastonia, NC – Training Center
EWA
• George South vs Masked B

April 28, 2004
Bluefield, WV – Concord College
• George South & Scotty McKeever vs Batten Twins

April 29, 2004
Rock Hill, SC – High School
EWA
• George South vs Scotty McKeever

April 30, 2004
Lancaster, SC – Middle School
EWA
• George South vs David Flair
Note: Special Referee Ricky "The Dragon" Steamboat

May 1, 2004
Greenville, NC – Fairgrounds
• George South vs Scotty McKeever

May 8, 2004
Charlotte, NC – Freedom Christian Center
EWA
• George South vs Jimmy Jack Funk Jr

May 13, 2004
Hartwell, GA
Preached at the Men's Prison

May 14, 2004
Hartwell, GA
• Radio Interview 8am
• Preached Hart Elementary School 11am
• Preached Middle School 2pm
• Youth Rally High School 6pm

May 15, 2004
Hartwell, GA – Middle School
EWA
• George South vs Scotty McKeever

May 22, 2004
St. Louis, MO
Harley Race Golf Tournament

May 29, 2004
Danville, VA – American Legion Hall
• George South vs Gladiator

June 5, 2004
Rockwell, TX – Rock Gym
• George South vs Jimmy Valiant w/ Ted DiBasie

June 12, 2004
Belfry, KY – 1st Baptist Church
• George South vs Scotty McKeever w/ Ted DiBasie

June 14, 2004
Dinner with Ole Anderson in Charlotte, NC

June 18, 2004
Morganton, NC – Rec Center
BCW
• George South vs Jeff Patton

June 20, 2004
Cherryville, NC – 1st Baptist Church
EWA
• George South vs Pastor Vince

June 24, 2004
St. Stephens, SC - Church
EWA
• George South vs Andy McDaniel

June 25, 2004
Summerville, SC – Baptist Church
• George South vs Ricky Morton

June 26, 2004
Charleston, SC – Naval Base
• George South vs Scotty McKeever

July 3, 2004
Scottsburg, VA – Fire Dept
• George South vs Scotty McKeever

July 9, 2004
Gastonia, NC – Training Center
• George South vs Ray Hudson

July 10, 2004
Danville, VA – Rec Center
• George South beat Student

July 12, 2004
Morganton, NC – Western Carolina Center
EWA
• George South vs Kenny Eaton

July 13, 2004
Marion, KY – Fairgrounds
• George South vs Gladiator

July 15, 2004
Morganton, NC – Skating Rink
BCW
• George South vs Jeff Patton

July 18, 2004
Odenton, MD – New Life Church
• George South vs Scotty McKeever

July 24, 2004
Wentworth, NC – Armory
• George South vs Chris Nelson

July 26, 2004
Dinner with Penny Banner

July 31, 2004
Morganton, NC – Rec Center
BCW
• George South vs Jeff Patton

August 7, 2004
Elizabethtown, KY – Elementary School
• George South vs Scotty McKeever

August 13, 2004
Meyers, PA – Fire Dept
• George South vs Eric Darkstorm

August 14, 2004
Fayetteville, NC – Rec Center
• George South vs Local

August 17, 2004
Aiken, SC – Conference Center
• Brad Armstrong w/ Mr. Wrestling II beat George South

August 18, 2004
Charlotte, NC – Church
EWA
• George South beat George South Jr

August 21, 2004
Colonial Heights, VA – Football Stadium
• George South beat The Gladiator

August 23, 2004
Belmont, NC – Grace Baptist Church
EWA
• George South beat Ray Hudson

August 26, 2004
Rock Hill, SC – Hickory Dock
• George South beat Student

August 28, 2004
Forest City, NC – Armory
• George South beat Black Angel

August 29, 2004
Decatur, GA - Church
• George South beat The Assassin

September 2, 2004
Rock Hill, SC - YMCA
EWA
• George South vs Jimmy Jack Funk Jr

September 3, 2004
Albemarle, NC – Bodyshop
George South beat Student

September 4, 2004
Marion, NC – Zip Car Wash
NAWA (Chad Bryd)
• George South vs Chad Byrd

September 5, 2004
Concord, NC – Training Center
• George South beat Jason Jones

September 9, 2004
Morganton, NC – Skating Rink
• George South vs Jeff Patton

September 11, 2004
Columbia, SC – Rec Center
• George South vs Local

September 15, 20004
Louisville, KY – Center
• George South beat John Noble

September 16, 2004
Louisville, KY – Center
• George South beat Gladiator

September 17, 2004
Florence, KY – Heritage Fellowship Hall
• George South vs Eric Darkstorm w/ Ted DiBasie

September 22, 2004
Princeton, WV – Memorial Hall
• George South vs Eric Darkstorm

September 23, 2004
Princeton, WV – Memorial Hall
• George South vs Shane White

September 25, 2004
Concord, NC – Training Center
EWA
• George South beat Student

September 26, 2004
Greenville, NC – Fairgrounds
• George South vs Local

October 2, 2004
Lancaster, SC – Middle School
EWA
• George South vs Ricky Morton

October 3, 2004
Lincolnton, NC – New Vision Ministries
EWA
• George South vs Ricky Morton

October 9, 2004
Columbia, SC – Rec Center
• George South vs Brad Armstrong

October 14, 2004
Morganton, NC – Fairgrounds
BCW
• George South vs Jeff Patton

October 16, 2004
Charlotte, NC – Charlotte Motor Speedway
EWA
• George South beat Jason Jones

October 18, 2004
Lincolnton, NC – Men's Prison
EWA
• George South vs Ricky Morton

October 19, 2004
Wrinder, GA – Elementary School
• George South beat The Gladiator

October 22, 2004
Ft. Myers, FL – Fathers House
• George South vs Eric Darkstorm w/ Ted DiBiase

October 23, 2004
Ft. Myers, FL – Fathers House
• George South vs Eric Darkstorm w/ Ted DiBiase

October 28, 2004
Granite Falls, NC – Haunted Trail
George South beat Jason Jones

October 30, 2004
Danville, VA – Wal-Mart
• George South w/ Ted DiBasie & Nikita Koloff beat Jason Jones

October 31, 2004
Salisbury, NC – Middle School
• George South beat Scotty McKeever

November 1, 2004
Lincolnton, NC – Freedom Christian Center
• George South beat The Body Guard

November 6, 2004
Lenoir, NC – Mulberry Rec
• George South beat George South Jr

Match # 5000
November 13, 2004
Danville, VA – American Legion
• George South beat Jimmy Jack Funk Jr

November 15, 2004
Marietta, GA – Cobb Co Civic Center
• George South vs Ronnie Gossett

November 18, 2004
Rock Hill, SC – Elementary School
• George South vs Jim Healer

November 20, 2004
Clover, SC - Savage Yard- 10am
• Ricky Morton beat George South

November 20, 2004
Kings Mountain, NC – Armory
• George South vs Ray Hudson

November 25, 2004
Kings Mountain, NC – Armory
• George South beat Ninja

November 27, 2004
Charlotte, NC -Hilton Ball Room
• George South Sr & Jr beat The Mack Brothers

December 4, 2004
Lenoir, NC – Mulberry Rec
CCW
• George South vs Brad Armstrong

December 9, 2004
Rock Hill, SC – Elementary School
• George South beat Jim Healer

December 11, 2004
Shelby, NC – Rec Center
• George South & Brad Anderson won the Anderson Brothers Classic

December 16, 2004
Boiling Springs, NC – Ripple Effect Club
- George South beat Jeff Victory

December 17, 2004
Beewood, NC – Community Center
- George South beat DL Kool

December 18, 2004
Albemarle, NC – Armory
EWA
- George South beat Jason Jones

December 25, 2004
Chesnee, SC – Shamrock Café
APW
- Jimmy Valiant beat George South

2005

January 1, 2005
Kings Mountain, NC – Armory
EWA
• George South vs Ray Hudson

January 7, 2005
Spindale, NC – Spindale House
EWA
• George South vs Ricky Morton

January 8, 2005
Lenoir, NC – Mulberry Rec
CCW
• George South vs Masked Superstar

January 14, 2005
Lancaster, SC – American Legion
EWA
• George South vs Scotty McKeever

January 15, 2005
Shelby, NC – Rec Center
CCW
• George South vs Jay Eagle

January 16, 2005
Morganton, NC – Collett St Rec
BCW
• George South vs Jeff Patton

January 19, 2005
Morganton, NC – Western Carolina Center
EWA
• George South vs Big Donnie Webb

January 22, 2005
Sugar Grace, WV – Naval Base
EWA
• George South vs Scotty McKeever

January 29, 2005
Tampa, FL – Double Tree Hotel
Wrestle Reunion
• George South vs Scotty McKeever

February 4, 2005
Lancaster, SC – American Legion
EWA
• Jimmy Valiant beat George South

February 5, 2005
Kings Mountain, NC – Armory
EWA
• George South beat Ray Hudson

February 11, 2005
Greenwood, SC – Civic Center
• George South vs Ronnie Gossett

February 12, 2005
Lenoir, NC – Mulberry Rec
CCW
• Brad Armstrong beat George South

February 19, 2005
Spartanburg, SC – Memorial Auditorium
CCW
• Brad Armstrong beat George South

February 25, 2005
Statesville, NC – Rec Center
• George South vs Scotty McKeever

February 26, 2005
Roseboro, NC – Middle School
• George South vs Carolina Dreamer

February 27, 2005
Forest City, NC – Armory
• George South beat Rex Rumble

March 1, 2005
Taylorsville, NC – Fire Dept
EWA
• George South beat Bobby Houston

March 5, 2005
Huntington, WV – Bethel Church
• George South beat Scotty McKeever w/ Nikita Koloff

March 12, 2005
Wichita Falls, TX – Evangel Temple
• George South beat Scotty McKeever

March 18, 2005
Greenwood, SC – Civic Center
• George South vs Ronnie Gossett

March 19, 2005
Kings Mountain, NC – Armory
EWA
• George South vs Ray Hudson

March 26, 2005
Statesville, NC – Rec Center
• George South vs Jimmy Jack Funk Jr

April 1, 2005
Albemarle, NC – Armory
• Cage Match: George South beat The Assassin

April 3, 2005
Radford, NC – Church
EWA
• George South beat Josh Boyd

April 9, 2005
Pickens, OH – Central High School
• George South vs Ronnie Byrd

April 10, 2005
Mooresville, NC – Armory
EWA
• George South beat The Assassin

April 16, 2005
Roseboro, NC – Middle School
• George South vs The G

April 23, 2005
Newton, NC – Rec Center
• George South vs Scotty McKeever

April 24, 2005
Greer, SC – Franklin Baptist Church
EWA
• George South vs Franklin's Finest

April 26, 2005
Princeton, WV – College
• George South, Scotty McKeever & Jason Kid beat
Eric Lester & The Batten Twins

April 29, 2005
Lancaster, SC – American Legion
EWA
• George South vs Masked Superstar

April 30, 2005
Spindale, NC – Gym
• George South beat Gladiator

May 1, 2005
Charlotte, NC – Grace Baptist Church
EWA
• George South beat Jimmy Jack Funk Jr

May 2, 2005
Morganton, NC – Western Carolina Center
EWA
• Big Donnie Webb beat George South

May 3, 2005
Charleston, SC -Minor League Baseball Stadium
• Refereed Midget Wrestling Show

May 6, 2005
Mt. Holly, NC – Hickory Grove Baptist Church
EWA
• George South beat Jimmy Jack Funk Jr

May 7, 2005
Gaffney, SC – Middle School
New Blood Championship Wrestling
• George South beat Rex Rumble

May 14, 2005
Charlotte, NC – Freedom Christian Center – 11am
EWA
• George South vs Jesse Morris

May 14, 2005
Roseboro, NC – Middle School – 8pm
• George South beat Gladiator

May 18, 2005
Meridian, MS – Highland Baptist Church
EWA (George South & Ted DiBiase)
• Robert Gibson beat George South

May 20, 2005
Greenwood, SC – Civic Center
• George South vs Ronnie Gossett

May 21, 2005
Charlotte, NC – Charlotte Motor Speedway – 10am
EWA
• George South beat Jimmy Jack Funk Jr

May 21, 2005
Statesville, NC – Rec Center – 8pm
• George South vs Chad Byrd

May 26, 2005
Charlotte, NC – Charlotte Motor Speedway – 10am
EWA
• George South beat Jimmy Jack Funk

May 27, 2005
Lancaster, SC – American Legion
EWA
• Ivan Koloff beat George South

June 4, 2005
Congers, GA – Community Center
• George South vs Burr Head Jones Jr

June 5, 2005
Spindale, NC – Spindale House
George South beat Ricky Morton

June 12, 2005
Chester, SC – Pleasant Grove Church
EWA
• George South beat Andy McDaniel

June 15, 2005
Red Cross, NC – New Faith Baptist Church
EWA
• George South beat Jimmy Jack Funk Jr

June 18, 2005
Statesville, NC – Rec Center
EWA
• George South beat Brad Anderson

June 24, 2005
Mooresville, NC – Armory
EWA
• George South beat Jimmy Jack Funk Jr

June 25, 2005
Summerville, SC – Miles Road Baptist
EWA
• Pastor Jim Palmer beat George South

June 26, 2005
Hudson, NC – Friendship Baptist Church
• Guest Preacher

June 30, 2005
Morganton, NC – Skating Rink
BCW
• George South beat Big Donnie Webb

August 5, 2005
Mooresville, NC – Armory
EWA
• George South beat Jimmy Jack Funk Jr

August 6, 2005
Canton, NC – Festival
• Bobby Fulton beat George South

August 7, 2005
Vienna, NC - Community Center
• George South beat Student

August 12, 2005
Clinton, MS – Morrison Heights Church
EWA
• George South beat Scotty McKeever w/ Ted DiBasie

August 13, 2005
Knightsdale, NC – Rec Center
EWA
• Jimmy Jack Funk Jr beat George South

August 14, 2005
Charleston, SC – New Beginnings Church
EWA
George South beat Jimmy Jack Funk Jr

August 16, 2005
Morganton, NC – Skating Rink
BCW
• George South vs Jeff Patton

August 20, 2005
Charlotte, NC – Hilton Hotel
Charlotte Fan Fest
George South beat Scotty McKeever

August 27, 2005
Mooresville, NC – Armory
EWA
Jimmy Valiant beat George South

August 28, 2005
Thomasville, NC – Armory – 2pm
EWA
• George South beat Jimmy Jack Funk

August 28, 2005
Asheville, NC – Civic Center
• George South vs Ronnie Gossett

September 3, 2005
Mooresville, NC – Armory
EWA
George South beat Gladiator

September 5, 2005
Troutman, NC – Fairgrounds
EWA
George South beat Tony Benge

September 10, 2005
Forest City, NC - Armory
• George South beat Student

September 11, 2005
Shelby, NC – Rec Center
• George South beat Jay Eagle

September 17, 2005
Statesville, NC – Grace Park Rec Center
• George South beat Gladiator

September 18, 2005
Yadkinville, NC – Church
EWA
• George South beat Andy McDaniel

September 22, 2005
Morganton, NC – Riverside Golf
BCW
• Big Donnie Webb beat George South

September 24, 2005
Asheboro, NC – Armory
EWA
• George South beat Jimmy Jack Funk Jr

September 27, 2005
Kinston, NC – Fairgrounds
• Bobby Fulton beat George South

October 1, 2005
Knightsdale, NC – Rec Center
• George South beat Assassin

October 4, 2005
Mooresville, NC – Armory
EWA
• George South beat Jimmy Jack Funk Jr

October 6, 2005
Morganton, NC – Fairgrounds
BCW
• Jeff Patton beat George South

October 8, 2005
Clyde, NC – Armory
• George South beat Assassin

October 14, 2005
Statesville, NC – Grace Park Rec Center
• George South beat Bobby Houston

October 15, 2005
Charlotte, NC - Charlotte Motor Speedway – 10am
EWA
• George South beat Jimmy Jack Funk Jr

October 15, 2005
High Point, NC – Boys & Girl Club
EWA
• George South beat Gladiator

October 20, 2005
Morganton, NC – Riverside Golf
BCW
• George South vs Jeff Patton

October 21, 2005
Thomasville, NC – Armory
EWA
• George South beat Henry Dean

October 22, 2005
Charleston, SC – New Beginnings Church
EWA
• George South beat Shawn Horn

October 27, 2005
Mooresville, NC – Armory
EWA
• George South beat Tony Benge

October 29, 2005
Waynesville, NC – High School
• George South beat Jake Manning

October 30, 2005
Salisbury, NC – Cross Roads Church
EWA
• George South vs Pastor Chris

October 30, 2005
Salisbury, NC – Haunted House – 10pm
• George South beat Jeff Patton

November 3, 2005
Rock Hill, SC - YMCA
• George South beat Jimmy Jack Funk Jr

November 4, 2005
Lincolnton, NC – Men's Prison
EWA
• Jimmy Valiant beat George South

November 11, 2005
Charlotte, NC – Rec Center
EWA
• George South beat Jimmy Jack Funk Jr

November 12, 2005
Danville, VA – Youth Rally
• George South beat Student

November 17, 2005
Statesville, NC – Grace Park Rec Center
• George South vs. Bobby Houston

November 18, 2005
Spindale, NC – Spindale House
• George South vs Ricky Morton

November 20, 2005
Spartanburg, SC – Memorial Auditorium
• George South beat Bobby Houston

November 24, 2005
High Point, NC – Boys & Girls Club
EWA
• George South beat Jimmy Jack Funk Jr

November 26, 2005
Mooresville, NC – Armory
EWA
• George South beat Jimmy Jack Funk Jr
December 3, 2005
Homestead, NC – High School
• George South beat Jay White

December 9, 2005
Statesville, NC – Grace Park Rec Center
• George South vs Bobby Ramone

December 10, 2005
Charlotte, NC – Coliseum
Queen City Clash
• George South beat Bobby Houston

December 25, 2005
Mooresville, NC – Armory
EWA
• George South beat Bobby Houston

2006

January 6, 2006
Newton, NC – Rec Center
• George South beat Rocky King

January 28, 2006
Hamlet, NC - Armory
• George South vs Tyrone Knox

February 4, 2006
Seagrove, NC – Elementary School
EWA
• George South beat Mike Lee

February 17, 2006
Shelby, NC
NGW
• George South Sr. vs. George South Jr.

February 18, 2006
Pickens, SC
NGW
• George South & Tracey Smothers vs. Dylan Eaton & Brad Thomas

February 25, 2006
Statesville, NC – Grace Park Rec Center
• George South vs Ricky Morton

February 26, 2006
Mooresville, NC – Armory
EWA
• George South Sr & Jr beat Jason Jones & Badstreet
• George South Sr & Jr vs Bobby Houston & Ethan Cage

March 4, 2006
High Point, NC – Boys Club
• George South beat Poco

March 17, 2006
Statesville, NC – Gracie Park Rec Center
• George South beat Jessie Moore

March 18, 2006
Randolph, NC – High School
• George South vs Jake Manning

March 25, 2006
Roseboro, NC – Middle School
• George South beat Hangman

March 26, 2006
Clinton, NC – APW Training Center
APW
• George South vs Ricky Morton

March 30, 2006
Mooresville, NC – Armory
EWA
• George South beat Bobby Houston

April 7, 2006
Lancaster, SC – American Legion
EWA
• George South vs Jason Jones

April 8, 2006
Conway, SC – High School
• George South vs Brad Armstrong

April 22, 2006
Hayes, VA – Rec Center
• George South vs Mark Fleming

April 23, 2006
Mooresville, NC – Armory
EWA
• George South vs Bobby Houston

April 27, 2006
Bluefield, WV - College
• George South vs Dillion Eaton

April 28, 2006
West Liberty, OH – Rec Center
• George South vs Ricky Morton

May 4, 2006
Columbia, SC – Temple
• George South vs Brad Armstrong

May 5, 2006
Lancaster, SC – American Legion
• George South vs Masked Superstar

May 6, 2006
Clayton, NC – Fitness Center
• George South vs Ivan Koloff

May 7, 2006
Arden, NC – Rec Center
• George South vs Bobby Houston

May 18, 2006
Mooresville, NC – Armory
• George South vs Bobby Houston

May 19, 2006
Concord, NC – Middle School
• George South vs Chris Goings

May 20, 2006
Louis, VA – New Life Comm Church
• George South vs Chris Goings

June 3, 2006
Statesville, NC – Gracie Park Rec Center
• George South vs Ernie Love

June 4, 2006
Arden, NC – Community Center
• George South vs Ricky Morton

June 11, 2006
Yanceyville, NC - Grace Church
• George South vs Jason Jones

June 17, 2006
Columbia, SC – Temple
• George South vs Masked Superstar

June 24, 2006
Mooresville, NC - Armory
• George South vs Bobby Houston

June 25, 2006
Harrisburg, NC – Ice Cream Bash
• George South vs Bobby Houston

July 4, 2006
Scottsburg, VA – Fire Dept
• George South vs Bobby Houston

July 7, 2006
Statesville, NC – Gracie Park Rec Center
• George South vs Ernie Ladd Jr

July 8, 2006
Charlotte, NC – Rec Center
• George South vs Ernie Ladd Jr

July 9, 2006
Mooresville, NC - Armory
• George South vs Bobby Houston

July 10, 2006
Morganton, NC – Western Carolina Center
• George South vs Bobby Houston

July 13, 2006
Lincolnton, NC – Men's Prison
• George South vs Bobby Houston

July 14, 2006
Jefferson, NC – Town Hall Gym
• George South vs Lodi

July 15, 2006
Charlotte, NC – Youth Rally VBS
EWA
• George South vs Bobby Houston

July 27, 2006
Mooresville, NC – Armory
• George South vs Bobby Houston

July 28, 2006
Taylorsville, NC – Birthday Party
• George South vs Bobby Houston

July 28, 2006
North Wilkesboro, NC – Cross Roads Harley Davidson
• George South vs Jake Manning

July 29, 2006
Kernersville, NC – Rec Center
• George South vs Ivan Koloff

July 30, 2006
Elkin, NC – Armory
• George South vs Jimmy Jack Funk Jr

August 4, 2006
Statesville, NC – Bentley Center
• George South vs Masked Superstar

August 5, 2006
Williamston, WV – Fieldhouse
• George South vs Bobby Houston

August 6, 2006
Huntington, WV – YMCA
• George South vs Bobby Houston

August 18, 2006
Jefferson, NC – Conway Baptist Church
• George South vs Jimmy Jack Funk Jr

August 19,2006
Burlington, NC – Boys Club – 12pm
• George South vs Tre G

August 19, 2006
Jefferson, NC - Town Hall Gym – 8pm
• George South vs Beautiful Bobby Eaton

August 20, 2006
Charlotte, NC – Plaza Rd Baptist Church
• George South vs Mike Lee

August 26, 2006
High Point, NC – Boys Club
• George South & Mike Lee vs Ricky Morton & Tony Benge

August 27, 2006
Mooresville, NC - Armory
• George South vs Beautiful Bobby Eaton

September 8, 2006
Lancaster, SC – American Legion
EWA
• George South vs Greg The Hammer Valentine

September 15, 2006
Charlotte, NC – Rec Center
EWA
• George South vs Ryan Stallone

September 16, 2006
Granite Quarry, NC – Fairgrounds – 2pm
• George South beat Mike Lee

September 16, 2006
Statesville, NC – Gracie Park Rec Center – 8pm
• George South beat Ryan Stallone

September 23, 2006
Memphis, TN – International Church
• George South beat Ryan Stallone
• Koko B Ware beat George South
• Koko B Ware & Ryan Stallone beat George South & Masked Superstar

September 28, 2006
Jefferson, NC – Town Hall
• George South vs Jason Jones

October 1, 2006
Elkin, NC – Armory
EWA
• George South beat Bobby Houston

October 7, 2006
Stafford, VA – Victory Baptist
EWA
- George South vs Jimmy Jack Funk Jr

October 13, 2006
Mt. Holly, NC – Church
- George South vs Jimmy Jack Funk Jr

October 14, 2006
Charleston, SC – New Beginnings Church
- George South vs Bobby Houston

October 19, 2006
Pageland, SC – Town Hall
- George South vs Jimmy Jack Funk Jr

October 25, 2006
Mooresville, NC – Armory
- George South vs Bobby Houston

October 26, 2006
Pageland, SC -Gym
- George South vs The Barbarian

October 28, 2006
Memphis, TN – Youth Rally
- Koko B Ware beat George South

October 29, 2006
Salisbury, NC – Comm Center
- George South vs Jimmy Jack Funk Jr

November 20, 2006
Mooresville, NC – Armory
EWA
- Cage Match: George South beat Masked Superstar

November 25, 2006
Kernersville, NC – Rec Center
- George South beat Mike Lee

December 1, 2006
Graham, NC – Elementary School
EWA
- George South vs Ricky Morton

December 2, 2006
Hamlet, NC – High School
- George South vs Larry Zbysko

December 9, 2006
Statesville, NC – Gracie Park Rec Center
- George South vs KC McKnight

December 17, 2006
Mooresville, NC – Armory
EWA
- George South beat Bobby Houston

2007

January 20, 2007
Sugar Grove, NC – Old Cove Creek Gym
EWA
• George South beat Jimmy Jack Funk Jr

January 24, 2007
Morganton, NC – Western Carolina Center
EWA
• George South beat The Chief

January 29, 2007
Mooresville, NC – Armory
EWA
• George South beat Bobby Houston

February 2, 2007
Matska, WV – Elementary School
• George South vs Assassin

February 3, 2007
Seagrove, NC – Elementary School
EWA
• Russian Chain Match: Ivan Koloff beat George South

February 9, 2007
Pageland, SC – High School
• George South vs Bobby Houston

February 17, 2007
Rockingham, NC – Elementary School
• George South vs Black Angel

February 23, 2007
Mooresville, NC - Armory
• George South vs Black Angel

March 9, 2007
Graver, NC – Elementary School
• George South vs Bobby Houston

March 17, 2007
Sugar Grove, NC – Old Cove Creek Gym
• George South vs Krazy Kane Adams

March 18, 2007
Mooresville, NC – Armory
EWA
• George South vs Bobby Houston

March 23, 2007
Chesnee, SC – Solid Rock Church
• George South vs James Clontz

April 5, 2007
Salisbury, NC - Armory
• George South vs Barbarian

April 6, 2007
Mooresville, NC – Armory
EWA
• George South vs Bobby Houston

April 7, 2007
Chester, SC – APW Arena
APW
• George South vs Jimmy Jack Funk Jr

April 12, 2007
Bluefield, WV – Concord College
• George South vs Eric Lester

April 13, 2007
Forest City, NC – Armory
• George South beat Brad Thomas

April 20, 2007
Winston-Salem, NC – Glen View Baptist Church
• George South vs Brad Thomas

April 21, 2007
China Grove, NC – Family Church
• George South vs Mr. USA

April 21, 2007
Mt. Pleasant, NC – High School
• George South vs Barbarian

April 22, 2007
Mooresville, NC – Armory
EWA
• George South vs Bobby Houston

May 5, 2007
Mooresville, NC – Armory
EWA
• George South vs Jimmy Jack Funk Jr

May 6, 2007
Charlotte, NC – Plaza Road Baptist Church
EWA
• George South vs Bobby Houston
• George South & Preacher Randy beat
Bobby Houston & Jimmy Jack Funk Jr

May 12, 2007
Charlotte, NC – Freedom Center
EWA
• George South vs Bobby Houston

May 19, 2007
Louis, VA – New Life Church
• George South vs Beautiful Bobby Eaton

May 25, 2007
Pageland, SC – Elementary School
• George South vs Jessie Morris

May 26, 2007
Charlotte, NC – Charlotte Motor Speedway – 11am
EWA
• George South beat Jimmy Jack Funk Jr

May 26, 2007
Elkin, NC – Armory
EWA
• George South vs Jimmy Jack Funk Jr

May 27, 2007
Mooresville, NC – Armory
EWA
- George South vs Jimmy Jack Funk Jr

June 6, 2007
Charlotte, NC - Freedom Center
- George South vs Jimmy Jack Funk Jr

June 8, 2007
Boiling Springs, NC - Campground
- George South vs Jimmy Jack Funk Jr

June 19, 2007
Mooresville, NC – Armory
EWA
- EWA World Title: The Barbarian beat Mr. Florida* to win the title.
Special Referee: Jimmy Valiant

June 23, 2007
High Point, NC – Boys Club
- George South vs Beautiful Bobby Eaton

June 24, 2007
Harrisburg, NC – Rec Center
- George South vs Jimmy Jack Funk Jr

June 29, 2007
Great Falls, SC – 1st Baptist
- George South vs Mike Lee

July 1, 2007
Louisville, KY – World Prayer Center
- George South vs Eric Darkstorm w/ Ted DiBasie

July 2, 2007
Louisville, KY – World Prayer Center
- George South vs Eric Darkstorm w/ Dr. Death Steve Williams

July 3, 2007
Louisville, KY – World Prayer Center
- George South vs Eric Darkstorm w/ Dr. Death Steve Williams

July 7, 2007
Elkin, NC - Armory
George South vs Jimmy Jack Funk Jr

July 14, 2007
Charlotte, NC – Durham Baptist Church – 12pm
EWA
- George South vs Bobby Houston

July 14, 2007
Morganton, NC – Fairgrounds – 8pm
BCW
- George South & Gorgeous Jeff Patton beat Big Donnie Webb & James Brody

July 15, 2007
Mooresville, NC – Armory
EWA
- George South vs Jimmy Jack Funk Jr

August 2, 2007
Rock Hill, SC - YMCA
- George South vs Charlie Dreamer

August 4, 2007
Rock Hill, SC – Birthday Party
• George South vs Jessie Morris
• George South vs Mike Lee

August 11, 2007
Charlotte, NC – Hilton Hotel
Mid Atlantic Fan Fest (Greg Price)
• George South vs Mark Tron
• George South Sr & Jr vs Randy & Bill Mulkey

August 18, 2007
Sophia, NC – 333 Flea Market
• George South vs Student
• George South vs Jimmy Jack Funk Jr
• Battle Royal

August 19, 2007
Mooresville, NC – Armory
EWA
• George South vs Carolina Dreamer

August 25, 2007
Elkin, NC – Armory
EWA
• George South vs Jimmy Jack Funk Jr

September 7, 2007
Lincolnton, NC – Men's Prison – 2pm
EWA
• George South vs Jimmy Jack Funk Jr

September 7, 2007
Gastonia, NC – Armory – 8pm
EWA
• George South vs Ricky Morton

September 8, 2007
Elkin, NC – Armory
EWA
• George South Sr & Jr beat Scotty McKeever & Jimmy Jack Funk Jr

September 15, 2007
Sophia, NC – 311 Flea Market
• George South vs Robert Sanchez

September 23, 2007
Stafford, VA – Widewater Elementary School
EWA
• George South & Jimmy Valiant beat Mike Williams & Rick Kelly

September 28, 2007
Mooresville, NC – Armory
EWA
• George South vs Jimmy Jack Funk Jr

October 6, 2007
Elkin, NC – Armory
EWA
• George South vs Scotty McKeever

October 12, 2007
Lincolnton, NC – Armory
EWA
• George South vs Charlie Dreamer

EWA PRESENTS

BOOGIE MAN JAM 2007

OLD SCHOOL FAMILY WRESTLING!

MR. NO. 1
GEORGE SOUTH

Special Appearance by **BOOGIE WOOGIE**
JIMMY VALIANT

SAT - SEPT 22 6PM BELLTIME

Widewater Elem. School STAFFORD, VA

5 BIG MATCHES WITH NWA LEGENDS MR. NO. 1 GEORGE SOUTH AND OTHER TOP STARS!

★ ★ ★ ★ ★ ★ ★ ★ ★ ★ ★

FREE! FREE! FREE!
★ ★ ★
CHURCH GROUPS WELCOME!

EWA
EXODUS WRESTLING ALLIANCE

FOR MORE INFO CALL 540-661-2558 or 704-577-5503

October 26, 2007
Mooresville, NC – Armory
EWA
• George South vs Jimmy Jack Funk Jr

October 27, 2007
Sophia, NC – 311 Flea Market
• George South vs Jimmy Jack Funk Jr

October 31, 2007
Meridian, MS – 11st Gym
• George South vs Charlie Dreamer

November 1, 2007
Mooresville, NC – Armory
EWA
• George South vs Jimmy Jack Funk Jr

November 3, 2007
North Wilkesboro, NC – High School
• George South vs Jimmy Jack Funk Jr

November 14, 2007
Meridian, MS – 11st Gym
• George South & Robert Gibson beat The Super Destroyers

November 17, 2007
Lenoir, NC – American Legion Hall
UWA (Roger Knight)
• George South vs Jason Jones

November 22, 2007
Pfafftown, NC – Community Center
• George South vs Jimmy Jack Funk Jr

November 24, 2007
Elkin, NC – Amory
EWA
• George South vs Jake Manning

December 1, 2007
Seagrove, NC – Elementary School
EWA
• George South vs Ricky Morton

December 8, 2007
Elkin, NC – Armory
NWA
• George South vs Preston Quinn

December 25, 2007
Mooresville, NC – Armory
EWA
• George South vs Jimmy Jack Funk Jr

December 29, 2007
Troutman, NC – VFW
• George South vs Charlie Dreamer

2008

January 16, 2008
Morganton, NC – Western Carolina Center
EWA
- George South beat Lil Donnie
- George South vs Jimmy Jack Funk Jr

January 20, 2008
Mooresville, NC -Armory
EWA
- George South vs Charlie Dreamer

February 2, 2008
Seagrove, NC – Elementary School
EWA
- George South vs Jimmy Jack Funk Jr

February 16, 2008
Morganton, NC – Fairgrounds
BCW
- George South vs Jimmy Jack Funk Jr

February 22, 2008
Mooresville, NC – Armory
EWA
- George South vs Student

February 23, 2008
Kings Mountain, NC – Armory
- George South vs Jimmy Jack Funk Jr

March 7, 2008
Grover, NC – Elementary School
- George South vs Jason Jones

March 28, 2008
Mooresville, NC – Armory
- George South vs Jimmy Jack Funk Jr

April 10, 2008
Athens, WV – Concord College
- George South vs Ricky Morton

April 12, 2008
Mooresville, NC – Armory
EWA
- George South vs Jimmy Jack Funk Jr

April 18, 2008
Pfafftown, NC – Community Center
- George South vs Jimmy Jack Funk Jr

April 19, 2008
Elkin, NC – Armory
EWA
- George South vs Ryan Will

April 25, 2008
Mooresville, NC -Armory
- George South vs Jimmy Jack Funk Jr
- George South vs Raymond Helms

April 26, 2008
Mooresville, NC – Armory
• George South vs Jimmy Jack Funk Jr

May 2, 2008
Charlotte, NC – Freedom Center
• George South vs Charlie Dreamer

May 3, 2008
Sophia, NC – 311 Flea Market – 12pm
• George South vs Charlie Dreamer

May 3, 2008
Elkin, NC – Armory
• George South vs Student

May 4, 2008
Charlotte, NC – Plaza Rd Church
• George South vs Charlie Dreamer

May 5, 2008
Charlotte, NC – Independence High School
Anderson Brothers Classic
• George South Sr & Jr beat Bobo Brazil Jr & Shawn White
• George South Sr & Jr beat Jacob Jones & Ryan Stallons
• George South Sr & Jr beat Jimmy Jack Funk Jr & Charlie Dreamer

May 6, 2008
Mooresville, NC – Armory
• George South vs Charlie Dreamer

May 8, 2008
Salisbury, NC – Armory
• George South vs Charlie Dreamer

May 16, 2008
Rhonda, VA – Church of God
• George South vs Jimmy Jack Funk Jr

May 22, 2008
Pageland, SC – Elementary School
• George South vs Charlie Dreamer
• George South & Masked Superstar vs Charlie Dreamer & Jim Heafer

May 23, 2008
Mooresville, NC – Armory
EWA
• George South vs Jake Manning

May 30, 2008
High Point, NC – Boys Club
• George South vs Jimmy Jack Funk Jr

June 11, 2008
Charlotte, NC – Freedom Center
EWA
George South vs Ricky Steamboat Jr
Note: This is Steamboat Jr's first pro match

June 14, 2008
Belmont, NC – Armory
EWA
• George South vs Ricky Steamboat Jr

June 15, 2008
Butler, PA – State Park
• George South vs Shane Matthews

255

June 19, 2008
Mooresville, NC – Armory
EWA
- George South vs Ricky Steamboat Jr

June 25, 2008
Polaski, VA – Central Gym
- George South vs Ricky Steamboat Jr

June 26, 2008
Boling Springs, NC – Circle J Ranch
- George South vs Ricky Steamboat Jr

June 27, 2008
War, WV – Old Gym
- George South vs Ricky Steamboat Jr

June 28, 2008
Mooresville, NC - Armory
- George South vs Ricky Steamboat Jr
- George South vs Jimmy Jack Funk Jr

June 29, 2008
Waterloo, IA - Church
- George South vs Jimmy Jack Funk Jr

July 2, 2008
Faith, NC - Fairgrounds
- George South vs Ricky Steamboat Jr

July 3, 2008
Faith, NC - Fairgrounds
- George South vs Ricky Steamboat Jr

July 5, 2008
Faith, NC – Fairgrounds
- George South beat Bobo Brazil Jr

July 10, 2008
Mooresville, NC – Armory
EWA
- George South vs Jimmy Jack Funk Jr

July 11, 2008
Salisbury, NC – Armory
- George South vs Charlie Dreamer

July 12, 2008
Belmont, NC - Armory
- George South vs Ivan Koloff

July 19, 2008
Forest City, NC - Armory
- George South vs Ricky Steamboat Jr

July 25, 2008
Statesville, NC – Gracie Park Rec Center
- George South vs Ricky Steamboat Jr

July 26, 2008
Mooresville, NC – Armory
EWA
- George South vs Ricky Steamboat Jr

July 27, 2008
Mooresville, NC - Armory
• George South vs Ricky Steamboat Jr

August 1, 2008
Kings Mountain, NC – Fairgrounds
• George South vs Ricky Steamboat Jr

August 2, 2008
Elkin, NC – Armory
EWA
• George South vs Ricky Steamboat Jr

August 9, 2008
Charlotte, NC – Sugar Creek Rec
EWA
• EWA Florida Title: Ricky Steamboat Jr. beat Mr. Florida* to win the title

August 16, 2008
Charlotte, NC – Hilton Hotel
NWA Mid-Atlantic Fan Fest
• George South vs Ricky Steamboat Jr

August 29, 2008
Mooresville, NC – Armory
• George South vs Ricky Steamboat Jr

August 30, 2008
Sophia, NC – 311 Flea Market
• George South vs Jake Manning

August 30, 2008
Belmont, NC – Armory – 8pm
• George South vs Ric Converse

September 12, 2008
Lincolnton, NC – Men's Prison
EWA
• George South vs Jason Jones

September 13, 2008
Charlotte, NC – Birthday Party
EWA
• George South vs Jason Jones
• George South vs Bobo Brazil Jr

September 20, 2008
Kings Mountain, NC - Armory
• George South vs Jimmy Jack Funk Jr

October 4, 2008
Kernersville, NC – Auditorium
• George South vs Tre G

October 17, 2008
Mooresville, NC – Armory
EWA
• George South vs Reid Flair
Note: Reid Flair's first pro match

October 25, 2008
Mt. Holly, NC – Cornerstone Church
• George South vs Dory Funk Jr
• George South vs Joel Deaton

October 31, 2008
Aiken, SC – Word of Life Church
• George South vs Joel Deaton Jr

November 6, 2008
Rock Hill, SC – YMCA
• George South vs Charlie Dreamer

November 13, 2008
Mooresville, NC – Armory
EWA
• George South vs Jake Manning

November 20, 2008
Hollywood, SC – St. Paul Academy
• George South & Beautiful Bobby Eaton beat
Jake Manning & Charlie Dreamer
• Battle Royal

November 25, 2008
Charlotte, NC – High School
• George South vs Jake Manning

November 26, 2008
Mooresville, NC – Armory
EWA
• George South & Ricky Steamboat Jr vs
Jake Manning & Charlie Dreamer

November 27, 208
Kings Mountain, NC – Armory
EWA
• George South & Ricky Steamboat Jr beat
Jimmy Jack Funk Jr & Bobo Brazil Jr

December 5, 2008
Greensboro, NC – Armory
• George South vs Ricky Steamboat Jr

December 6, 2008
Charlotte, NC – Vance High School
• George South vs Charlie Dreamer

December 12, 2008
Grover, SC – High School
• George South vs Charlie Dreamer

December 13, 2008
Statesville, NC – Gracie Park Rec Center
• George South vs Jake Manning

2009

January 3, 2009
Mooresville, NC – Armory
EWA
- George South vs Jake Manning

January 10, 2009
Anderson, NC – High School
- George South vs Mike Lee

January 17, 2009
Mooresville, NC - Armory
- George South vs Shawn Halen

January 24, 2009
Salisbury, NC - Armory
- George South vs Jimmy Jack Funk Jr

January 25, 2009
Concord, NC – Parkwood Church
- George South vs Jake Manning

January 31, 2009
Seagrove, NC – Elementary School
- George South vs Mr. Florida

February 7, 2009
Gun, AL – High School
- George South vs Charlie Dreamer

February 8, 2009
Yadkinville, NC – NWA Building
NWA
- George South vs Jimmy Jack Funk Jr

February 15, 2009
Yadkinville, NC – NWA Building
NWA
- George South vs Jimmy Jack Funk Jr

February 19, 2009
Mooresville, NC - Armory
- George South vs Mike Lee

February 20, 2009
Arcadia, NC - VFW
- George South vs Charlie Dreamer

February 27, 2009
Mooresville, NC - Armory
- George South vs Shawn Halen

February 28, 2009
Lexington, NC - Armory
- George South vs Jake Manning

March 6, 2009
Statesville, NC – Gracie Park Rec Center
- George South vs Charlie Dreamer

March 7, 2009
Robbins, NC – Middle School
- George South vs Jimmy Jack Funk Jr

March 13, 2009
Pageland, SC – Elementary School
- George South vs Charlie Dreamer

March 14, 2009
Mooresville, NC - Armory
- George South vs Chad Aaron

March 19, 2009
Mooresville, NC - Armory
- George South vs Jack Manning

March 20, 2009
Raleigh, NC – High School
- George South &? vs Midnight Express w/ Jim Cornette

March 21, 2009
Wilmington, NC – Armory
- George South vs Ricky Morton

April 4, 2009
Fort Mills, SC – Rays – 2pm
- George South vs Barbarian

April 4, 2009
Asheboro, NC – Boys Club – 8pm
- George South vs Henry Dean

April 9, 2009
Knoxville, NC – Jacobs Building
- George South & Masked Superstar vs Greg Valentine & Honkey Tonk Man

April 10, 2009
Charlotte, NC – Grady Cole Center
- George South & Masked Superstar vs David & Reid Flair

April 11, 2009
Trinity, NC - Braxton School
- George South vs Henry Dean

April 16, 2009
Mooresville, NC - Armory
- George South vs Jake Manning

April 17, 2009
Mooresville, NC – Armory
- George South vs Charlie Dreamer

April 18, 2009
Winston-Salem, NC – Coliseum
- George South vs Chris Hamrick

April 25, 2009
Bluefield, WV – Armory
- George South vs Eric Lester

May 2, 2009
Robbins, NC – Middle School
- George South vs Jimmy Jack Funk Jr

May 3, 2009
Charlotte, NC – Plaza Rd Church
• George South vs Jake Manning

May 8, 2009
Charlotte, NC – High School
• George South vs Ricky Steamboat Jr

May 9, 2009
Lexington, NC - Armory
• George South vs Henry Dean

May 11, 2009
Thomasville, NC – Elementary School
EWA
• George South beat Matt Houston

May 15, 2009
Mooresville, NC – Armory
• George South vs Raymond Helms

May 16, 2009
Charlotte, NC – Freedom Center – 8pm
• George South vs Raymond Helms

May 16, 2009
Sharon, SC – Fire Dept – 8pm
• George South vs Charlie Dreamer

May 23, 2009
Gaffney, SC – Middle School
• George South vs Jimmy Jack Funk Jr

June 13, 2009
Salisbury, NC – Armory
• George South vs Jimmy Jack Funk Jr

June 20, 2009
Mooresville, NC – Armory
• George South vs Henry Dean

June 26, 2009
Trinity, NC – Church
• George South vs Raymond Helms

June 28, 2009
Mooresville, NC – Armory
• George South vs Jake Manning

July 4, 2009
Athens, TX – Civic Center
• George South vs Charlie Dreamer

July 18, 2009
Goldsboro, NC – Clayton Homes
• George South vs Henry Dean

July 22, 2009
Princeton, WV – 4 H Club
• George South vs Eric Lester

July 24, 2009
Spartanburg, SC – Eastside Baptist Church
• George South vs Jimmy Jack Funk Jr
• George South vs Pastor Mike

July 25, 2009
Durham, NC – Baptist Church
• George South vs Jimmy Jack Funk Jr

July 29, 2009
Charlotte, NC – Freedom Center
• George South vs Jake Manning

July 30, 2009
Mooresville, NC – Armory
• George South vs Jake Manning

August 1, 2009
Spartanburg, SC – APW Arena
APW
• George South & Jay Eagle vs Mike Foley & Thor

August 8, 2009
Charlotte, NC – Hilton Hotel
NWA Mid Atlantic Fan Fest
• George South beat Charlie Dreamer

August 15, 2009
Summerville, SC – Mills Road Baptist Church
• George South vs Barbarian w/ Baby Doll

August 21, 2009
Mooresville, NC – Armory
• George South beat Raymond Helms

August 22, 2009
Wentworth, NC – Armory
• George South beat Cedric Reed

August 29, 2009
Lexington, NC -Armory
• George South beat Henry Dean

September 11, 2009
Lincolnton, NC – Men's Prison
• George South vs Cedric Reed

September 12, 2009
Huntersville, NC – Birthday Party
• George South vs Cedric Reed
• Battle Royal

September 18, 2009
Mooresville, NC – Armory
• George South Sr & Jr vs Jason King & Jimmy Jack Funk Jr

September 22, 2009
Albemarle, NC - Fairgrounds
• George South vs Jimmy Jack Funk Jr

September 24, 2009
Albemarle, NC – Fairgrounds
• George South vs Jimmy Jack Funk Jr

September 25, 2009
Albemarle, NC – Fairgrounds
• George South vs Captain Thunderdome

September 26, 2009
High Point, NC – Boys Club
• George South vs Cedric Reed

Highway Run into the Midnight Sun

October 3, 2009
Clayton, NC – Fitness Center
• George South beat Jesse Moore

October 10, 2009
Lexington, NC – Armory
• George South beat Bobo Brazil Jr

October 16, 2009
Mooresville, NC – Armory
• George South beat Ninja

October 17, 2009
Charlotte, NC – Charlotte Motor Speedway – 11am
EWA
• George South vs Shawn Halen

October 17, 2009
Kings Mountain, NC – Armory – 8pm
• George South vs Ray Hudson

October 30, 2009
Charlotte, NC – Birthday Party
• George South vs Cedric Reed

November 5, 2009
Rock Hill, SC – YMCA
• George South beat Cedric Reed

November 7, 2009
Pfafftown, NC – Community Center
• George South vs Ricky Steamboat Jr

November 13, 2009
Mooresville, NC – Armory
• George South beat Raymond Helms

November 19, 2009
Lancaster, SC -American Legion
• George South vs Ivan Koloff

November 20, 2009
Rock Hill, SC – Middle School
• George South beat Jake Manning

November 26, 2009
Lexington, NC – Armory
• George South vs Henry Dean

November 27, 2009
Newton, NC – Armory
• George South & Rocky King beat Bobo Brazil Jr & Cedric Reed

November 28, 2009
Griffin, GA – Church
• George South vs Chic Donovan

November 29, 2009
Bluefield, WV – Armory
WVCW TV Taping
• George South vs Shawn Russell
• George South vs Mad Dog David Lynch
• George South vs Eric Lester

December 2, 2009
Meridian, MS – 11th Street Gym
• George South vs Shane Halen

December 4, 2009
Laurens, SC – Club
• George South vs Ricky Steamboat Jr

December 5, 2009
Clayton, NC – Fitness Center
• George South vs Bobo Brazil Jr

December 14, 2009
Mooresville, NC – Armory
• George South vs Ricky Steamboat Jr

December 15, 2009
Lexington, NC – Armory
• George South vs Shane Helms

December 18, 2009
Shelby, NC – Middle School
• George South vs American GI

December 27, 2009
Bluefield, WV – Armory
WVCW TV Taping
• George South vs Mad Dog David Lynch
• George South vs Ricky Morton

2010

January 2, 2010
Pfafftown, NC - Gym
• George South vs Jake Manning

January 16, 2010
Lexington, NC - Armory
• George South vs Henry Dean

January 23, 2010
Salisbury, NC - Armory
• George South vs Jerry Nash

January 25, 2010
Princeton, WV – Cole Center
WVCW
• George South vs Chase Owens

January 29, 2010
Mocksville, NC - Armory
• George South vs Jimmy Jack Funk Jr

January 30, 2010
Mocksville, NC – Armory
• George South vs Adam James
Note: Paul Jones Training Day

January 31, 2010
Salisbury, NC – Church
• George South vs Pastor Chris

February 6, 2010
Robbins, NC Middle School
• George South vs Ricky Steamboat Jr

February 7, 2010
Salisbury, NC – Baptist Church
• George South vs Pastor Chris

February 13, 2010
Lexington, NC - Armory
• George South vs Henry Dean

February 20, 2010
Kings Mountain, NC - Armory
• George South vs Ray Hudson

February 26, 2010
Lexington, NC – Armory
• George South vs Jimmy Jack Funk Jr

February 27, 2010
Clayton, NC – Fitness Center
Ivan Koloff Tag Team Tournament
• George South Sr & Jr vs AWOL

February 28, 2010
Charlotte, NC – Expo Center
• George South vs Local

March 6, 2010
Spartanburg, SC – Arena
APW
• George South vs Jay Eagle

March 12, 2010
Laurens, SC – Exchange Club
• George South vs Deon Johnson

March 13, 2010
Lexington, NC - Armory
• George South vs Henry Dean

March 14, 2010
Charlotte, NC – Hilton Hotel
• George South vs Local

March 19, 2010
Salisbury, NC - Armory
• George South vs Gerry Nash

March 20, 2010
High Point, NC – Boys Club
• George South vs Local

March 21, 2010
Gastonia, NC - Armory
• George South vs Texas Ranger

March 25, 2010
Lancaster, SC – American Legion
• George South vs Masked Superstar

March 26, 2010
Mocksville, NC - Armory
• George South vs Jimmy Jack Funk Jr

March 27, 2010
Winston-Salem, NC - Armory
• George South vs Jason Jones

April 10, 2010
Lexington, NC - Armory
• George South vs Henry Dean

April 16, 2010
Mocksville, NC - Armory
• George South vs Gerry Nash

April 17, 2010
Monroe, NC - Fairgrounds
• George South vs Baron Bullard

April 23, 2010
Mocksville, NC - Armory
• George South vs Ricky Steamboat Jr

April 24, 2010
Lincolnton, NC – High School
• George South vs Ring Lord Speedy

April 30, 2010
Gastonia, NC – Birthday Party
• George South vs Local

May 1, 2010
High Point, NC – Boys Club
• George South vs Baron Bullard

May 2, 2010
Charlotte, NC – Plaza Rd Church
EWA
• George South vs Jessie Morris

May 7, 2010
Laurens, SC – Exchange Club
• George South vs Local

May 8, 2010
Charlotte, NC – Freedom Center
EWA
• George South vs Jimmy Jack Funk Jr

May 8, 2010
Mocksville, NC – Armory
• Jake The Snake Roberts beat George South

May 15, 2010
Chesnee, SC – Arena
APW
• George South vs Jay Eagle

May 21, 2010
Mocksville, NC – Armory
• George South vs Jimmy Jack Funk Jr

May 22, 2010
Charlotte, NC – Charlotte Motor Speedway – 10am
EWA
• George South beat Gladiator

May 22, 2010
Burlington, NC – Armory – 8pm
• George South beat Bobby Houston

May 28, 2010
Mocksville, NC - Armory
• George South vs Jimmy Valiant

May 29, 201
Charlotte, NC – Charlotte Motor Speedway – 11am
EWA
• George South vs Student

May 29, 2010
Winston-Salem, NC – Armory – 8pm
George South vs Jimmy Valiant

June 5, 2010
Elkin, NC – Armory
EWA
• George South vs Reid Flair

June 6, 2010
Monroe, NC – Hopewell Baptist Church
EWA
Anderson Brothers Tag Team Tournament
• The Assassins beat George South & Mr. Florida

June 12, 2010
Gastonia, NC – Family Dollar
• George South vs Ray Hudson

June 18, 2010
Mocksville, NC - Armory
•   George South vs Gerry Love

June 19, 2010
Clayton, NC – Fitness Center
• George South & Mr. Florida vs Demolition

June 25, 2010
Roma, GA – Civic Center
• George South vs Ronnie Gossett

June 26, 2010
Belmont, NC – Armory
• George South beat Buzz

June 30, 2010
Faith, NC – Smokey Mountain Fairgrounds
• George South vs Ricky Steamboat Jr

July 1, 2010
Faith, NC – Smokey Mountain Fairgrounds
• George South vs. Jimmy Jack Funk Jr

July 2, 2010
Faith, NC – Smokey Mountain Fairgrounds
• George South vs. Local

July 3, 2010
Faith, NC – Smokey Mountain Fairgrounds
• George South vs. Ricky Steamboat Jr

July 10, 2010
Spartanburg, SC – Arena
APW
• George South vs Jay Eagle

July 14, 2010
Charlotte, NC – Freedom Center
• George South vs Cedric Alexander

July 16, 2010
Mocksville, NC - Armory
• George South vs Local

July 17, 2010
Sumter, SC – Baptist Church
EWA
• George South vs Jimmy Jack Funk Jr

July 21, 2010
Princeton, WV – 4 H Camp
• George South vs Eric Lester

July 22, 2010
Chesnee, SC – APW Arena
APW
• George South vs Jay Eagle

July 23, 2010
Mocksville, NC - Armory
• George South vs Charlie Murdoch

July 24, 2010
Kings Mountain, NC - Armory
• George South vs Ray Hudson

July 30, 2010
Spartanburg, SC – Eastside Baptist
• Jimmy Valiant beat George South

July 31, 2010
Newberry, SC – St. Andrews Church
• George South beat Deon Johnson

August 1, 2010
Newberry, SC – St. Andrews Church
• George South vs Deon Johnson

August 7, 2010
Charlotte, NC - Hilton Hotel
Mid Atlantic Fan Fest (Greg Price)
• George South vs Local

August 12, 2010
Lancaster, SC – Wal Mart Parking Lot
EWA
• George South beat Cedric Alexander

August 14, 2010
Belmont, NC – Armory
• George South vs Student

August 20, 2010
Mocksville, NC - Armory
• George South vs Gerry Nash

August 21, 2010
Kings Mountain, NC - Armory
• George South vs Ray Hudson

August 27, 2010
Laurens, SC – Exchange Club
• George South vs Ricky Morton

August 28, 2010
Snellville, GA – South Gwinnett High School
EWA
• George South beat Southern Flame

September 3, 2010
Lexington, NC – Fairgrounds
• George South vs Jimmy Jack Funk Jr

September 11, 2010
Troutman, NC - Fairgrounds
• George South vs Local

September 12, 2010
Morganton, NC – Fairgrounds
BCW
• George South vs James Brody

September 18, 2010
Kings Mountain, NC - Armory
• George South vs Ray Hudson

September 24, 2010
Monroe, NC – Armory
NWA Carolinas (Eldon Speer)
• George South vs Jimmy Jack Funk Jr

September 25, 2010
Shelby, NC - Fairgrounds
• George South vs Local

October 1, 2010
Salisbury, NC – Armory
• George South vs. Ricky Morton

October 2, 2010
Boling Springs, SC – Rock City Church
• George South vs. DL Kool

October 2, 2010
Chesnee, SC – APW Arena
APW (Jay Eagle) – 8pm

October 8, 2010
Laurens, SC – Exchange Club
• George South vs. Deon Johnson

October 9, 2010
Clayton, NC – Fitness Center
• George South vs. Lewis Moore

October 14, 2010
Morganton, NC – Western Carolina Center
BCW
• George South beat Big Donnie Webb

October 15, 2010
Marion, NC – Rec Center
• Jimmy Valiant beat George South

October 16, 2010
Charlotte, NC – Charlotte Motor Speedway – 11am
EWA – 10am
• George South beat Gladiator

October 16, 2010
Lincolnton, NC – North Lincolnton High School – 8pm
George South vs. The Barbarian

October 22, 2010
Mocksville, NC – Armory
• George South vs Referee Chad

October 23, 2010
Bessemer City, NC – Armory
• George South beat DL Kool

October 24, 2010
Kings Mountain, NC – Armory
• George South vs Ray Hudson

November 4, 2010
Rock Hill, SC - YMCA
• George South vs Jimmy Jack Funk Jr

November 12, 2010
Eden, NC - Mall
• George South vs Local

November 13, 2010
Lexington, NC – Armory
• George South vs Henry Dean

November 19, 2010
Pageland, SC -Elementary School
• George South vs Jim Hefner

November 20, 2010
Lincolnton, NC – High School
• George South vs Jimmy Jack Funk Jr

November 21, 2010
Harrisburg, NC – Church
EWA
• George South vs Jimmy Jack Funk Jr

November 25, 2010
Asheboro, NC – Old Gym
• George South vs Local

November 26, 2010
Mocksville, NC - Armory
• George South vs Local

November 27, 2010
Mooresboro, NC – Old Gym
EWF
• George South vs Chris Thunder Anderson

December 3, 2010
Mocksville, NC - Armory
• George South vs Jimmy Jack Funk Jr

December 4, 2010
Cashers, NC – Elementary School
• George South vs Ricky Steamboat Jr

December 10, 2010
Lexington, NC – Armory
• George South vs Henry Dean

December 11, 2010
Lincolnton, NC – Oakwod Homes – 2pm
• George South vs The Barbarian

December 11, 2010
Clayton, NC – Fitness Center – 8pm
• George South vs Lewis Moore

December 17, 2010
Kings Mountain, NC – Middle School
• George South vs American GI

December 18, 2010
Lancaster, SC – Birthday Party
• George South vs Jimmy Jack Funk Jr

December 25, 2010
Kings Mountain, NC – Armory
• George South vs Ray Hudson

2011

January 1, 2011
Asheboro, NC – Community center
• George South vs Jimmy Jack Funk Jr

January 8, 2011
Shelby, NC – Clayton Homes - 2pm
• George South vs The Barbarian

January 8, 2011
Smithfield, NC – Aggie Center – 8pm
• George South vs Local

January 15, 201
Kings Mountain, NC - Armory
• George South vs Ray Hudson

January 21, 2011
Mocksville, NC – Armory
• George South vs Jimmy Jack Funk Jr

January 22, 2011
Lincolnton, NC – High School
• George South vs Reid Flair

January 23, 2011
Morganton, NC – North Morganton Baptist
EWA
• George South vs Jimmy Jack Funk Jr

January 28, 2011
Eden, NC – Event Center
• George South vs Local

February 5, 2011
Asheboro, NC – Community Center
• George South vs Jimmy Jack Funk Jr

February 10, 2011
Hamburg, NC – Church
EWA
• George South Sr & Jr vs Cedric Alexander & Jake Manning

February 12, 2011
Villa Rocca, GA – Bay Springs School
• George South vs Ricky Morton

February 18, 2011
Mocksville, NC – Armory
• George South vs Jimmy Jack Funk Jr

February 19, 2011
Lincolnton, NC – High School
• George South & Buddy Landel vs Ricky Morton & Deon Johnson

February 25, 2011
Kings Mountain, NC – Middle School
• George South Sr & Jr vs Rock & Roll Express

February 26, 2011
Clayton, NC – Fitness Center
• George South Sr & Jr vs Rock & Roll Express

Highway Run into the Midnight Sun

February 27, 2011
Lexington, NC – High School
• George South vs. Nick Richards

March 5, 2011
Gaffney, SC – Boys Club
• George South vs Rex Rumble

March 12, 2011
Yanceyville, NC – Armory
• George South vs Jimmy Love

March 18, 2011
Charlotte, NC – Freedom Church – 2pm
• George South & Gorge South Jr beat Cedric Alexander & Jake Manning

March 18, 2011
Mocksville, NC – Armory – 8pm
• George South vs Reid Flair

March 19, 2011
Hickory, NC - Armory
• George South vs Student

March 26, 2011
Lincolnton, NC – High School
• George South vs The Barbarian

April 1, 2011
Mocksville, NC – Armory
• George South vs Jimmy Jack Funk Jr

April 2, 2011
Goldsboro, NC – Pawn Shop – 2pm
• George South vs Buzz

April 2, 2011
Asheboro, NC – Boys Club – 8pm
• George South vs Jimmy Jack Funk Jr

April 9, 2011
Philadelphia, PA - Ramada
• George South vs Local w/ Molly Holly

April 10, 2011
Shelby, NC – Baptist Church
EWA
• George South vs Pastor Chris

April 14, 2011
Forest City, NC – Armory
• George South vs Ray Hudson

April 16, 2011
Gastonia, NC – High School
• George South & Baron Bullard vs The Rock & Roll Express

April 22, 201
Laurens, SC - Fairgrounds
• George South vs Deon Johnson

April 23, 2011
Gaffney, SC – Boys Club
• George South vs Rex Rumble

April 29, 2011
Jefferson, SC -Old Gym
• George South vs Patrick Rebel

April 30, 2011
Clayton, NC – Fitness Center
• George South vs Lewis Moore

May 1, 2011
Charlotte, NC – Plaza Road Baptist Church
EWA
• George South vs Jimmy Jack Funk Jr

May 5, 2011
Charlotte, NC – Charlotte Motor Speedway
EWA
• George South vs Baron Bullard

May 6, 2011
Newton, NC – Armory
• George South vs Local

May 7, 2011
Charlotte, NC – Charlotte Motor Speedway
EWA
• George South vs Baron Bullard

May 7, 2011
Asheboro, NC – Boys Club
• George South vs Baron Bullard

May 14, 2011
Charlotte, NC – Freedom Center
EWA
• George South vs Jimmy Jack Funk Jr

May 15, 2011
Gastonia, NC – Birthday Party
• George South vs Jeff Hart

May 19, 2011
Mocksville, NC - Armory
• George South vs Ricky Steamboat Jr

May 20, 2011
Mocksville, NC – Armory
• George South vs Baron Bullard

May 21, 2011
Charlotte, NC – Charlotte Motor Speedway – 11am
EWA
• George South vs Jimmy Jack Funk Jr

May 21, 2011
Charleston, SC – New Beginnings Church
EWA
• George South vs Pastor Shawn

May 28, 2011
Charlotte, NC – Charlotte Motor Speedway – 11am
EWA
• George South vs Jimmy Jack Funk Jr

May 28, 2011
Fletcher, NC – Middle School
• George South vs Ricky Steamboat Jr

Highway Run into the Midnight Sun

May 29, 2011
Mocksville, NC – Armory
• George South vs Local

June 4, 2011
Smithfield, NC – Aggie Center
• George South vs Baron Bullard

June 5, 2011
Monroe, NC – Baptist Church
• George South & Baron Bullard beat David Flair & George South Jr

June 11, 2011
Roseboro, NC – Middle School
• George South vs Charlie Dreamer

June 15, 2011
Charlotte, NC – Freedom Center
EWA
• George South vs Mike Lee

June 17, 2011
Sugar Grove, NC – Old Cove Creek Gym
• George South beat Myles Long

June 18, 2011
Gretta, VA – Birthday Party – 11am
• George South vs Student

June 18, 2011
Pelham, NC – High School – 8pm
• George South vs Jimmy Love

June 24, 2011
Mocksville, NC – Armory
• George South vs Gary Good

June 25, 2011
Belmont, NC – Armory
• George South vs Local

June 29, 2011
Faith, NC – Fairgrounds
• George South vs Baron Bullard

June 30, 2011
Faith, NC – Fairgrounds
• George South vs Ricky Steamboat Jr

July 2, 2011
Faith, NC – Fairgrounds
• George South vs Johnny Smooth

July 3, 2011
Faith, NC – Fairgrounds
• George South vs Ricky Steamboat Jr

July 13, 2013
Charlotte, NC – Freedom Center
• George South vs Gladiator

July 16, 2011
Lincolnton, NC – Baptist Church
• George South vs Baron Bullard

July 16, 2011
Morganton, NC – Fairgrounds – 8pm
BCW
• George South vs Big Donnie Webb

July 17, 2011
Rock Hill, SC – Birthday Party
• George South vs Student

July 20, 2011
Princeton, WV – 4 H Camp
• George South vs Eric Lester

July 22, 2011
Mocksville, NC - Armory
• Battle Royal

July 23, 2011
Monroe, GA – Ford Dealership
• George South vs Baron Bullard

July 29, 2011
Lenoir, NC – Armory
• George South vs The Barbarian

July 30, 2011
Mt. Airy, NC - Armory
• George South vs Henry Dean

August 5, 2011
Atlanta, GA – Hilton Hotel
Georgia Wrestling Fan Fest
• George South vs Local

August 6, 2011
Roseboro, NC – Middle School
• George South vs Carolina Dreamer

August 13, 2011
Mt. Airy, NC – Armory – 3pm
• George South vs Henry Dean

August 13, 2011
Kings Mountain, NC – Armory – 8pm
• George South vs Ray Hudson

August 19, 2011
Mocksville, NC – Armory
• George South vs Baron Bullard

August 20, 2011
Greensboro, NC – Potters House – 11am
• George South vs Local

August 20, 2011
Lincolnton, NC – High School
• George South vs The Barbarian

August 24, 2011
Charlotte, NC – Freedom Center
EWA
• George South vs Baron Bullard

August 27, 2011
Mt. Airy, NC - Armory
• George South vs Local

September 3, 2011
Asheboro, NC – Boys Club
• George South vs Gladiator

September 10, 2011
Reidsville, NC – Rec Center
• George South vs Jim Love

September 17, 2011
Mt, Airy, NC – Armory – 3pm
• George South vs Henry Dean

September 17, 2011
Kings Mountain, NC – Armory – 8pm
• George South vs Ray Hudson

September 24, 2011
Clayton, NC – Fitness Center
• George South vs Local

October 1, 2011
Asheboro, NC – Boys Club
• George South vs Baron Bullard

October 7, 2011
Charlotte, NC – Expo Center
NWA
• George South beat Jimmy Jack Funk Jr

October 9, 2011
Gastonia, NC – Freightliner
• George South vs Ray Hudson

October 13, 2011
Morganton, NC – Fairgrounds
BCW
• George South vs Jeff Patton

October 15, 2011
Charlotte, NC – Charlotte Motor Speedway – 11am
EWA
• George South vs Gladiator

October 15, 2011
Fisher, VA - Expo Center – 8pm
• George South vs Jake Manning

October 21, 2011
Mocksville, NC – Armory
• George South vs Referee Chad

October 22, 2011
Lexington, NC - Armory
• George South vs Henry Dean

October 29, 2011
Greatra, VA – Midway Baptist
EWA
• George South vs Student

November 5, 2011
Rock Hill, SC – YMCA
• George South vs Jimmy Jack Funk Jr

November 12, 2011
Denver, NC – Birthday Party – 12pm
• George South vs Avenger

November 12, 2011
Belmont, NC – Armory – 8pm
• George South vs Texas Ranger

November 19, 2011
Kannapolis, NC – River Church of God – 11am
EWA
• George South vs Student

November 19, 2011
Spartanburg, SC – APW Arena – 8pm
APW
• George South vs Jay Eagle

November 20, 2011
Charlotte, NC – Belk Community Center
• George South vs Jake Manning

November 24, 2011
Asheboro, NC – Boys Club
• George South vs Baron Bullard

November 25, 2011
Monroe, NC – Back to Bethel Church
• George South vs Local

November 26, 2011
Kings Mountain, NC – Armory
• George South vs Tim Hunter

December 2, 2011
Hickory, NC – Freedom Center
• George South vs Randy Sledge

December 3, 2011
Yanceyville, NC – High School
• Ricky Morton beat George South

December 9, 2011
Lexington, NC – High School
• Jake The Snake Roberts w/ The Perfect 10 Bab Doll beat George South

December 10, 2011
Shallotte, NC – Armory
• George South vs Bad Brad

December 15, 2011
Shelby, NC – Burns Middle School
• George South vs American GI

December 17, 2011
Mt. Airy, NC – Armory
• George South vs Henry Dean

December 18, 2011
Monroe, NC – Birthday Party
• George South vs Avenger

December 25, 2011
Kings Mountain, NC – Armory
• George South vs Ray Hudson

December 30, 2011
Mooresville, NC – Armory
• George South vs Bobby Houston

December 31, 2011
Spartanburg, SC – APW Arena
APW
• George South vs Jay Eagle

2012

January 6, 2012
Marion, NC – Armory
• George South vs Local

January 7, 2012
Asheboro, NC – Boys Club
• George South vs Jimmy Jack Funk Jr

January 14, 2012
Hickory, NC – Freedom Center
• George South vs Randy Sledge

January 21, 2012
Kings Mountain, NC – Armory
• George South vs Russian Assassin

February 4, 2012
Seagrove, NC – Elementary School
EWA
• Ricky Morton beat George South

February 10, 2012
Hickory, NC – Freedom Center
• George South vs Baron Bulalrd

February 11, 2012
Villia Rica, GA – High School
• George South vs Local

February 18, 2012
Gaffney, SC – Boys Club
• George South vs Local

February 25, 2012
Clayton, NC -Fitness Center
• Jerry Lawler beat George South

March 2, 2012
Icard, NC – East Burke High School
NAWA (Chad Bryd)
• George South vs. Chad Bryd

March 3, 2012
Thomasville, NC – High School
• George South vs Matt Houston

March 8, 2012
Summerville, SC – Middle School
• George South vs Bobby Eaton

March 10, 2012
Belmont, NC – Armory
ECCW
• Robert Gibson & Willie Clay Sr. beat George South & Texas Ranger

March 11, 2012
Belmont, NC – Armory
• George South vs Jimmy Jack Funk Jr

March 12, 2012
Thomasville, NC – Armory
• George South beat Lewis Moore

March 17, 2012
Liberty, NC – High School
• George South vs Ivan Koloff

March 24, 2012
Mooresboro, NC – Old Gym
EWF
• George South vs Local

March 24, 2012
Kings Mountain, NC – Armory – 8pm
• George South vs Local

March 31, 2012
Tarboro, NC – Church
• George South vs Ricky Morton

April 5, 2012
Kings Mountain, NC – Adult Center
• George South vs Jake Manning

April 7, 2012
Union, SC – Fairgrounds
• George South vs Jake Manning

April 8, 2012
Mooresville, NC – Armory
• George South vs Chad Bryd

April 11, 2012
Greensboro, NC - Gym
• George South vs Student

April 14, 2012
Gaffney, SC – Boys Club
• George South vs Russian Assassin

April 20, 2012
Burnsville, NC – Old Gym
• George South vs Jimmy Valiant

April 21, 2012
Smithfield, NC – Rec Center
• George South vs Lewis Moore

April 27, 2012
Mocksville, NC – Armory
• George South vs Local

April 28, 2012
Gastonia, NC – High School
• George South vs Baron Bullard

May 5, 2012
Taylorsville, NC – Armory
• George South vs Texas Ranger

May 6, 2012
Charlotte, NC – Plaza Road Church – 12pm
EWA
George South vs Jimmy Jack Funk Jr

May 6, 2012
Charlotte, NC – Freedom Center – 6pm
EWA
• George South vs Jimmy Jack Funk Jr

May 12, 2012
Gaffney, SC – High School
• George South vs Local

May 19, 2012
Charlotte, NC – Charlotte Motor Speedway – 11am
EWA
• George South vs Avenger

May 19, 2012
Kings Mountain, NC – Armory – 8pm
• George South vs Ray Hudson

May 26, 2012
Charlotte, NC – Charlotte Motor Speedway
EWA
• George South vs Student

May 26, 2012
Mt. Airy, NC – Armory
• George South vs Local

May 27, 2012
Mt. Airy, NC – VFW Park
• George South vs Double Trouble

June 1, 2012
Rahway, NJ – Rec Center
PWS
• Koko B Ware beat George South

June 9, 2012
Bluefield, WV – Auditorium
• George South vs Eric Lester

June 10, 2012
Maxon, NC – Birthday Party
• George South vs Student

June 14, 2012
Kings Mountain, NC – Armory
• George South vs Shane Austin

June 16, 2012
Winston-Salem, NC – Frank Myers Auto – 2pm
• George South vs Local

June 16, 2012
Ware Shoals, SC – Baseball Field
• George South vs Avenger

June 23, 2012
Spartanburg, SC – APW Arena
APW
• George South vs Jay Eagle

June 24, 2012
Charlotte, NC - Gym
• George South vs The Barbarian

June 27, 2012
Concord, NC – Friendship Baptist Church
EWA
• George South vs Jake Manning

June 28, 2012
Faith, NC – Fairgrounds
• George South vs Local

June 30, 2012
Huntington, WV - Riverfront Park
NWA
• George South beat Stan Lee
Note: Met Mils Mascaras

July 4, 2012
Faith, NC - Fairgrounds
• George South vs Ricky Steamboat Jr

July 6, 2012
Eden, NC – Event Center
• George South vs Local

July 7, 2012
Union, SC – Fairgrounds
Trans South
• George South vs Deon Johnson

July 13, 2012
Chester, SC – APW Arena
APW
• George South vs Local

July 14, 2012
Lincolnton, NC – Baptist Church – 2pm
• George South vs Jeff Victory

July 14, 2012
Gaffney, SC – Peach Festival
• George South vs Jeff Victory

July 17, 2012
Rock Hill, SC – Birthday Party
• George South vs Student

July 18, 2012
Princeton, WV – 4 H Camp
• George South vs Eric Lester

July 20, 2012
St. Allen, WV – High School
• George South & Jeff Victory vs Ricky Morton & Eric Lester

July 21, 2012
Kings Mountain, NC - Armory
• George South vs Local

July 27, 2012
Charleston, IN – Civic Center
• George South vs Local

July 28, 2012
Clayton, NC – Fitness Center
• George South vs Reid Flair

August 1, 2012
Welister, WV – State Park
• George South vs Eric Lester

August 4, 2012
Mt. Gilead, NC – Inn
• George South vs Jake Manning

August 8, 2012
Charlotte, NC – Freedom Church
EWA
• George South beat Cedric Alexander

August 11, 2012
Gaffney, SC – Boys Club
• George South Cedric Alexander

August 12, 2012
Spartanburg, SC – APW Arena
APW
• George South vs Jay Eagle

August 17, 2012
Eden, NC – Event Center
• George South vs Corey Edesill

August 18, 2012
Winston-Salem, NC – Frank Myers Auto – 12pm
• George South vs Baron Bullard

August 18, 2012
Lincolnton, NC – Baptist Church – 4pm
• George South vs Baron Bullard

August 18, 2012
Hudson, NC – Rec Center – 8pm
NAWA
• George South vs Chad Byrd

August 24, 2012
Thomasville, NC – High School
• George South vs Reid Flair

August 25, 2012
Belmont, NC – Armory
• George South vs Texas Ranger

August 31, 2012
Eden, NC – Event Center
• George South vs Rob McBride

September 1, 2012
Covington, VA – Jackson River Complex
• George South vs Henry Dean

September 8, 2012
Union, SC – Fairgrounds
Trans South
• George South vs Deon Johnson

September 14, 2012
Rahway, NJ – Rec Center
PWS
• George South vs The Barbarin

September 15, 2012
Newton, NC – VFW
• George South vs DL Kool

September 22, 2012
Hickory, NC – Birthday Party – 2pm
• George South vs Cedric Alexander

September 22, 2012
Mocksville, NC – Brock Gym – 8pm
• George South vs Local

September 29, 2012
Eden, NC – Fairgrounds
• George South vs Baron Bullard

October 6, 2012
Silva, NC – Railroad Days – 11am
• George South vs Lewis Moore

October 6, 2012
Thomasville, NC – Middle School
• George South vs Matt Houston

October 11, 2012
Simpsonville, SC – 5 Forks Church
EWA
• George South vs DL Kool

October 12, 2012
Charlotte, NC – Charlotte Motor Speedway – 11am
EWA
• George South vs Avenger

October 12, 2012
Chesnee, SC – APW Arena – 8pm
APW
• George South vs Jay Eagle

October 19, 2012
Mooresville, NC – Armory
EWA
• George South vs Bad Chad

October 20, 2012
Tarboro, NC - Armory
• George South vs Ricky Morton

October 26, 2012
Eden, NC – Event Center
• George South vs Local
October 27, 2012
Spartanburg, SC – APW Arena
APW
• George South vs Jay Eagle

October 31, 2012
Concord, NC – 1st Baptist Church
EWA
• George South vs Jake Manning

November 1, 2012
Rock Hill, SC – YMCA
• George South vs Local

November 2, 2012
Stanley, NC – Birthday Party
• George South vs Baron Bullard

November 3, 2012
Hudson, NC – Rec Center
NAWA
• George South vs Chad Bryd

November 10, 2012
Shelby, NC – High School
• George South vs Mark Henderson

November 17, 2012
Boone, NC – Watauga High School
• George South vs Al Snow

November 22, 2012
Asheboro, NC – Boys Club
• George South vs Local

November 23, 2012
Monroe, NC – Bethel Church
• George South vs Local

November 24, 2012
Kings Mountain, NC – Armory
• George South vs Shane Austin

November 25, 2012
Winston-Salem, NC – Benton Convention Center
WrestleCade SuperShow
AML
• Jimmy Valiant & Manny Fernandez beat George South & Masked Superstar w/ Baby Doll

November 30, 2012
Forest City, NC – Armory
• George South vs Local

December 1, 2012
Belmont, NC - Armory
• George South vs DL Kool

December 2, 2012
Knoxville, TN – Elementary School
• George South vs Dr. Tom Prichard

December 7, 2012
Elkin, NC - Armory
• George South vs Baron Bullard

December 8, 2012
Clayton, NC – Fitness Center
• George South vs Lewis Moore

December 14, 2012
Shelby, NC – Burns Middle School
• American GI beat George South

December 15, 2012
Middletown, OH – Arena
• Bobby Fulton & Tom McClare beat George South & Jake Manning

December 21, 2012
Mooresville, NC - Armory
• George South vs Jake Manning

December 25, 2012
King Mountain, NC – Armory
• George South vs Shane Austin

December 29, 2012
Chesnee, SC – APW Arena
APW
• George South vs Jay Eagle

2013

January 5, 2013
Lexington, VA – Rodeo Arena
• George South vs Zane Riley

January 12, 2013
Roscommon, MI – Bama Lake Club
• George South vs Local

February 2, 2013
Seagrove, NC – Elementary School
• George South & Baron Bullard vs Dawson Brothers

February 9, 2013
Supply, NC – Fire Dept
• George South vs Tre G

February 15, 2013
Lincolnton, NC – Community Center
• George South vs The Barbarian

February 16, 2013
Atlanta, GA – Middle School
• George South vs Kyle Matthews

February 22, 2013
North Wilkesboro, NC – Elementary School
• George South vs Local

February 23, 2013
Clayton, NC – Fitness Center
• George South vs Bunkhouse Buck (Jimmy Golden)

March 1, 2013
Marion, NC – Armory
• George South vs Local

March 2, 2013
Troy, NC – Agee Center
• George South vs Local

March 9, 2013
Princeton, WV – Rec Center
WVCW
• George South vs Eric Lester

March 10, 2013
Dallas, NC – Birthday Party
• George South vs Avenger

March 23, 2013
Thomasville, NC – High School
• George South vs Matt Houston

March 30, 2013
Wentworth, NC – Armory
• George South vs Jimmy Valiant

April 5, 2013
Union, SC – Fairgrounds
Trans South
• George South vs Local

April 6, 2013
Franklin, NC – Elementary School
• George South vs Local

April 13, 2013
South Boston, VA – High School
PXW
• Jimmy Valiant & Zane Riley beat George South & John Skyler

April 19, 2013
Lincolnton, NC – VFW
• George South vs Baron Bullard

April 20, 2013
Randleman, NC – High School
• George South vs Capt. Lou

April 27, 2013
Gastonia, NC – High School
• George South vs Local

May 3, 2013
Charleston, WV – Haunted Barn
• George South vs Local

May 4, 2013
Union, SC - Fairgrounds
• George South vs Local

May 5, 2013
Shawsville, VA – Boogie's Wrestling Camp – 12pm
• George South vs Student

May 5, 2013
Charlotte, NC – Plaza Road Church
• George South vs Student

May 10, 2013
Kings Mountain, NC – Armory
• George South vs Local

May 11, 2013
Gastonia, NC – Birthday Party
• George South vs Jeff Hart

May 11, 2013
Hudson, NC – Rec Center – 8pm
NAWA
• George South vs Chad Bryd

May 18, 2013
Charlotte, NC – Charlotte Motor Speedway – 11am
EWA
• George South vs Avenger

May 18, 2013
Asheboro, NC – Boys Club – 8pm
• George South vs Local

May 24, 2013
Newland, NC – Avery High School
• George South vs Russian Assassin
Note: Special Referee Jimmy Valiant

Highway Run into the Midnight Sun

May 25, 2013
Charlotte, NC – Charlotte Motor Speedway – 11am
EWA
- George South vs Student

May 25, 2013
Kings Mountain, NC – Armory – 8pm
- George South vs Shane Austin

June 1, 2013
Bluefield, WV – City Auditorium
WVCW
- George South & Baron Bullard vs Bunkhouse Boys

June 5, 2013
Wise, VA – Fairgrounds
SSW
- George South vs Beau James

June 6, 2013
Kingsport, TN – Fairgrounds
SSW
- Jimmy Valiant & Ricky Morton beat George South & John Skyler

June 8, 2013
Hudson, NC – Rec Center
NAWA
- George South & Chad Byrd vs The Rock & Roll Express

June 14, 2013
Concord, NC – El Patron Club
- George South vs Local

June 15, 2013
Princeton, WV – Rec Center
WVCW
- George South vs Eric Lester

June 16, 2013
Knoxville, TN – Chilhowee Park
- Tim Horner & Dr. Tom Prichard beat George South & Bob Orton Jr (12:05)
Special Referee: JJ Dillion

June 20, 2013
Morganton, NC - Fairgrounds
BCW
- George South vs Big Donnie Webb

June 22, 2013
Kings Mountain, NC – Church – 11am
- George South vs Shane Austin

June 22, 2013
Kings Mountain, NC – Armory – 8pm
- George South vs Ray Hudson

June 27, 2013
Faith, NC – Fairgrounds
- George South vs Baron Bullard

June 29, 2013
North Wilkesboro, NC – Aarons Renal
- George South vs Chad Byrd

July 4, 2013
Faith, NC - Fairgrounds
- George South vs Ricky Steamboat Jr

July 7, 2013
Cherokee, NC – Gym
• George South vs Ricky Morton

July 13, 2013
Gaffney, SC – Peach Festival
• George South vs Deon Johnson

July 17, 2013
Princeton, WV – 4 H Camp
• George South vs Eric Lester

July 20, 2013
Mocksville, NC – Brock Gym - 2pm
• George South vs Local

July 20, 2013
Asheboro, NC – Boys Club – 8pm
• George South vs Student

July 27, 2013
Clayton, NC -Fitness Center
• George South vs Lewis Moore

August 3, 2013
Charlotte, NC – Hilton Hotel
Mid Atlantic Fan Fest (Greg Price)
• George South vs Jake Manning

August 10, 2013
Princeton, WV – Rec Center
WVCW
• George South vs Eric Lester

August 16, 2013
Charlotte, NC – Freedom Church
EWA
• George South beat Jake Manning

August 17, 2013
Mocksville, NC – Brock Gym
• George South vs Local

August 23, 2013
Winston- Salem, NC – Uncle Frank's Used Cars
• George South vs Ricky Morton

August 24, 2013
Matthews, NC – Eastwood Baptist Church – 12pm
EWA
• George South vs Baron Bullard

August 24, 2013
Kings Mountain, NC – Armory – 8pm
• George South vs Local

August 31, 2014
McAdenville, NC – Armory
• George South vs Ivan Koloff

September 7, 2013
Union, SC – Fairgrounds
Trans South Wrestling
• Deon Johnson beat George South
Note: Special Referee Terry Funk

Highway Run into the Midnight Sun

September 11, 2013
Asheville, NC – Fairgrounds
• George South vs Chad Bryd

September 13, 2013
War, WV – Town Festival
• George South vs Eric Lester

September 14, 2013
Randleman, NC – High School
• George South vs Capt. Lou

September 15, 2013
Knoxville, TN – State Fairgrounds
Tennessee Mountain Wrestling (Terry Landell)
• George South & Tom Prichard vs Bob & Steve Armstrong

September 21, 2013
Asheboro, NC – Southwest High School
• George South vs Jimmy Valiant

September 28, 2013
Hendersonville, NC – High School
• George South vs Viper

October 4, 2013
Tamp, FL – Crossover Church
• George South vs. Bulldog Chad Byrd

October 12, 2013
Charlotte, NC – Charlotte Motor Speedway – 11am
EWA
• George South vs Student

October 12, 2013
Princeton, WV – Rec Center – 8pm
WVCW
• George South vs Eric Lester

October 19, 2013
Troy, NC – Civic Center
• George South vs Johnny Smooth

October 20, 2013
Hudson, NC – Community Center
NAWA (Chad Bryd)
• George South vs. Bulldog Chad Byrd

October 26, 2013
Tarboro, NC – Street Festival
• Ricky Morton beat George South

November 2, 2013
Gauley Bridge, WV – Community Center
WVCW
• George South vs Eric Lester

November 7, 2013
Rock Hill, SC – YMCA
• George South vs Jake Manning

November 9, 2013
Charlotte, NC – Birthday Party – 2pm
• George South beat Barron Bullard

November 9, 2013
Mooresboro, NC – Old Gym – 8pm
EWF
• George South beat Local

November 16, 2013
Rome, GA – High School
• George South vs Local

November 22, 2013
Hickory, NC – Community Center
NAWA
• George South vs Chad Bryd

November 23, 2013
Mooresville, NC – Benchwarmers
• George South beat Tony Benge

November 28, 2013
Asheboro, NC – Boys & Girls Club
• George South vs Local

November 30, 2013
Winston-Salem, NC – Benton Convention Center
WrestleCade SuperShow
AML
• Tag Team Gauntlet: Caprice Coleman & Cedric Alexander beat George South & Manny Fernandez,
Demolition, Powers of Pain, The Head Bangers &The Rock & Roll Express w/ Jimmy Valiant (58:02)

December 1, 2013
Albemarle, NC – Waddell Center
• George South vs Local

December 7, 2013
Clayton, NC – Fitness Center
• George South & B Brian Blair vs The Rock & Roll Express

December 13, 2013
Lincolnton, NC Elementary School
• George South vs Jim Heafner

December 14, 2013
Fallston, NC – Burns Middle School
• George South vs Tim Hunter

December 21, 2013
Spartanburg, SC – Fire Dept
• George South beat Jake Manning

December 25, 2013
Kings Mountain, NC – Armory
NMCW
George South vs Local

December 28, 2013
Mooresboro, NC – Old Gym
EWF
• George South vs Local

2014

January 4, 2014
Asheboro, NC – Boys Club
• George South vs Baron Bullard

January 11, 2014
Princeton, WV – Rec Center
• George South vs Eric Lester

February 1, 2014
Seagrove, NC – Elementary School
EWA
• George South vs Baron Bullard

February 8, 2014
Princeton, WV – Rec Center
• George South vs Eric Lester

February 9, 2014
Asheboro, NC – Boys Club
• George South vs Baron Bullard

February 28, 2014
Spartanburg, SC – Memorial Auditorium
Big Time Wrestling
• Kenny James beat George South

March 1, 2014
Mooresboro, NC – Old Gym
EWF
• George South vs Local

March 8, 2014
Thomasville, NC – High School
• George South vs Matt Houston

March 15, 2014
Rhonda, NC – Community Center
NEW
• George South vs Local

March 29, 2014
Clayton, NC – Fitness Center
Ivan Koloff Tag Team Tournament

April 5, 2014
Bluefield, WV – Auditorium
WVCW
• George South vs Eric Lester

April 11, 2014
War, WV – Elementary School
WVCW
• George South vs Eric Lester

April 12, 2004
Princeton, WV - Rec Center
WVCW TV Taping
• George South vs Eric Lester

April 19, 2014
Rhonda, NC – Community Center
NEW
• George South vs. Lil Donnie

April 25, 2014
Fayetteville, NC – Rock Shop
• George South vs Rob McBride

April 26, 2014
Gastonia, NC – High School
• George South vs John Skyler

May 2, 2014
Fort Mill, SC – Walter Elisha Park
Strawberry Festival (Chad Adams)
• George South vs American GI

May 3, 2014
Fort Mill, SC – Walter Elisha Park
Strawberry Festival (Chad Adams)
• George South & Barbarian vs Rock & Roll Express

May 4, 2014
Charlotte, NC – Player Road Church
EWA
• George South beat Jimmy Jack Funk Jr

May 8, 2014
Denver, NC – Elementary School
• George South vs Local

May 10, 2014
Princeton, WV – Rec Center
• George South vs Benny Conley

May 17, 2014
Charlotte, NC – Charlotte Motor Speedway
EWA
• George South vs Baron Bullard

May 24, 2014
Charlotte, NC – Charlotte Motor Speedway
EWA
• George South vs Student

May 31, 2014
Bluefield, WV – Auditorium
WVCW
• George South vs Eric Lester

June 1, 2014
Hickory, NC – LP Frans Stadium
Big Time Wrestling
• Rock & Roll Express & Jimmy Valiant beat George South, Danny Mills & Tiny Lester

June 6, 2014
Lumberton, NC – POW Arena
• George South vs. Ty Tyson

June 7, 2014
Wallace, NC – Rec Center
• George South vs Baron Bullard

June 14, 2014
Rhonda, NC – Community Center
NEW
• George South vs Local

June 21, 2014
Kings Mountain, NC - Armory
• George South vs Ray Hudson

June 22, 2014
Asheville, NC – Tato Express
• George South vs Ricky Morton

July 4, 2014
Faith, NC – Fairgrounds
• George South vs Baron Bullard

July 5, 2014
Union, SC – Fairgrounds
Trans South
• George South vs Local

July 11, 2014
Matska, WV – Rec Center
• George South vs Eric Lester

July 12, 2014
Princeton, WV – Church of God – 2pm
• George South vs Eric Lester

July 12, 2014
Princeton, WV – Rec Center
• George South vs Hobo Joe

July 13, 2014
Knoxville, TN – Civic Center
• George South vs The Juicer

July 18, 2014
Fayetteville, NC – Rock Shop
• George South vs The G

July 19, 2014
Gaffney, SC – Peach Festival
• George South vs Deon Johnson

July 23, 2014
Princeton, WV – 4 H Camp
• George South vs Eric Lester

July 24, 2014
Somerset, KY – Fairgrounds
SSW
• George South vs Scott Cash

July 26, 2014
Kings Mountain, NC – Armory
• George South vs Local

August 8, 2014
Rhonda, NC – Community Center
NEW
• George South vs James Brody

August 9, 2014
Gaffney, SC - Auditorium
• George South vs Local

August 16, 2014
Dallas, NC – Birthday Party
• George South vs Carl Styles

August 16, 2014
Clayton, NC – Fitness Center – 8pm
NCWA
• Rock & Roll Express beat George South & George South Jr

August 22, 2014
Hickory, NC – Fairgrounds
• George South vs Adam James

August 23, 2014
Summerville, SC – Mills Road Baptist Church
• George South vs Local

August 28, 2014
Morganton, NC – Fairgrounds
BCW
• George South & Bobby Eaton beat Big Donnie Webb & James Brody

August 30, 2014
Elkin, NC – Armory
EWA
• George South drew Tessa Blanchard (60:00)

September 6, 2014
Union, SC – Fairgrounds
Trans South
• George South vs Anthony Henry

September 10, 2014
Concord, NC – Friendship Church
EWA
• George South vs Jake Manning

September 13, 2014
Princeton, WV – Rec Center
• George South vs Roger Hamm

September 14, 2014
Charlotte, NC – AME Church
EWA
• George South vs Baron Bullard

September 20, 2014
Bridge, MI – High School
• George South vs Bobby Fulton

September 27, 2014
Clayton, NC – Fitness Center
• George South vs Lewis Moore

October 3, 2014
North Wilkesboro, NC – Fairgrounds
NEW
• George South vs Local

October 4, 2014
Mocksville, NC - Armory
• George South vs Gladiator

October 5, 2014
Charlotte, NC – Birthday Party
• George South vs Student

October 9, 2014
Union, SC - Armory
• George South vs Deon Johnson

October 11, 2014
Charlotte, NC – Charlotte Motor Speedway – 10am
• George South vs Gladiator

October 11, 2014
Asheboro, NC – Boys Club – 8pm
• George South vs

October 17, 2014
Union, SC – Fairgrounds
Trans South
• George South vs Deon Johnson

October 18, 2014
Rhonda, NC – Community Center
NEW
• George South vs Local

October 25, 2014
Forest City, NC - Armory
• George South vs Local

October 31, 2014
Tarboro, NC – Piggy Wiggly – 2pm
• George South vs Ricky Morton

October 31, 2014
Tarboro, NC - Church
• George South vs Robert Gibson

November 1, 2014
Williamston, NC – 1st Baptist Church
EWA
• George South vs Ricky Morton

November 8, 2014
Princeton, WV – Rec Center
• George South vs Eric Lester

November 15, 2014
Gaffney, SC – Auditorium
• George South vs Mick Foley
• George South & Baron Bullard vs Mick Foley & Deon Johnson

November 22, 2014
Kings Mountain, NC – Armory
• George South vs Ray Hudson

November 27, 2014
Asheboro, NC – Boys Club
• George South vs Bobby Fulton

November 29, 2014
Winston-Salem, NC – Benton Convention Center
WrestleCade SuperShow
AML
• Fatal Four Way Tag Team: Rick & Scott Steiner beat George South & Dr. Tom Prichard, The Rock & Roll Express &The Faces of Fear
(Meng & The Barbarian)

December 5, 2014
Laurens, SC – Exchange Building
• George South vs Jaxon James

December 6, 2014
Jonesville, SC – Old Gym
• George South vs Local

December 13, 2014
Clayton, NC – Fitness Center
• George South vs Local

December 19, 2014
Shelby, NC – Burns Middle School
• George South vs Chris Thunder Anderson

December 27, 2014
Rhonda, NC – Community Center
NEW
• George South vs Local

2015

January 9, 2015
Morganton, NC – Collett St. Rec
Big Time Wrestling
• George South beat Cousin Larry

January 10, 2015
Spartanburg, SC – Memorial Auditorium
Big Time Wrestling
• George South beat Cousin Larry

January 25, 2015
Winston-Salem, NC – AML Arena
AML (Tracey Myers)
• Bunkhouse Buck (Jimmy Golden) beat George South

January 31, 2015
Seagrove, NC – Elementary School
EWA
• George South beat Jake Manning

February 7, 2015
Union, SC - Fairgrounds
Trans South
• George South vs Chase Brown

February 15, 2015
Winston-Salem, NC – AML Arena
AML
• Tracey Smothers beat George South

February 20, 2015
Bristol, TN – Vance Middle School
Big Time Wrestling
• Jimmy Valiant beat George South

February 22, 2015
Bluefield, WV – Armory
Big Time Wrestling
• Jimmy Valiant beat George South

February 27, 2105
Albemarle, NC – Rec Center
• George South vs Freight Train

February 28, 2015
Spindale, NC – Armory
EWF
• George South vs Chris Hamrick

March 6, 2015
Senera, SC – Baptist Church
• George South vs Jake James

March 7, 2015
Thomasville, NC – Middle School
• George South vs Jimmy Valiant

March 14, 2015
Shelby, NC – Crest High School
• George South vs Deon Johnson

March 22,2015
Winston-Salem, NC – Johnny & Junes
AML
• Managed Zane Dawson

March 28, 2015
Gastonia, NC - Birthday Party
• George South beat Gladiator

April 4, 2015
Clayton, NC – Fitness Center
• George South vs Bobby Fulton

April 11, 2015
Kernersville, NC – Community Center
• George South beat The G

April 18, 2015
Gastonia, NC – High School
• The Barbarian beat George South

April 19, 2015
Winston-Salem, NC – Johnny & Junes
AML
• Managed Zan Dawson

April 24, 2015
Lincolnton, NC - High School
• Jimmy Valiant & Jim Heafer beat George South & Baron Bullard

April 25, 2015
Rhonda, NC – Community Center
NEW
• George South vs James Brody

May 1, 2015
Fort Mill, SC – Walter Elisha Park
Strawberry Festival (Chad Adams)
• George South & The Barbarian vs AWOL

May 2, 2015
Fort Mill, SC – Walter Elisha Park
Strawberry Festival (Chad Adams)
• George South & The Barbarian vs The Rock & Roll Express

May 8, 2015
Oakwood, VA – Middle School
• George South vs Ricky Morton

May 9, 2015
Lawrenceville, VA – High School
• George South vs The Patriot

May 16, 2015
Charlotte, NC – Charlotte Motor Speedway – 10am
EWA
• George South vs Carl Styles

May 16, 2015
Rhonda, NC – Rec Center
NEW
• George South vs James Brody

May 23, 2015
Charlotte, NC – Charlotte Motor Speedway
EWA
• George South vs Carl Styles

May 24, 2015
Winston-Salem, NC – Johnny & Junes
AML
• Managed The Heatseekers

May 29, 2015
Dallas, NC – AME Zion Church
• George South vs Johnny Smooth

May 30, 2015
Lenoir, NC – WPHC – 3pm
• George South vs DL Kool

May 30, 2015
Gastonia, NC – Armory – 8pm
• George South vs Baron Bullard

June 6, 2015
Bluefield, WV – Auditorium
WVCW
• George South vs Joey Morton

June 13, 2015
Cheraw, NC – Armory
• George South vs American GI

June 19, 2015
Rhonda, NC – Rec Center
NEW
• George South vs. Wildman James Brody

June 26, 2015
Faith, NC - Fairgrounds
• George South vs Carl Styles

June 27, 2015
Clayton, NC – Fitness Center
NCWA
• George South vs. Ricky Steamboat

June 28, 2015
Winston-Salem, NC – Johnny & Junes
AML
• Managed Zane Dawson

July 4, 2015
Faith, NC – Fairgrounds
• George South vs Eric Lester

July 11, 2015
Princeton, WV – Church of God – 11am
WVCW
• George South vs Eric Lester

July 11, 2015
Princeton, WV – Rec Center – 8pm
WVCW
• George South vs Frank Parker

July 21, 2015
Gastonia, NC – Armory
• George South & The Barbarian beat George South Jr &?

July 23, 2015
Somerset, KY – Fairgrounds
SSW
• George South vs Scott Cash

July 24, 2015
Rhonda, NC – Rec Center
NEW
• George South vs. White Mike

July 26, 2015
Winston-Salem, NC – Johnny & Junes
AML
• Managed Zane Dawson

August 1, 2015
Princeton, WV – Rec Center
WVCW
• George South vs Jason Kincaid

August 8, 2015
Forest City, NC – Armory
EWF
• George South vs Student

August 15, 2015
Hickory, NC - Fairgrounds
• George South & Chad Bryd vs Adam James & Randy Sledge

August 16, 2015
Huntington, WV – Roller Rink
• George South vs Al Snow
• George South vs Dan Severn

August 22, 2015
Charlotte, NC – AME Zion Church
EWA
• George South vs Student

August 30, 2015
Winston-Salem, NC – AML Arena
AML
• George South w/ Barron Bullard, De Mack & Zane Dawson beat George South Jr (10:04)

September 5, 2015
Union, SC – Fairgrounds
Trans South
• George South vs Deon Johnson

September 11, 2015
Troutman, NC – Fairgrounds
EWA
• George South vs Mr. Florida

September 19, 2015
Mocksville, NC - Armory
• George South vs Local

September 24, 2015
Ellenburg, NC - Fairgrounds
• George South vs Ricky Steamboat Jr

September 26, 2015
Rhonda, NC – Community Cener
NEW
• George South vs Mitch Blake

September 27, 2015
Winston-Salem, NC – Johnny & Junes
AML
• George South vs Local

Highway Run into the Midnight Sun

September 30, 2015
Shelby, NC – Fairgrounds
• George South vs Local

October 2, 2015
Alma, GA – High School
• George South vs Local

October 3, 2015
Hartsville, SC – TB Thomas Sports Center
• George South vs Tommy Rich

October 7, 2015
Shelby, NC - Dixie Co Fairgrounds
EWF
• George South vs Local

October 10, 2015
Charlotte, NC – Charlotte Motor Speedway – 10am
EWA
• George South vs Darius Lockhart

October 10, 2015
Stuart, VA – High School
• George South vs Stan Lee

October 17, 2015
High Point, NC – Rec Center
AML
• Managed Zane Dawson

October 24, 2015
Drexel, NC – R.O. Huffman Center
Western Carolina Pro Wrestling (Jason Freeman)
• George South beat Man Scout Jake Manning

October 25, 2015
Winston-Salem, NC – Johnny & Junes
AML
• George South vs George South Jr

October 28, 2015
Concord, NC – Friendship Church
EWA
• George South vs Jake Manning

October 31, 2015
West Oak, SC – Middle School
• George South vs Ricky Morton

November 13, 2015
Chester, SC – APW Arena
APW
• George South &? vs Rock & Roll Express

Match # 6,000
November 14, 2015
Shelby, NC – Crest Middle School
Hardcore Championship Wrestling (Rex Rumble)
• George South beat Chris Anderson

November 20, 2015
Norfolk, VA – The Scope
Big Time Wrestling
• George South vs Terry Morris

November 21, 2015
Powhatan, VA – High School
Big Time Wrestling
• George South & Bam Bam Shaw vs Rock & Roll Express

November 26, 2015
Asheboro, NC – Rec Center
• George South vs Jake Manning

November 28, 2015
Winston-Salem, NC – Benton Convention Center
WrestleCade Supershow
• George South vs Masked Superstar

December 4, 2015
Concord, NC – CC Griffin Middle School
EWA
• George South beat Jake Manning

December 12, 2015
Drexel, NC – R.O. Huffman Center
WCPW/NAWA (Jason Freeman)
• George South & Elliott Russell beat Movie Myk & Big Time Yah

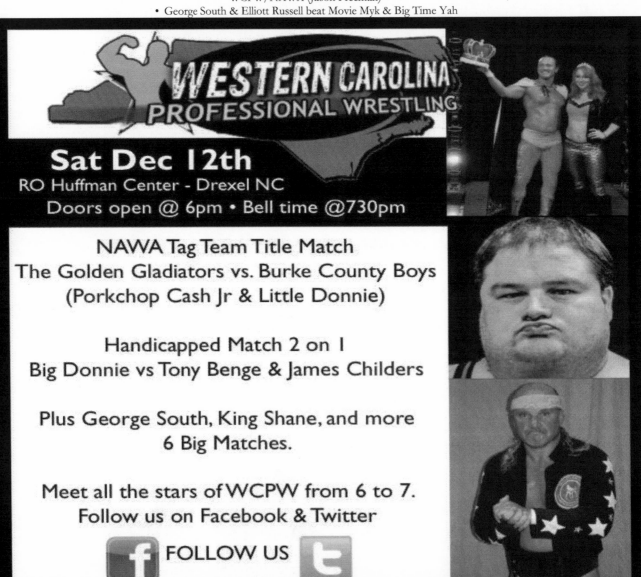

2016

January 3, 2016
Asheboro, NC – Boys & Girl Club
• George South vs Bobby Fulton

January 8, 2016
Rhonda, NC – Community Center
NEW
• George South beat White Mike

January 30, 2016
Winston-Salem, NC – Fairgrounds
AML
• Managed: Zane Dawson vs. Damien Wayne
• Managed: Barron Bullard & Dee Mack vs. The Washington Bullets

February 6, 2016
Seagrove, NC – Elementary School
EWA
• George South vs Jimmy Valiant

February 26, 2016
Raleigh, NC – Dorton Arena
Big Time Wrestling
• George South vs Gladiator

February 28, 2016
High Point, NC – Southside Rec Center
AML
• Loser Leaves Town: George South & Zane Dawson beat Baron Bullard & Dee Mack

March 5, 2016
Drexel, NC – R.O. Huffman Center
NAWA
• George South beat Bulldog Chad Bryd w/ The Perfect 10 Baby Doll

March 12, 2016
Pickens, SC – Middle School
• George South vs Local

March 18, 2016
Thomasville, NC – Middle School
• George South vs Chase Stevens

March 19, 2016
Gastonia, NC – Westend Hardware
EWA
• George South vs Ian Maxwell

March 20, 2016
Clayton, NC – Fitness Center
• George South vs Dave Dawson

March 26, 2016
Yadkinville, NC – Elementary School
AML
• Managed Zane Dawson

April 1, 2016
Dallas, NC – Zion AME Church
EWA
• George South vs Gladiator

April 2, 2016
Drexel, NC – R.O. Huffman Center
NAWA
• George South & Deon Johnson beat Bryson Willis & Masked Intern # 3

April 9, 2016
Mocksville, NC – Armory
• George South vs. Adam James
Note: Terry Funk Day

April 16, 2016
Gastonia, NC – High School
• George South & Barron Bullard vs The Rock & Roll Express

April 23, 2016
Winston-Salem, NC – High School
AML
• Managed Zane Dawson

April 30, 2016
Cylde, NC – Armory
George South beat American GI

May 6, 2016
Fort Mill, SC – Walter Elisha Park
Strawberry Festival (Chad Adams)
• George South vs Deon Johnson

May 7, 2016
Fort Mill, SC – Walter Elisha Park
Strawberry Festival (Chad Adams)
• George South & The Sheik vs The Rock & Roll Express

May 13, 2016
Shelby, NC – Burns High School
New Blood (Rex Rumble)
• George South vs Chris Thunder Anderson

May 14, 2016
Lincolnton, NC – High School
New Blood
• George South &? vs Rock & Roll Express

May 15, 2016
Hickory, Nc – Convention Center
AML
• Managed Zane Dawson

May 21, 2016
Charlotte, NC – Charlotte Motor Speedway – 10am
EWA
• George South vs Randall Eaton

May 21, 2016
Drexel, NC – R.O. Huffman Center
NAWA
• George South beat Masked Intern # 4

May 28, 2016
Charlotte, NC – Charlotte Motor Speedway
EWA
• George South vs Joe Greene

June 5, 2016
High Point, NC – Birthday Party
• George South vs Movie Mky

June 19, 2016
Cheoapeke, WV – Memorial Complex
• George South vs Eric Darkstorm

June 25, 2016
Morganton, NC – Rec Center
• George South vs Barron Bullard

June 26, 2016
High Point, NC – Boys & Girls Club
AML
• Managed Zane Dawson

July 27, 2016
Princeton, WV – 4-H Camp
• George South vs Eric Lester

July 29, 2016
Rhonda, NC – Community Center
NEW
• George South beat Mitch Blake

July 30, 2016
Conedella, GA – Rec Center
George South vs Tracer X

July 31, 2016
Clemmons, NC – Old Gym
AML
• Managed Zane Dawson

August 3, 2016
Tazwell, VA – Fairgrounds
• Jimmy Valiant beat George South

August 6, 2016
Charlotte, NC – Hilton Hotel
Mid Atlantic Fan Fest (Greg Price)
• George South vs Jared Frity

August 13, 2016
Spring Hill, WV – Mnt. Heights Church
• George South vs Brad Thomas

August 17, 2016
Charlotte, NC – Freedom Church
EWA
• George South beat Jake Manning

August 20, 2016
Lenoir, NC – Armory
NAWA
• George South beat Golden Gladiator # 2

August 27, 2016
Mocksville, NC – High School
AML
• Managed Zane Dawson

September 1, 2016
Morganton, NC – Burke Co Fairgrounds
NAWA
• Tony Benge beat George South

September 10, 2016
Seneca, SC – 1st Baptist Church
• George South & Barron Bullard vs Lodi & Scotty Matthews

September 18, 2016
Albemarle, NC – Waddell Center
• Freight Train beat George South

September 22, 2016
Morganton, NC – Rec Center
Big Time Wrestling
• George South vs Golden Gladiator

September 23, 2016
Raleigh, NC – Dorton Arena
Big Time Wrestling
• Jimmy Valiant & The Rock & Roll Express beat George South, Mr. TA & Gladiator

September 24, 2016
Clayton, NC – Bike Fest
• Ricky Morton & Jimmy Valiant beat George South &?

October 1, 2016
Drexel, NC – R.O. Huffman Center
NAWA
• Big Time Yah beat George South

October 8, 2016
Lenoir, NC – Armory
NAWA
• 6 Man Tag: George South, Big Donnie & Zack Jackson beat The Phoenix Brothers & Little Donnie

October 22, 2016
High Point, NC – Southside Rec Center
AML
• 4 on 3 Handicap Match: The Expendables (George South, Matt Sigmon, Elliott Russell & Zane Dawson
beat Cam Carter, James Ryan & LaBron Kozone

November 5, 2016
Drexel, NC – R.O. Huffman Center
NAWA
• George South & Big Donnie beat Logan Murphy & Colt Belk

November 12, 2016
Sugar Grove, NC – Old Cove Creek Gym
NAWA
• Golden Gladiator # 2 & Tony Benge beat George South & James Brody

November 18, 2016
Beech Mountain, NC – Rec Center
• George South vs Ricky Morton

November 19, 2016
Cherryville, NC – Nixon Gym
• George South vs Ricky Morton

November 24, 2016
Asheboro, NC – High school
• George South beat Harley Dean

November 26, 2016
Winston-Salem, NC – Benton Convention Center
WrestleCade SuperShow
AML
• CW Anderson, Jack Victory, Steve Corino & The Geordie Bulldogs beat George South, Zane Dawson, Elliott Russell, Matt Sigmon &
Zane Riley
• 3rd Annual George South Battle Royal: winner George South

December 3, 2016
Drexel, NC – R.O. Huffman Center
NAWA
- 6 Man Tag: George South, Jimmy Valiant & Deon Johnson beat Golden Gladiator # 2, Thurston Cogdell III & Logan Murphy

December 17, 2016
High Point, NC – Southside Rec Center
EWA
- George South & Brian Hawks beat The Golden Gladiators

2017

January 28, 2017
Winston-Salem, NC – Fairgrounds
AML
• Managed: The Expendables (Zane Dawson, Elliott Russell & Matt Sigmon) vs. Shane Williams & The Geordie Bulldogs

February 4, 2017
Seagrove, NC – Elementary School
EWA
• EWA World Title: George South* beat Johnny Smooth

February 10, 2017
Raleigh, NC – Dorton Arena
Big Time Wrestling
• Wildfire Tommy Rich beat George South

February 11, 2017
Spartanburg, SC – Memorial Auditorium
Big Time Wrestling
• Wildfire Tommy Rich beat George South

February 12, 2017
Rock Hill, SC – American Legion
• Ricky Morton beat George South

February 25, 2017
Winston-Salem, NC – Fairgrounds
AML
• Managed: Zane Dawson vs. King Shane Williams w/ Queen Taylor
Note: Dawson won the AML Heavyweight Title

March 4, 2017
Drexel, NC – R.O. Huffman Center
NAWA
• George South beat Little Donnie

March 10, 2017
Morganton, NC – Collett St. Rec
Big Time Wrestling
• Tony Atlas beat George South

March 11, 2017
Bluefield, WV – Armory
Big Time Wrestling
• Tony Atlas beat George South

March 17, 2017
Thomasville, NC – Middle School
• Shane Douglas beat George South

March 18, 2017
Clayton, NC – Fitness Center
NCWA
• George South beat Dave Dawson

March 25, 2017
Thomasville, NC – East Davidson High School
AML
• Ian Maxwell, Big Time Yah & Caprice Coleman beat George South, Elliott Russell & Matt Sigmon
• Managed: Zane Dawson

March 26, 2017
Franklinton, NC Middle School
• George South beat Student

April 22, 2107
Gastonia, NC – High School
• George South vs Chris Hamrick

April 23, 2017
Winston-Salem, NC – Armory
AML
• Managed: Zane Dawson

April 28, 2017
Fayetteville, NC – Rock Shop
• George South beat James Drake

April 29, 2017
Drexel, NC – R.O. Huffman Center
NAWA
• George South beat Big Time Yah

May 5, 2017
Fort Mill, SC – Walter Elisha Park
Strawberry Festival (Chad Adams)
• George South beat Deon Johnson

May 6, 2017
Fort Mill, SC – Walter Elisha Park
Strawberry Festival (Chad Adams)
• Al Snow & The Rock & Roll Express beat George South, The Barbarian & Zane Riley

May 19, 2017
Asheboro, NC – High School
• George South vs Matt Houston

May 20, 2017
Lenoir, NC – Armory
NAWA
• NAWA Tag Team Title: George South & Golden Gladiator # 2* w/ Thurston Cogdell III
beat Sweet Dreamz & Myles Long

May 21, 2017
Burlington, NC – Youth Center
• George South vs. Rob McBride

May 22, 2017
Lincolnton, NC – North Brook Elementary School
• George South beat Jim Heafner

May 27, 2017
Charlotte, NC – Charlotte Motor Speedway
EWA
• George South beat Jake Manning

May 28, 2017
Yadkinville, NC – Elementary School
AML
• Managed Zane Dawson

June 3, 2017
Bluefield, WV – Auditorium
WVCW
• George South vs Benny Conley

June 16, 2017
Hickory, NC – Church Softball Field
EWA
• George South beat Jake Manning

June 25, 2017
Hickory, NC – Convection Center
AML
• Managed The Heatseekers
• Managed Zane Dawson

July 26, 2017
Princeton, WV – 4-H Club
• George South vs Eric Lester

July 30, 2017
Lexington, NC – Middle School
AML
• Managed The Heatseekers
• Managed Zane Dawson

August 4, 2017
Lenoir, NC – American Legion Hall
NAWA
• NAWA Tag Team Title: Big Donnie & James Brody beat George South & Golden Gladiator # 2*
and Bunkhouse Buck & KL3 to win the tag team titles.

August 11, 2017
Dallas, NC – AME Zion Church
EWA
• George South beat Yoda

Match # 6,1000
August 12, 2017
Salem, VA – Salem Red Sox Baseball Stadium
Big Time Wrestling
• Ricky Morton & Jimmy Valiant beat George South & Ian Brown

August 26, 2017
Lexington, NC – Middle School
AML
• Managed The Heatseekers
• Managed Zane Dawson

September 8, 2017
War, WV – Main Street
WVCW
• George South vs. Brad Thomas

September 22, 2017
Raleigh, NC – Dorton Arena
Big Time Wrestling
• Tommy Rich beat George South

September 23, 2017
Spartanburg, SC – Memorial Auditorium
Big Time Wrestling
• Jimmy Valiant, Ian Brown & Danny Miles beat George South, Zane Riley & Elite 19

September 30, 2017
Thomasville, NC – High School
AML
• Managed The Heatseekers
• Managed Zane Dawson

October 7, 2017
Charlotte, NC – Charlotte Motor Speedway – 11am
• EWA
George South vs Super Destroyer

October 7, 2017
Clayton, NC – Fitness Center – 8pm
• George South vs Dave Dawson

October 28, 2017
Winston-Salem, NC – Fairgrounds
AML
• Managed The Heatseekers
• Managed Zane Dawson

November 4, 2017
Kinston, NC – Armory
• George South vs The G

November 24, 2017
Winston-Salem, NC – Benton Convention Center
3rd Annual Showcase of Champions
AML
Managed: Zane Dawson vs. Bu Ku Dao

November 25, 2017
Winston-Salem, NC – Benton Convention Center
WrestleCade SuperShow
AML
• Jerry Lawler beat George South (8:13)

December 2, 2017
Drexel, NC – R.O. Huffman Center
NAWA
• George South beat Chris "Thunder" Anderson

December 15, 2017
Charlotte, NC – CC Griffin Middle School
EWA
• George South Sr, George South Jr & Dallas South beat White Mike, Timmy Lou & Ian Brown

December 23, 2017
Forest City, NC – Armory
EWF
• George South beat Cruiser Lewis

2018

January 27, 2018
Winston-Salem, NC – Benton Convention Center
AML
- Managed: Zane Dawson
- Managed The Heatseekers

February 3, 2018
Seagrove, NC – Elementary School
EWA
George South beat Manscout Jake Manning

February 23, 2018
Chase, NC – Chase High School
EWF
- Jimmy Valiant & Mickey Richards beat George South & Deon Johnson

February 25, 2018
Winston-Salem, NC – Benton Convention Center
AML
- Managed: Zane Dawson
- Managed: The Heatseekers

March 2, 2018
Pembroke, NC – Boys Club
Wrestling With Purpose (Barron Bullard)
- George South beat Johnny Smooth

March 3, 2018
Roanoke Rapids, NC – High School
- George South vs. Preston Quin

March 10, 2018
Madison, WV – Civic Center
ASW
- George South vs. Al Snow

March 24, 2018
Clayton, NC – Fitness Center
NCWA
- George South vs. Dave Dawson

March 31, 2018
Yadkinville, NC – Elementary School
AML
- Managed: AML World Champion Zane Dawson

April 13, 2018
Thomasville, NC – Middle School
North Carolina Wrestling Alliance
- Shane Douglas beat George South

April 14, 2018
Gastonia, NC – Forest View High School
Super Star Wars Wrestling
- George South & Chris Hamrick beat Barron Bullard & Johnny Smooth

April 20, 2018
Walhalla, SC – Middle School
- George South vs. Stan Lee

April 27, 2018
Maxton, NC – Elementary School
Wrestling With Purpose (Barron Bullard)
• George South beat Chief Red Thunder

April 28, 2018
Dallas, NC – Ole Dallas Brewery
Carolina All-Star Wrestling (Mike Ramsey)
EWA World Title: Movie Myk beat George South* (count out)

April 29, 2018
Thomasville, NC – East Davidson High School
AML
• Managed: AML World Champion Zane Dawson beat Fallah Bahh

May 4, 2018
Fort Mill, SC – Walter Elisha Park
Strawberry Festival (Chad Adams)
• George South beat Deon Johnson

May 5, 2018
Fort Mill, SC – Walter Elisha Park
Strawberry Festival (Chad Adams)
• Rock & Roll Express, Jimmy Valiant & Bobby Fulton beat George South, Zane Riley, The Barbarian & Elliott Russell
• George South & Elliott Russell beat The Soul Patrol

May 12, 2018
Denton, NC – South Davidson High School
EWA
• George South beat Movie Myk

May 18, 2018
Winston-Salem, NC – Fairgrounds
AML
• Managed: The Heatsekers vs. Extreme Horsemen (CW Anderson& Damien Wayne)
• Managed: Zane Dawson vs. Caleb Konley

May 19, 2018
Charlotte, NC – Charlotte Motor Speedway
EWA
• George South beat J. D. Dirt

May 26, 2018
Charlotte, NC – Charlotte Motor Speedway
EWA
• George South beat The Assassin

June 2, 2018
Bluefield, WV – Auditorium
WVCW
George South & vs. Ricky Morton & CW Anderson

June 9, 2018
Lenoir, NC – American Legion Hall
NAWA
• Golden Gladiator # 2 beat George South (12:03)

June 24, 2018
Winston-Salem, NC - Benton Convention Center
AML
• Managed: Dawson Brothers & Zane Riley vs.

June 30, 2018
Dallas, NC – Ole Dallas Brewery
Carolina All-Star Wrestling (Mike Ramsey)
• George South Sr & George South Jr beat Mean Mark& Yoda

July 18, 2018
Princeton, WV – 4-H Camp
WV TV Title Tournament:
- George South beat Eric Laster
- Finals: George South beat David Anthony to win the WV TV Title.

July 21, 2018
Hudson, NC – Hometown Pharmacy – 11am
NAWA
- Battle Royal

July 21, 2018
Marion, NC – Southeast Fitness – 7pm
NAWA
- Battle Royal

July 29, 2018
Greensboro, NC – Triad Stage
AML/ IMPACT
- Managed: Zane Dawson vs. Fallah Bahh

August 4, 2018
Morganton, NC – Burke Co. Fairgrounds
NAWA
- George South beat Golden Gladiator # 2 (0.06)
- George South beat Golden Gladiator # 2 (0.12)
- George South beat Golden Gladiator # 2 (7:09)

August 10, 2018
Pembroke, NC – Middle School
WWP
- George South vs. Chief Red Thunder

August 11, 2018
Madison, WV – Civic Center
ASW
- George South vs. Blazin' Eagle

August 18, 2018
Lenoir, NC – American Legon Hall
NAWA
- Golden Gladiator # 2 & Boris Baronov beat George South & Lucky Ali

August 26, 2018
Lexington, NC – Parks & Rec
AML
- Managed Zane Dawson

September 28, 2018
Casear, NC – Men's Center
EWA
- George South beat Randy Sledge

September 29, 2018
Charlotte, NC – Charlotte Motor Speedway
EWA
- George South beat Joe Dirt

October 6, 2018
Lenoir, NC – American Legion
NAWA
- Managed Stuart Snodgrass
- Loser Wears a Dress: George South beat Golden Gladiator # 2
- Phoenix Brothers Battle Royal

October 20, 2018
Clayton, NC – Fitness Center
• Managed Dawson Brothers

Match # 6,165
October 27, 2018
Winston-Salem, NC – Armory
AML
• George South vs Elliott Russell

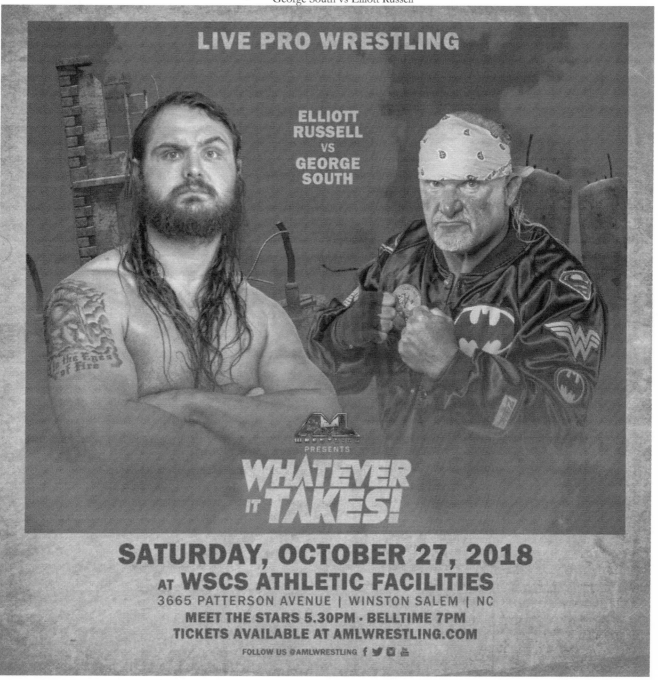

Quotes about George…..

" I always considered George a 4- Horseman, we beat him up every week. " -
J.J. Dillon   October 22, 2018

The 3 things that matter in George Souths life:
1) God
2) Family
3) Wrestling
I'm very proud to call him a friend, and I know if I ever needed anything, he'd be there without hesitation.
Ricky " The Dragon " Steamboat

"Between me and Chuck Coates, we've got about 5 matches" (gimmicks)

"I love wrestling, but I love telling fans about Jesus more"

"Stallion, you better not hit me like that or I'll work with the lady in the front row for 30 minutes"

"There might be a foot of snow out there, but this is a sold out show. We ain't canceling JACK"!

One of the wrestlers on a show was doing a psycho mad man type gimmick and George said
"Brother with the hatchet asked me to pray for him, then he tried to cast a spell on me"

Talking to me one night after a show "Maxx, the House was down tonight and we can't pay you,but we did hook you a live Christmas tree"
This is a shoot 😅

Chuck Coates- Mad Max - Russian Assassin - etc etc etc

In 43 years of wrestling…George has remained one of my best friends….We had some knock down dragouts thru the years and I would have not missed a minute of it,,,,,…love you brother…..Eagle
Chief Jay Eagle

I was there the day George started. He has always been a real sweetheart and a very talented pro grappler. Everyone love to work with him then and almost 40 years later that's still true. I remember when he worked Channel 17 TBS Superstation in Atlanta. That cable went all over the world. George South had a barn-burning with world champion, Ric Flair. Angel and I just love him and appreciate the work that you both give us. Most of all we're proud to call him our loyal friend.
Jimmy Boogie Woogie Man Valiant

George South had Mabel and I in a back corner of the dressing room in 1993 Kings Mountain National Guard Armory. He was always saying go to Memphis boys that's where it starts, Italian Stallion walks in and says George whatta u doing boii? Lol (Stallion didn't like George encouraging us to leave. But we left anyways. We always tell people it was George who was instrumental in us getting to WWE. He taught us all of our tag team combinations.
Sir Mo WWF Tag Team Champion

When I first met George South I knew he would make it big in our sport. He had the drive and determination that very few rookies exhibit…and by the thousands upon thousands of his matches proves my point not to mention how many world championship and big names requested him for their opponent, including Ric Flair…he is a true credit to pro wrestling, in more ways than one as he is not ashamed to tell you about his Lord and Savior Jesus Christ….proud to call Mr. #1 a brother and a friend…….
Beast Master Rick Link

I started working with George in 1991-92 with the PWF. From the first time I met him I knew there was gonna be a bond and not just in the wrestling business. I am also a Christian first who just happens to wrestle. George, as most people in the business know, is all about getting everything done (setting up the ring/chairs) in a timely manner. He would then disappear for a while and have his alone time with Jesus. That was when I knew we had a bond, a brotherhood that some might not understand. He is still one of my best friends (in and out of the ring) today…..
Richie Scruggs American GI

PWF Story….sitting in PWF Training center in Charlotte on a Thursday night. George sitting next to me. Doc Feel Good an Pony(Carolina Dreamer) having words…George an I sitting there getting dressed. George says.look at them…Goofs….then they started throwing blows…..I remember this like it was yesterday…George reaches over ….puts his hand on my boot and says…."Don't look up Gossett don't put them over.. look at em ….. dad burn idiots….. don't put them over God's it just keep putting on your boots… Idiots!!! PWF Training Center story Charlotte North Carolina… true story!!!!
Black Angel

George told me once, "Bullet No matter what you do in life even if you are living under a bridge. As long as you know how to work you will always have money in your pocket". But because of George teaching me how to work I'm a home owner.
Jake Manning

When I first walked into George's wrestling school I knew he would further my wrestling education and make me a better wrestler. What I didn't realize after countless miles, matches, discussions and prayers, George would help make me a better person as well. George not only taught me about wrestling but about life as well. He truly became not only my trainer, mentor, friend but my second father as well. I could never be able to repay George for all that he has done for me. I am truly thankful and blessed to know this great man of God.
Baron Bullard

In 1985 we were working for Ole in Atlanta — I was doing a thing where I spray painted George's hair on tv to lead to match with Tommy rich where I wud try & do it to him - George did it the right way putting me over and me gettin heat coloring his hair pink with spray and Tommy rich coming out to save George & put heat on me ... George did it right ... u gotta b a team player with right attitude to help draw a crowd ... George had correct attitude & was great to work with ...
Rip Rogers

I have known George South since I was 12 years old. He has always stood by his faith!! I am blessed because he was a part of my life.
Missey Childers

I'm a George south girl. George is my hero.
Barbara Rhyne

George South is a wrestler's wrestler. He has taken his craft and used it to educate the future of our sport and to spread the word of our lord Jesus Christ. I'm honored to have been a partner, an opponent, and most importantly a friend of one of the true legends of the sport of professional wrestling. God bless you George South, my friend.
Austin Steele

"If you look up the word "Journeyman" in the dictionary, you'll see a picture of George South. The guy has been everywhere, and I firmly believe he has wrestled everyone that has ever laced up a pair of boots. His passion for the history and the sport of professional wrestling is un-matched, his love for his faith and family too, is also a sight to behold.

When I was younger in the business, I used to get irritated by George and his critiques, but then I realized the information he was giving me was not only valuable information but it was coming from a place of George wanting to see me grow as a professional. He truly has always had me, and every young man and woman with a sign of potentials best interest in mind.

Young men and women should consider it a privilege and blessing to share a locker room with George South. Lend him your ears, you may just learn a thing or two."
John Skylar

George South may not remember but it happened in Gastonia and was one of the first times that I met Queen Taylor. Chase Stevens and I traveled in from Nashville, TN...I showed up to the rasslin' event in Gastonia mad & upset about a rib gone wrong on me..I think I yelled at about everyone in the locker room and I went to an opposite room to get dressed by myself...I threw a chair in the corner and started getting dressed when I bent over to tie my boots, George South came into the room and simply sat by me..I knew the history of Mr. George South in the Mid Atlantic territory and this was the first time I ever met him, he simply took the time to talk to this young and dumb kid..I will never forget that, if I had a time machine, I would travel back in time and be trained the right way by a true professional wrestler... George South!
King Shane Williams

One of, if not the last of the true professionals in the business. The love that he has for the art of professional wrestling and the men and women in it, can't be measured in words. George South is a gift to us all.
Adam James

What we have they can't have what they have we don't want
I love you Pop
Chad Bryd

George South: A motivator, a man of knowledge and wisdom, and a man whether he's a competitor or a trainer is a genuine credit to his craft Was definitely a privilege to perform in the ring with him.
Jeff Victory - Rev Slim

Have known George almost 30 years and he has been a great friend, dance partner and more than anything a guy that's always tried to help guys whether they were rookies or veterans that he helped do something the right way. Thanks for sharing your life and wisdom with us all.
Big Donnie Webb

I remember teaming with George against Big Donnie and James Brody. I had James in a chin lock. I looked at George and yelled I got him now. He smiled at me. That was one of the my fondest memories in my career.
Jeff Patton

George gave me a black leather ring vest with USA on it which I've worn the past 2 tours of japan I've done. He signed the inside of the vest WrestleCade 2016 I love you

Elliott Russell

Two things that stick out with George while working he would always say when working a match slow down never rush, you don't rush the story to get to the ending. Always praying for everyone in the locker room which meant a lot. And the Funniest that sticks out to me is we worked a show at Paw Creek outside near a set of Rail Road tracks I think it was George and stallion, they went to lock up, Train came by hit the whistle and Scared George so bad he bumped himself without being touch. Funniest thing I ever seen. Awesome teacher and trainer.

Jerry Scruggs - Dozer

Ever since I was introduced to George around 1986 and started working shows with him and traveling with him, he has not changed one bit to this day. George is always positive and encouraging. He takes his craft very seriously and from the top guys to the bottom, he is well respected. He loves Jesus and loves to share the good news! It was early on in my career and walk with the Lord that George started encouraging me and I know for certain it kept my life from going off the rails like so many of our late brothers in the business. I am blessed to call George South my friend.

Tommy Angel

George is a classic old school worker and probably the easiest guy (next to Rip Rogers maybe?) to have a match with... If you get hurt while in the ring with George, IT'S YOUR FAULT because you won't feel a thing he does to you! George is a true pro who still has a passion for the business and is always a pleasure to work with.

Dr. Tom Pritchard

George South Thank you for all you've done and continue to do. You have the biggest heart for being the biggest/best heel ever. I have inserted in my life something you teach all of your future wrestling stars and that is "sometimes when you lose you really win". I really won something when we became friends. God bless you and I love you my buddy. "Don't stop believing " ever.

Dean Archer

Well, One good story that I have about George is.. At one of the shows we were doing during the PWF days. We were at a school in WV. Not really sure which one it was and I'm thinking it was in the winter of 1991-92. We used to do shows all in WV during school for the kids. It was a stay off of drugs type of thing. Stallion would come out and do his stay off drugs speech and of course Geore would come out and tell them that they wasnt gonna listen to him blah blah blah, ya know just be the heel.. Well, After they done their thing the matches would start it was usually George, Myself, Italian Stallion, Mark Canterbury and Michael Mcreynolds. Mike and mark would usually open the show with Mike as the Juicer and mark doing the Russian gimmick. Michael always used the silly string to get the big pop from the kids at the school. he would get it out of his pocket and spray whoever then put it back up but on this day he dropped his can of silly string after he sprayed the bad guy (The Russian)... What we didn't see was one of the students pick the can up and hold onto it.. After Mike and mark get finished its time for George and myself to work. George comes out and has everybody in the building wanting to kill him as usual. we have a good match and those kids are hot after he pins me. Time for the main event which was the Italian Stallion vs Mean Mark Canterbury.. The work for about 20 mins and do their finish and Stallion gets the win George starts doing his typical routine and running his mouth when all of a sudden he turns to say something to this one kid and the kid lets him have it.. Right in the face with a full can of silly string..He was aiming right for his face and it literally filled George's mouth full of silly string. He was trying to yell but it was hard with his mouth full. I was running the music and I was dying. I was laughing so hard that I had tears streaming down my face. Finally one of the teachers got the can from the kid .. Needless to say once we got in the locker room it wasnt a good day for Michael because he didnt hold on to his can of silly string. I have never heard somebody get chewed out like he did that day and it happend all too often with Mike. We all learned from mistakes though and had a laugh about it afterwards...I can hear George right now.. MICHAEL!!!!!! ALWAYS MAKE SURE TO HOLD ON TO THAT JUNK,, YA FRUIT!!!!!.... If I can think of anything else Ill message ya again..hope this helps

Joey Morton

George South was a great worker in the business of wrestling and always as we say a night off. George was also one of the best to get along with inside the ring and out. Always a smile and joke or two. I admire his faith in the lord. He never wavered.

Ravishing Randy Rose

George South is "The Last Rassler"! He is the true meaning of the word wrestler! When lm around George he's always entertaining and knowledgeable at the same time and funny thing about it is l don't think he knows it! Lol lm all my countless matches with its always a thrill and learning experience! He's always tells me that l "GET" it and that l can dance! We need more George Souths in this business! George you have made Paul Jones proud!

Deon Johnson

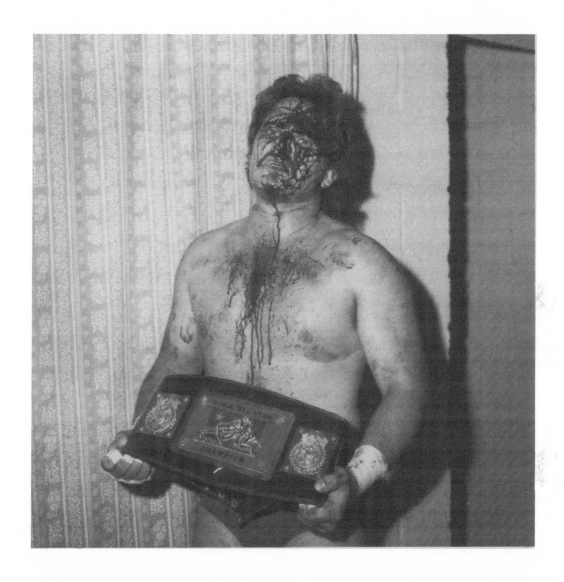

PRO-WRESTLING
SAT. - JUNE 22
8:15 P. M.

COW PALACE
Air Conditioned
LEXINGTON, NORTH CAROLINA
SPONSOR: AMVETS POST 855

6 BIG EVENTS

★ 6 MAN TAG TEAM MATCH ★
JOHNNY HUNTER & RICK LINK
AND CHIEF EAGLE
vs.
IRONMAN "SOUTH" & MASK INFERNOS I & II

★ ★ TEXAS DEATH MATCH ★ ★
CHIEF JAY EAGLE
vs.
"IRONMAN" SOUTH

MASK ASSASSIN vs. BOB STABLER

JIM TUCKER vs. THE ISLANDER

THE FABULOUS BLONDE vs. JOSE COLON

GEORGE DARBY vs. JOE BLEVINS

PRO-WRESTLING EVERY SAT. NITE AT COW PALACE